CASEBOOKS PUBLISHED AND IN PRINT

Jane Austen: *Emma* DAVID LODGE
Jane Austen: *'Northanger Abbey' & 'Persuasion'* B. C. SOUTHAM
Jane Austen: *'Sense and Sensibility', 'Pride and Prejudice' & 'Mansfield Park'* B. C. SOUTHAM
William Blake: *Songs of Innocence and Experience* MARGARET BOTTRALL

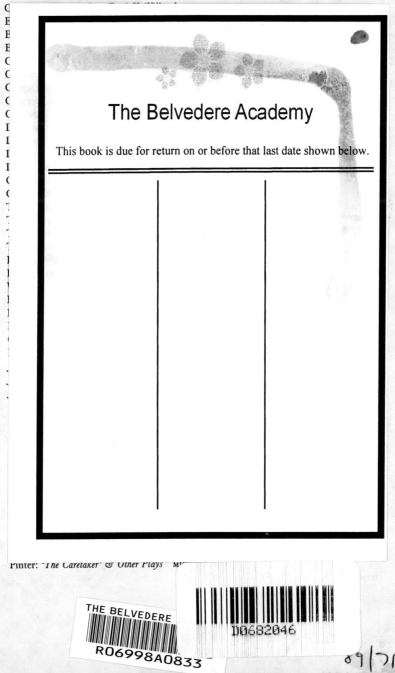

The Belvedere Academy

This book is due for return on or before that last date shown below.

Pinter: *'The Caretaker' & Other Plays* M

Pope: *The Rape of the Lock* JOHN DIXON HUNT
Shakespeare: *A Midsummer Night's Dream* ANTONY PRICE
Shakespeare: *Antony and Cleopatra* JOHN RUSSELL BROWN
Shakespeare: *Coriolanus* B. A. BROCKMAN
Shakespeare: *Hamlet* JOHN JUMP
Shakespeare: *Henry IV Parts I and II* G. K. HUNTER
Shakespeare: *Henry V* MICHAEL QUINN
Shakespeare: *Julius Caesar* PETER URE
Shakespeare: *King Lear* FRANK KERMODE
Shakespeare: *Macbeth* JOHN WAIN
Shakespeare: *Measure for Measure* G. K. STEAD
Shakespeare: *The Merchant of Venice* JOHN WILDERS
Shakespeare: *'Much Ado About Nothing' & 'As You Like It'* JOHN RUSSELL BROWN
Shakespeare: *Othello* JOHN WAIN
Shakespeare: *Richard II* NICOLAS BROOKE
Shakespeare: *The Sonnets* PETER JONES
Shakespeare: *The Tempest* D. J. PALMER
Shakespeare: *Troilus and Cressida* PRISCILLA MARTIN
Shakespeare: *Twelfth Night* D. J. PALMER
Shakespeare: *The Winter's Tale* KENNETH MUIR
Shelley: *Shorter Poems & Lyrics* PATRICK SWINDEN
Spenser: *The Faerie Queene* PETER BAYLEY
Sheridan: *Comedies* PETER DAVISON
Swift: *Gulliver's Travels* RICHARD GRAVIL
Tennyson: *In Memoriam* JOHN DIXON HUNT
Thackeray: *Vanity Fair* ARTHUR POLLARD
Trollope: *The Barsetshire Novels* T. BAREHAM
Webster: *'The White Devil' & 'The Duchess of Malfi'* R. V. HOLDSWORTH
Wilde: *Comedies* WILLIAM TYDEMAN
Virginia Woolf: *To the Lighthouse* MORIS BEJA
Wordsworth: *Lyrical Ballads* ALUN R. JONES & WILLIAM TYDEMAN
Wordsworth: *The Prelude* W. J. HARVEY & RICHARD GRAVIL
Yeats: *Poems 1919–35* ELIZABETH CULLINGFORD
Yeats: *Last Poems* JON STALLWORTHY

Medieval English Drama PETER HAPPÉ
Elizabethan Poetry: Lyrical & Narrative GERALD HAMMOND
The Metaphysical Poets GERALD HAMMOND
Poetry of the First World War DOMINIC HIBBERD
Poetry Criticism and Practice: Developments since the Symbolists A. E. DYSON
Thirties Poets: 'The Auden Group' RONALD CARTER
Comedy: Developments in Criticism D. J. PALMER
Drama Criticism: Developments since Ibsen ARNOLD P. HINCHLIFFE
Tragedy: Developments in Criticism R. P. DRAPER
The English Novel: Developments in Criticism since Henry James STEPHEN HAZELL
The Language of Literature NORMAN PAGE
The Pastoral Mode BRYAN LOUGHREY
The Romantic Imagination JOHN SPENCER HILL

OTHER CASEBOOKS ARE IN PREPARATION

Thomas Hardy

Three Pastoral Novels

Under the Greenwood Tree
Far from the Madding Crowd
The Woodlanders

A CASEBOOK

EDITED BY

R. P. DRAPER

MACMILLAN
EDUCATION

First published 1987

Published by
MACMILLAN EDUCATION LTD
*Houndmills, Basingstoke, Hampshire RG21 2XS
and London
Companies and representatives
throughout the world*

*Typeset by
Wessex Typesetters
(Division of The Eastern Press Ltd)
Frome, Somerset*

Printed in Hong Kong

British Library Cataloguing in Publication Data
Thomas Hardy: three pastoral novels: Under
the greenwood tree, Far from the madding
crowd, The woodlanders: a casebook.
1. Hardy, Thomas, *1840–1928*—Criticism
and interpretation
I. Draper, R. P.
823'.8   PR4754
ISBN 0–333–38339–7
ISBN 0–333–38340–0 Pbk

CONTENTS

General Editor's Preface   7
Introduction   8

Part One: *Comments by Hardy*

1. Prefaces from Editions of the Novels   25

   Under the Greenwood Tree (1896 edn), p. 25; (1912 edn),
   p. 26 – *Far from the Madding Crowd* (1895 & 1902 edns),
   p. 27 – *The Woodlanders* (1895 edn), p. 29; (1912 edn),
   p. 30.

2. Extracts from *The Life of Thomas Hardy*   31

   On the Stinsford Choir, p. 31 – On *Far from the Madding
   Crowd*, p. 33 – Comments during composition of *The
   Woodlanders*, p. 37 – On the ending of *The Woodlanders*,
   p. 39.

Part Two: *Reviews and Early Criticism*

HORACE MOULE (1872), p. 43 – HENRY JAMES (1874),
p. 46 – ANONYMOUS (1875), p. 50 – ANONYMOUS (1887),
p. 56 – J. M. BARRIE (1889), p. 59 – JOSEPH WARREN
BEACH (1922), p. 64 – VIRGINIA WOOLF (1928) p. 83.

Part Three: *Modern Studies on Individual Novels*

1. *Under the Greenwood Tree*   89

   JOHN F. DANBY: 'The Individual and the
        Universal' (1959)   89
   MICHAEL MILLGATE: 'Elements of Several Literary
        Modes' (1971)   97
   NORMAN PAGE: Hardy's Dutch Painting (1976)   106
   PETER J. CASAGRANDE: 'Man's Goodnesse': A
        Comedy of Forgiveness (1982)   111

2. *Far from the Madding Crowd*   116

   ROY MORRELL: A Novel as an Introduction
     to Hardy's Novels   (1965)   116
   JOHN LUCAS: 'Bathsheba's Uncertainty of Self'
     (1977)   128
   ALAN SHELSTON: 'Narrative Security'   (1979)   137
   ANDREW ENSTICE: The Farming Community
     (1979)   146

3. *The Woodlanders*   157

   DOUGLAS BROWN: 'Transcience Intimated in
     Dramatic Forms'   (1954)   157
   MERRYN WILLIAMS: 'A Post-Darwinian Viewpoint
     of Nature'   (1972)   170
   MICHAEL SQUIRES: Arcadian Innocents   (1974)   180
   SHELAGH HUNTER: 'The Implications of
     Impressionism'   (1984)   194

Select Bibliography   203

Notes on Contributors   205

Acknowledgements   207

Index   208

GENERAL EDITOR'S PREFACE

The Casebook series, launched in 1968, has become a well-regarded library of critical studies. The central concern of the series remains the 'single-author' volume, but suggestions from the academic community have led to an extension of the original plan, to include occasional volumes on such general themes as literary 'schools' and genres.

Each volume in the central category deals either with one well-known and influential work by an individual author, or with closely related works by one writer. The main section consists of critical readings, mostly modern, collected from books and journals. A selection of reviews and comments by the author's contemporaries is also included, and sometimes comment from the author himself. The Editor's Introduction charts the reputation of the work or works from the first appearance to the present time.

Volumes in the 'general themes' category are variable in structure but follow the basic purpose of the series in presenting an integrated selection of readings, with an Introduction which explores the theme and discusses the literary and critical issues involved.

A single volume can represent no more than a small selection of critical opinions. Some critics are excluded for reasons of space, and it is hoped that readers will pursue the suggestions for further reading in the Select Bibliography. Other contributions are severed from their original context, to which some readers may wish to turn. Indeed, if they take a hint from the critics represented here, they certainly will.

A. E. DYSON

8

INTRODUCTION

In December 1872, Hardy received a request from Leslie Stephen, the celebrated editor of the *Cornhill*, for a story which might be serialised in that publication. Stephen had been led to read *Under the Greenwood Tree* by Horace Moule's review [*] in the *Saturday Review* and, like Moule, had found it a congenial 'prose idyl' of the kind which he thought would please his middle-class readership. Sensing that this was the nature of the interest he had aroused, Hardy replied, as recorded in *The Life of Thomas Hardy* [ch. 7], that, although he was currently engaged on *A Pair of Blue Eyes*, he would make his next novel available to Stephen; and 'he had thought of making it a pastoral tale with the title of *Far from the Madding Crowd* . . .'. [*]

Hardy does not define what he means by 'pastoral'. The only details he gives – 'that the chief characters would probably be a young woman-farmer, a shepherd, and a sergeant of cavalry' – leave the possibilities wide open. At this stage Hardy himself probably knew very little more. He had no elaborately worked-out plan; and even when it came to writing the tale for serialisation he found himself, with some anxiety, caught up in a commitment to monthly instalments and able only to keep two or three months ahead. But the three main figures thus adumbrated (they were to become Bathsheba Everdene, Gabriel Oak and Sergeant Troy) already hint at both a specifically sheep-rearing meaning of 'pastoral' and a wider treatment of agricultural life; while the 'sergeant of cavalry' suggests a glamorous figure impinging on this life from outside, including perhaps – since there are two men to one woman – the theme of conflict between rival wooers which is also a long-established feature of that kind of pastoral which blends bucolic matters with love romance.

Such speculation is reasonable since it points in the direction that Hardy had already gone in his admired rural tale of *Under the Greenwood Tree*; and the proposed new title, *Far from the Madding Crowd*, carried with it associations which, like the earlier title,

---

*An asterisk within square brackets in the text of this Introduction indicates an item included in the present Casebook.

implied that the work would take its place in the great English tradition of pastoral literature. 'Under the greenwood tree' is the song sung by Amiens to the exiled Duke and those of his court who have followed him to the forest of Arden in Act II, scene v of *As You Like It*: a play which, according to Michael Millgate [*], 'seems to have had a special fascination for Hardy'. The song celebrates the delight and leisure and freedom from hostility (though not from the harshness of the elements) which characterise the word 'pastoral' in the wider sense of an idealised version of country life lived in harmony with nature:

> Under the greenwood tree
> Who loves to lie with me,
> And turn his merry note
> Unto the sweet bird's throat,
> Come hither, come hither, come hither.
> Here shall he see
> No enemy
> But winter and rough weather.

And 'far from the madding crowd' is a phrase which occurs in Gray's well-known 'Elegy Written in a Country Church-Yard', which similarly contrasts the humble lot of country characters living and dying in village obscurity with the public glory of those whose names and deeds are recorded in national history. The meaning of 'pastoral' is here extended still further to include an implicit claim for the moral superiority of a life of rural retirement and anonymity:

> Far from the madding crowd's ignoble strife,
> Their sober wishes never learn'd to stray;
> Along the cool sequester'd vale of life
> They kept the noiseless tenor of their way.

Such a version of 'pastoral' may also, however, subtly flatter the vanity of the more sophisticated audience to which it is directed. It at once appeals to their nostalgia for lost innocence and allows them to assume an attitude of patronage towards the attractive, but simple-minded, inhabitants of the idealised world which is being created. The success of both *Under the Greenwood Tree* and *Far from the Madding Crowd* with their original readership probably owed a great deal to this combination. The resulting ambivalence is certainly reflected in the comments made by early reviewers. Henry James [*], for example, whose own fiction was to become the very acme of sophisticated consciousness and narrative technique, found *Far from the Madding Crowd* both naive and over-extended: 'Mr

Hardy's novel is very long, but his subject is very short and simple
. . .' . James holds himself slightly aloof; and where he does give
something like warm praise for the sympathetic handling of what
he calls the 'rural phenomena', he accompanies it with a faintly
condescending air: 'The most genuine thing in [Hardy's] book, to
our sense, is a certain aroma of the meadows and lanes – a natural
relish for harvesting and sheep-washings. He has laid his scene in
an agricultural county, and his characters are children of the soil –
unsophisticated country-folk.'

The unsigned review in the *Saturday Review* of January 1875 [*] is
more generous, welcoming *Far from the Madding Crowd* as a further
contribution by Hardy to the exploration of 'the pleasant byways of
pastoral and agricultural life which he made familiar to his readers
in his former novels, *Under the Greenwood Tree* and *A Pair of Blue
Eyes*'. Nevertheless, it questions the plausibility of many of his
episodes and magisterially rebukes him for disfiguring 'his pages by
bad writing, by clumsy and inelegant metaphors, and by
mannerism and affectation' – thus anticipating what was to become
a standard criticism of Hardy's supposedly inept and ungainly
language.

Later critics have developed a less patronising attitude towards
Hardy both as stylist and as observer of the rural world, and have
come to recognise that his pastoral novels show not a sentimental
but a tough response to the realities of country life, and that they are
coloured by a complex awareness of the interplay between innocence
and experience. *Under the Greenwood Tree* in particular has come to
be taken more seriously than it was formerly (though there are still
a number of critics whose judgement of its status as 'idyll' remains,
consciously or unconsciously, pejorative).

John F. Danby [*] leads the way to this more recent revaluation
in his *Critical Quarterly* article of 1959. He begins by quoting
Hardy's own comment [*], in the Preface to the 1912 Wessex
edition, which reveals the author himself succumbing to the general
tendency to underestimate the novel with the apology that
'circumstances would have rendered any aim at a deeper, more
essential, more transcendent handling inadvisable at the date of
writing'. Danby observes, however, that 'Makers are notoriously
bad judges of their own creations', and he reverses this judgement:
'It has no obvious design on depth or transcendence, but achieves
profundity nevertheless'. The means by which this is done are
essentially imaginative. The general is inferred from the particular.
A precise and vivid vignette, such as that of Dick Dewy appearing
in profile against the night sky 'like the portrait of a gentleman in

black cardboard', has the effect of universalising the individual so that he becomes a symbol of humanity, but without assuming the portentousness of a figure deliberately endowed with mythical significance. Hardy's art plays round his rustics, even at times giving them a somewhat whimsical literary decoration, but keeping them always in firm relation to a larger community which both substantiates them and subordinates them to its own perspectives. The result is a novel which has the structure of a comedy, founded on the stability of the Mellstock community. The complexity is increased, however, by the recognition that the stability is already vanishing; and, while celebrating Mellstock, the novel also 'dramatises the first shocks to its structure'. But in *Under the Greenwood Tree*, none of this is solemnly underlined. The theme of the old order changing, which is given such prominence in Hardy's later fiction, is present also in this novel, but with the difference that it is never thrust obtrusively upon the reader. The method is one of suggestion rather than statement, requiring the kind of attention to tone and texture which is usually given to a poem rather than a novel.

In his consideration of *Under the Greenwood Tree* (in his 1971 study of Hardy) Michael Millgate [*] follows up Danby's re-assessment with a careful and attractively reasonable analysis which capitalises on the debt to *As You Like It* mentioned above. Millgate argues that the essence of Shakespeare's treatment of pastoral is that it establishes an easy dialectic between conventional assumptions and down-to-earth realities; a critical 'touchstone' is incorporated within the golden world of the Forest of Arden to achieve a mocking anti-romanticism which still leaves unimpaired whatever is genuinely and emotionally valid in the time-honoured appeal of romance. It would be an exaggeration to suggest that Hardy creates an equally well-balanced synthesis in *Under the Greenwood Tree*, nor does Millgate make such a claim; what he finds there is a similarly Shakespearean mingling of genres and a similar flexibility of manner: 'While it displays elements of several literary modes it does not fully exemplify any one of them, and nothing in the book is more impressive than Hardy's refusal to allow it to become wholly predictable along the lines of a single formal precedent.'

The relationship between Fancy Day and Dick Dewy, though they themselves are not very complex characters, is also presented in a complex way which prevents labelling, and even allows for apparent inconsistency. Thus Fancy Day behaves sometimes like a social climber, disturbing the settled ways of Mellstock, and sometimes as a pious traditionalist; and Dick seems both to merge himself in the group-consciousness of the church quire and to stand out from them as an independent individual, even welcoming the new attitudes. The future of the newly married pair, as it is hinted at in the close of the novel, is again adroitly ambiguous and ironic. Dick's naive belief in the 'full confidence' existing between himself and Fancy seems to be confirmed by the shining of a romantic moon that 'was just over the full, rendering any light from lamps or their own beauties quite unnecessary to the pair'. But its culmination in their question, 'We'll have no secrets from each other, darling, will we ever?', is qualified by Fancy's reply, 'None from to-day', and her suppression of Parson Maybold's proposal of marriage. Moreover, the 'loud, musical, and liquid voice' of the nightingale crying, 'Tippiwit! swe-e-e-t ki-ki-ki! Come hither, come hither!' which accompanies this exchange, makes a comment on their marriage which readers are left to construe for themselves. (It alludes, of course, to the song we quoted above, with its 'Come hither' refrain, but is also probably meant to echo Jaques's sardonic parody which he uses 'to call fools into a circle'.) The ending is one of happy innocence for those who want to see it as such; but for those who have attended to the sceptical tone which provides the substratum of experience running throughout the novel, it is a somewhat more brittle compromise.

For Peter J. Casagrande [*], *Under the Greenwood Tree*, despite its intimations of a fallen world, remains 'Comedy of Forgiveness'. Pastoral usually does, in fact, imply a fundamentally tolerant and optimistic view of life. In his other two exercises in this complex genre, *Far from the Madding Crowd* and *The Woodlanders*, Hardy respectively confirms and subverts this optimism. *Far from the Madding Crowd* in the main shows continuity with *Under the Greenwood Tree*, as its compositional origins suggest. It, too, comes finally to rest in a marriage which is achieved after threatening rivalry has been circumvented; and it may even be said that it is more optimistic than *Under the Greenwod Tree* in that the loving voyage of Gabriel and Bathsheba seems victualled for a longer period than that of Dick and Fancy. But the interruptions to the smooth progress of their love are also much more serious, and the elegiac note struck by the tale of Fanny's seduction by Sergeant Troy is something new compared with *Under the Greenwood Tree*. More especially, the spectacle of the seemingly rock-like Boldwood shaken to his foundations by so frail an instrument as a valentine, and the admittedly melodramatic, but still tragically dimensioned, course of his passion for Bathsheba, disturbs the pastoral world more radically than anything in the earlier novel.

The Woodlanders was first thought of as an immediate successor to *Far from the Madding Crowd*, and perhaps if it had actually been written in the 1870s, it might have kept a similar tenor, qualified only by catastrophes which could be contained within a still essentially optimistic feeling; but the idea was laid aside and not realised till 1887, by which time Hardy's tragic vision had deepened, through *The Return of the Native* (1878) and *The Mayor of Casterbridge* (1886), into a more radical conviction of the hostility of circumstance to human happiness. Consequently, *The Woodlanders*, though retaining its place in the pastoral tradition, became what David Lodge, in his Introduction to the New Wessex edition, has called 'a novelistic adaptation of the pastoral elegy' in which the customary modulation from grief to consolation (and in English literature a consolation which has strongly Christian overtones) is 'split into two' – Grace finding an ultimate renewal of her marriage with Fitzpiers, which, even though it is still more unstable than that of Dick and Fancy, could nevertheless be regarded as conforming to the same pattern of rest after disturbance; while Marty South, still faithful to Giles's memory, continues to represent that more profound sense of tragic loss which can only find comfort in its own threnodic rehearsal.

Criticism of these two novels thus divides into the comic and the tragic. For example, in his richly savoured, if now slightly old-fashioned-seeming study, *The Technique of Thomas Hardy* (1922), Joseph Warren Beach [*] gives a genial and benign account of Hardy's Wessex and the Wessex characters who throng the pages of *Far from the Madding Crowd*. Recalling the 1912 Preface, in which Hardy [*] states that *Far from the Madding Crowd* was the novel in which he 'first ventured to adopt the word "Wessex" from the pages of early English history' and which for him belonged to 'the horizons and landscapes of a partly real, partly dream-country', Beach interprets the world of that novel as at once idyllic and practical. He cites the precedents from classical pastoral literature which are somewhat self-consciously echoed in *Far from the Madding Crowd*, but he sets the true source of Hardy's inspiration, particularly the speech of his rustics, in 'the large grave manner of Scripture pastorals'. 'They remind us', Beach says, 'of characters in the Old Testament – in the story of Joseph or of Ruth, of King David or of Queen Esther.' Consequently they move with a dignified impressiveness which comes, especially in the case of Gabriel Oak, from an innate moral seriousness which, even if it is an idealisation of the tone and temper of country life, is not to be dismissed as mere nostalgic fantasy. Moreover, the medium within which this dignity exists, and with which it is so interconnected that the one is virtually inseparable from the other, is composed of both the physical environment and the social customs of 'Wessex'; and these again, if they are idealised, have their idealisation based firmly in a closely observed and faithfully reproduced culture. It is a medium which, as in *Under the Greenwood Tree*, has a slightly derivative, Shakespearean flavour (Beach notes, for example, that the conversation of the rustics is 'largely of a reminiscential sort, like that of Justice Shallow'), and this has caused less sympathetic critics to condemn the pastoral scenes in *Far from the Madding Crowd* as too coy, or sentimental. To Beach, however, they form part of a realism modified by the tonal qualities of Hardy's artistic predilections: his country pictures suggest 'the less sublime among the Dutch masters' and, still more, 'the deep and eloquent chiaroscuro of Rembrandt'. They are both shrewd and indulgent.

Roy Morrell [*], in his chapter on the novel in *Thomas Hardy – The Will and the Way* (1965), takes what seems to be an altogether more tough-minded, no-nonsense view. 'The end of *Far from the Madding Crowd*', he says, 'is emphatically not a romantic happy-ever-after affair'. What Gabriel and Bathsheba face is 'a reality that Hardy represents as more valuable, a reality of hard and good work on the two farms'. But for Morrell, too, the novel is essentially a comedy precisely because it demonstrates that 'where there's a will there's a way'. The opposition between romance and reality is dramatised in Bathsheba's choice between the flashy, uniformed Troy and the solid, oak-like Oak, and their contrasting values are reflected in their respective actions when faced with the gargoyle spouting on Fanny's grave and the storm which threatens to destroy Bathsheba's harvest ricks. Troy is sentimental, but negative, and finally futile; Oak is positive and practical, and his ultimate virtue is his ability to adapt quietly and sensibly to changing circumstances. Such a view may leave out the poetic resonance which other admirers of *Far from the Madding Crowd* find to be its greatest charm, but it is a useful reminder of the sound, prosaic common sense which forms the necessary foundation of Hardy's rural world.

John Lucas's approach [*] is likewise one that stresses the prose rather than the poetry. His theme is Bathsheba's psychological-cum-social uncertainty about herself and its manifestation in her relationships with her three lovers: Gabriel Oak appeals to the country girl aspect of her personality, Boldwood to the social climber in her, and Troy to her unstable romanticism. And each of these relationships also involves a false image that has to be brought down to more prosaic reality, two of these being idealised visions of Bathsheba held by Gabriel and Boldwood, and the third being Bathsheba's own bedazzled image of the dashing Sergeant Troy. Only when these have been shattered by the events of the story is it possible for the sane relationship of Oak and Bathsheba – based on 'an attained, and a rare, balance of social and economic quality as well as an unvisionary forbearance towards one another' – to lead the novel to its happy but sober ending.

Still in the same vein, Andrew Enstice's discussion [*] of *Far from the Madding Crowd* in terms of 'The Farming Community' pays detailed attention to the novel's setting and the occupations of its characters. Bathsheba's farmhouse, Warren's Malthouse and the Corn Exchange at Casterbridge are all considered in relation to their functions within the active business of the rural world; and the characters of Oak and Bathsheba, and the episodes in which they participate, are presented in terms of their agricultural roles. This approach is almost pragmatic; as in Roy Morrell's treatment, the sensational episode of the storm [chs. 37–8] is seen as one which puts the emphasis on Gabriel Oak's country skills and his ability to deal with practical problems in an efficient manner. The effect, however, is not reductively prosaic. Oak still emerges as something of an heroic figure, but his heroism is manifested in his instinctive adjustment to the needs of a situation which calls as much for co-operation with nature as resistance to it. In this respect he is the chief representative of a rural tradition which in Hardy's later work, including *The Woodlanders*, is under threat of extinction, but which still flourishes in *Far from the Madding Crowd*, notwithstanding the influence of the alien intruder, Sergeant Troy, and is able to establish its own kind of quiet, cannily realistic order at the end. Shrewdness and practical good sense thus occupy much more of the foreground for both Enstice and Morrell than they do for Beach, but they all three agree in finding evidence in *Far from the Madding Crowd* of an integrated rural society which remains strong enough to cope with the forces threatening it. The tradition is a vital one, whether it is looked at from an idyllic or a practical standpoint.

However, by the time he came to write *The Woodlanders*, Hardy seems to have lost some of this confidence in the rural world. Paradoxically, he was at once more distant from it and more nostalgically involved with it. In the General Preface to the 1912 Wessex edition of his novels and poems, Hardy speaks of his care to authenticate details in his work 'in order to preserve for [his] own satisfaction a fairly true record of a vanishing life'; and this sense of an old way of life disappearing, with corresponding nostalgia for what was lost, or in the process of being lost, may account for the comment he made on *The Woodlanders* when he was re-reading it and preparing its text for inclusion in that same edition: 'On taking up *The Woodlanders* and reading it after many years I think I like it, *as a story*, the best of all. Perhaps that is owing to the locality and scenery of the action, a part I am very fond of. It seems a more quaint and fresh story than the *Native*, and the characters are very distinctly drawn' [*Life*, p. 358].

If by liking it '*as a story*' Hardy meant that he particularly admired the plot-structure of *The Woodlanders*, his judgement seems a little odd, and is not in general borne out by later critical comment. He can be a very good story-teller, but of the three novels here being considered it is *Far from the Madding Crowd* rather than *The Woodlanders* which shows his narrative skill at its most effective, as Alan Shelston [*] demonstrates in his essay, 'The Particular Pleasure of *Far from the Madding Crowd*'. Nevertheless, the reference to 'locality and scenery' and his fondness for this district (the north-western corner of Dorset) suggest that it was the atmosphere of the woodlands which really appealed to Hardy; and on this there is much greater critical agreement. Douglas Brown [*], for example, is particularly enthusiastic about Hardy's treatment of the setting of *The Woodlanders*: he insists that it is not merely 'a collection of private descriptive set pieces', but that 'the feeling towards the woods wells up from within the frame of the narrative'. For Brown, *The Woodlanders*, as its title implies, is of all Hardy's novels the one in which the relationship between dweller and place of dwelling acquires the greatest importance, and, as he states uncompromisingly at the beginning of his discussion, it is 'the novel that most comprehensively expresses Hardy's feeling towards agricultural life, and his sense of its resistance to despair'.

'Resistance' is not, perhaps, the most precise word – as Merryn Williams [*] points out (in her chapter on the novel in *Thomas Hardy and Rural England*), 'one of the saddest things about *The Woodlanders* is that the community, unlike those in earlier novels, seems to have almost no capacity for resistance'. All the same, there is ample evidence for Brown's claim that it is Hardy's 'most fluid book'; the powerful sense of organic continuity between man and nature which surges through so much of the descriptive writing makes *The Woodlanders* the most attractively readable of the pastoral novels and endows it with a special imaginative appeal.

Brown also argues that Hardy evaluates his characters according to the degree of their affinity with nature. Thus Marty South is the most admirable because she is the one most gifted with innate sensitivity to her natural surroundings; Giles is next in order of merit; Grace comes next, though she begins to show the dangerously alienating influence of education and social ambition; and Fitzpiers and Mrs Charmond are the least sympathetic – Mrs Charmond, in particular, being invested with a banal power 'to dissolve old local ties and commitments' which threatens the very existence of a living and sustaining relationship between man and nature. Merryn Williams again disagrees with this view. It is 'much too simple', she maintains. The woodlands are presented as 'productive and fruitful in certain seasons and under certain aspects, but they are also seen from a more sceptical, 'post-Darwinian viewpoint' as manifestations of the 'Unfulfilled Intention'.

There is, in fact, a 'scientific' as well as an 'imaginative' dimension to the treatment of nature in *The Woodlanders*, and this other dimension is responsible for an occasional quality of cool abstraction in the language of the novel ('Dead boughs were scattered about like icthyosauri in a museum . . .', which prompted the Victorian poet, Coventry Patmore, to comment distastefully on Hardy's use of the 'detestable lingo of the drawing-room "scientist" (*St James's Gazette*, 2 April 1887), but which the modern novelist and critic, David Lodge, associates with its 'evolutionary pessimism' (Introduction to New Wessex edition, p. 24). This is part of a pervasive irony and detachment which gives the pastoralism of *The Woodlanders* a very different tone and temper from *Under the Greenwood Tree* or *Far from the Madding Crowd*.

Comparing *The Woodlanders* with its predecessors, Michael Squires [*] comments: 'If they are on the whole charming and idyllic, *The Woodlanders* is gloomy and ironic. If they express full confidence in the strength of the pastoral world to sustain itself, *The Woodlanders* expresses doubt and anxious melancholy . . .'. Division, which is incidental, and subordinate to a more optimistic unity in *Under the Greenwood Tree* and *Far from the Madding Crowd*, here becomes a basic principle of organisation. This perception leads Squires to an unusually detailed analysis of the special kind of pastoral world that is created in *The Woodlanders*. With the aid of the traditional terms of pastoral literature, he distinguishes between the idyllic *eclogue* of pastoral poetry, which concentrates on the leisure and loves of shepherds and shepherdesses, and the *georgic*, which is a didactic poem about the real world of farming and productive country pursuits, geared to the hard, physical labour that must be performed on the land to make it yield its crops. Both are present in *The Woodlanders*. Thus Giles in *eclogue* fashion can rise upon

Grace's sentimental memory 'as the fruit-god and the wood-god in alternation', a figure whom, as Squires luxuriantly expresses it, 'Hardy immerses ... in the harvest, perfuming Giles's visual exterior with the redolent atmosphere of crops'. On the other hand, Marty South's spar-making is presented in more realistic *georgic* terms: it is hard, unpleasant work which gives her little satisfaction, but it is recognised as a basic skill essential to the woodland industry, and one at which she excels and which gives her a valuable place in the rural economy.

Another example which might be used to extend Squires's emphasis on the *georgic* aspect of *The Woodlanders* is the episode with which the novel opens – the cutting of Marty's hair. This is symptomatic of her role in the rest of the book. Marty at first resists the bargain which would deprive her of her one claim to romantic attraction (Barber Percomb cruelly diagnoses her reluctance to part with her locks: 'you've got a lover yourself, and that's why you won't let it go!'); but when she learns that Giles is intended for Grace she cuts off her locks with her own hands and lays them out symbolically, as though they were a corpse, 'Upon the pale scrubbed deal of the coffin-stool table ... like waving and ropy weeds over the washed white bed of a stream'. The language here creates a starkness of effect altogether different from the celebrated passage which later glamorises Giles; it signifies that renunciation of *eclogue* values which is to constitute the essence of Marty's character.

It is in the ending of the novel that one sees the ultimate outcome of this. Grace settles for the unpropitious compromise of renewed marriage to Fitzpiers, and Marty alone remains faithful to Giles's memory. According to Squires, the speech which she intones over his grave is 'a muted pastoral elegy', and its function is the time-honoured pastoral one of 'assuaging sorrow and revealing to man his place in the universe'. It is a kind of musical coda, signing off the novel in an artistically appropriate minor key. But the fact that Marty and the woodlands – Marty, indeed, is here almost the voice of the woodlands – are Giles's only commemoration quietly emphasises the lack of traditional consolation and the failure to bring man and nature into harmony. The final elegy, moving as it is, only serves to underline the extent to which pastoral in *The Woodlanders* has become identified with nostalgia and regret for a vanished virtue; and the detached, anti-pastoral dimension in which the natural world is also presented not only reminds us of the real, as opposed to the ideal (that, after all, was effectively done in the earlier novels as well), but compels us to recognise the co-existence of a distinctively modern version of country life which, if it knows anything of pastoral, knows it simply as a classical convention without felt relationship to an actual community. This is what makes Marty's speech seem to mean so much more than it says. It is spoken for the dead and to the dead, by that which, if it is not itself yet dead, is regretfully dying.

The entire approach to these three novels which is implicit in labelling them as 'pastoral novels' carries with it a recognition that the manner of their presentation counts as much as the matter. They include close, and at times sociologically precise, observation of rural life, and the degree of realism with which the agricultural community is rendered is a proper and important part of our critical concern. But realism is not adequate to account for their full effect. Even the avowedly pictorial *Under the Greenwood Tree* is not simple portrait-painting. Norman Page [*], for example, is not prepared to accept the view that its mode is straightforward realism. He sees the fact that its title alludes to *As You Like It* and its subtitle to the Dutch masters as evidence of a deliberate counterpointing of romance and realism; and he also suggests that the influence of other schools of painting, and the particular circumstances of its composition (Hardy's return to Dorset from London and his recent marriage to Emma), combine to make it a novel of highly subjective emotion.

In the period leading up to *The Woodlanders*, Hardy grew increasingly interested in the non-realistic style of painting associated with the late work of the great English artist, J. M. W. Turner. In January 1887 he jotted down the following comment:

After looking at the landscape ascribed to Bonington in our drawing-room I feel that Nature is played out as a Beauty, but not as a Mystery. I don't want to see landscapes, i.e., scenic paintings of them, because I don't want to see the original realities – as optical effects, that is. I want to see the deeper reality underlying the scenic, the expression of what are sometimes called abstract imaginings.

The 'simply natural' is interesting no longer. The much decried, mad, late-Turner rendering is now necessary to create my interest. The exact truth as to material fact ceases to be of importance in art – it is a student's style – the style of a period when the mind is serene and unawakened to the tragical mysteries of life; when it does not bring anything to the object that coalesces with and translates the qualities that are already there, – half hidden, it may be – and the two united are depicted as the All.

[*Life*, p. 185]

Shelagh Hunter [*] refers to this passage in her illuminating discussion of the quality of Hardy's narrative writing in *The*

Woodlanders, and she uses it as the basis for her argument that the elusive 'shimmer' of this novel is a fictional equivalent of the impressionist method employed by Turner. Landscape, or, more exactly, the fluctuating images of woodland scene and arboreal phenomena, become as important as any of the individual characters. What Hardy set out to do in *The Return of the Native* (where Egdon Heath is such an impressive prelude) but failed to realise in the main body of that novel, is actually accomplished in *The Woodlanders* by treating the setting as a pervasive reflector of tragic feeling. The narrative method becomes one in which the registering of impressions plays a continually varying part. Nothing exists except as it is reflected in some particular consciousness, either that of a character within the novel or of an implied narrator; and ultimately these media are simply extensions of the larger, more complex registering consciousness which is that of the author himself expressing his 'abstract imaginings'.

The Woodlanders is as far as Hardy goes in this direction within his fiction; the rendering of narrative as consciousness is given its fullest development in his subsequent epic drama, *The Dynasts* (1904–08). (See 'Comments Made During Composition of *The Woodlanders*' [*]) But each of the pastoral novels involves some mingling of realistic observation and subjective impressionism. These, in fact, are the poles between which criticism of the three novels continually wavers; and Hardy himself seems to have shared in the uncertainty. As some of the remarks which have already been quoted from him indicate, he can be seen as a supporter of both realistic and non-realistic approaches. On balance he is probably more inclined to the non-realistic, though this may simply be the result of a tendency, increasingly marked in later years, to react against the dominant realism of nineteenth-century critical opinion. In comments on his poems, for example, he becomes emphatic that they are to be understood as subjective impressions only. What he says about his novels, however, is more variable, and the variability in their actual tone and temper seems to reflect a Janus-like attitude. Fortunately, the pastoral tradition, which itself embraces both realism and idealism, offered a congenially adaptable form which he could use for the expression of this complex response to country life.

Nothing is more typical of Hardy's own wry awareness of the ambiguous status of what he creates than the way he welcomes his contemporaries' readiness to join him 'in the anachronism of imagining a Wessex population living under Queen Victoria; – a modern Wessex of railways, the penny post, mowing and reaping

machines, union workhouses, lucifer matches, labourers who could
read and write, and National school children' (Preface to *Far from
the Madding Crowd*). The bizarre list is deliberately selected in order
to highlight modern agricultural realities which ought to be
incompatible with an ancient, almost mythical, 'Wessex', while
author and reader conspire together in enjoying the anachronistic
contradiction. It is in this spirit, and with the desire to satisfy this
complex pleasure in seeming incompatibilities, that the pastoral
novels are written.

As a final example one may point to the closing paragraph of *Far
from the Madding Crowd*, where the long-awaited union of Oak and
Bathsheba, which meets the romantic requirements for a happy
ending, is nonetheless spoken of in such unromantic terms:

Theirs was that substantial affection which arises (if any arises at all)
when the two who are thrown together begin first by knowing the rougher
sides of each other's character, and not the best till further on, the romance
growing up in the interstices of a mass of hard prosaic reality. This good-
fellowship – *camaraderie* – usually occurring through similarity of pursuits,
is unfortunately seldom superadded to love between the sexes, because
men and women associate, not in their labours, but in their pleasures
merely. Where, however, happy circumstance permits its development, the
compounded feeling proves itself to be the only love which is strong as
death – that love which many waters cannot quench, nor the floods drown,
beside which the passion usually called by the name is evanescent as
steam.   [ch. 56]

Here, too, is the best available definition of Hardy's particular
version of pastoral: 'romance growing up in the interstices of a
mass of hard prosaic reality'. The modification which remains to be
made is that, in *Under the Greenwood Tree* and *Far from the Madding
Crowd* the romance continues somehow to grow, but in *The
Woodlanders* an elegiac sadness tacitly admits its failure to do so.

PART ONE

Comments by Hardy

1. PREFACES FROM EDITIONS OF THE NOVELS

Under the Greenwood Tree   (first published 1872)

Edition of 1896

This story of the Mellstock Quire and its old established west-gallery musicians, with some supplementary descriptions of similar officials in *Two on a Tower*, *A Few Crusted Characters*, and other places, is intended to be a fairly true picture, at first hand, of the personages, ways, and customs which were common among such orchestral bodies in the villages of fifty or sixty years ago.

One is inclined to regret the displacement of these ecclesiastical bandsmen by an isolated organist (often at first a barrel-organist) or harmonium player; and despite certain advantages in point of control and accomplishment which were, no doubt, secured by installing the single artist, the change has tended to stultify the professed aims of the clergy, its direct result being to curtail and extinguish the interest of parishioners in church doings. Under the old plan, from half a dozen to ten full-grown players, in addition to the numerous more or less grown-up singers, were officially occupied with the Sunday routine, and concerned in trying their best to make it an artistic outcome of the combined musical taste of the congregation. With a musical executive limited, as it mostly is limited now, to the parson's wife or daughter and the school-children, or to the school-teacher and the children, an important union of interests has disappeared.

The zest of these bygone instrumentalists must have been keen and staying, to take them, as it did, on foot every Sunday after a toilsome week through all weathers to the church, which often lay at a distance from their homes. They usually received so little in payment for their performances that their efforts were really a labour of love. In the parish I had in my mind when writing the present tale, the gratuities received yearly by the musicians at Christmas were somewhat as follows: From the manor-house ten shillings and a supper; from the vicar ten shillings; from the farmers five shillings each; from each cottage-household one shilling; amounting altogether to no more than ten shillings a head annually – just enough, as an old executant told me, to pay for their fiddle-strings, repairs, rosin, and music-paper (which they mostly ruled themselves). Their music in those days was all in their own manuscript, copied in the evenings after work, and their music-books were home-bound.

It was customary to inscribe a few jigs, reels, hornpipes, and ballads in the same book, by beginning in at the other end, the insertions being continued from front and back till sacred and secular met together in the middle, often with bizarre effect, the words of some of the songs exhibiting that ancient and broad humour which our grandfathers, and possibly grandmothers, took delight in, and is in these days unquotable.

The aforesaid fiddle-strings, rosin, and music-paper were supplied by a pedlar, who travelled exclusively in such wares from parish to parish, coming to each village about every six months. Tales are told of the consternation once caused among the church fiddlers when, on the occasion of their producing a new Christmas anthem, he did not come to time, owing to being snowed up on the downs, and the straits they were in through having to make shift with whipcord and twine for strings. He was generally a musician himself, and sometimes a composer in a small way, bringing his own new tunes, and tempting each choir to adopt them for a consideration. Some of these compositions which now lie before me, with their repetitions of lines, half-lines, and half-words, their figures and their intermediate symphonies, are good singing still, though they would hardly be admitted into such hymn-books as are popular in the churches of fashionable society at the present time.

August 1896

Wessex Edition of 1912

Under the Greenwood Tree was first brought out in the summer of 1872 in two volumes. The name of the story was originally intended to be, more appropriately, *The Mellstock Quire*, and this has been appended as a sub-title since the early editions, it having been thought unadvisable to displace for it the title by which the book first became known.

In rereading the narrative after a long interval there occurs the inevitable reflection that the realities out of which it was spun were material for another kind of study of this little group of church musicians than is found in the chapters here penned so lightly, even so farcically and flippantly at times. But circumstances would have rendered any aim at a deeper, more essential, more transcendent handling unadvisable at the date of writing; and the exhibition of the Mellstock Quire in the following pages must remain the only extant one, except for the few glimpses of that perished band which I have given in verse elsewhere.

April 1912

Far from the Madding Crowd   (first published 1874)

Editions of 1895 and 1902

In reprinting this story for a new edition I am reminded that it was in the chapters of *Far from the Madding Crowd*, as they appeared month by month in a popular magazine, that I first ventured to adopt the word 'Wessex' from the pages of early English history, and give it a fictitious significance as the existing name of the district once included in that extinct kingdom. The series of novels I projected being mainly of the kind called local, they seemed to require a territorial definition of some sort to lend unity to their scene. Finding that the area of a single county did not afford a canvas large enough for this purpose, and that there were objections to an invented name, I disinterred the old one. The region designated was known but vaguely, and I was often asked even by educated people where it lay. However, the press and the public were kind enough to welcome the fanciful plan, and willingly joined me in the anachronism of imagining a Wessex population living under Queen Victoria; – a modern Wessex of railways, the penny post, mowing and reaping machines, union workhouses, lucifer matches, labourers who could read and write, and National school children. But I believe I am correct in stating that, until the existence of this contemporaneous Wessex in place of the usual counties was announced in the present story, in 1874, it had never been heard of in fiction and current speech, if at all, and that the expression, 'a Wessex peasant', or 'a Wessex custom', would therefore have been taken to refer to nothing later in date than the Norman Conquest.

I did not anticipate that this application of the word to modern story would extend outside the chapters of these particular chronicles. But it was soon taken up elsewhere, the first to adopt it being the now defunct *Examiner*, which, in the impression bearing date July 15, 1876, entitled one of its articles 'The Wessex Labourer', the article turning out to be no dissertation on farming during the Heptarchy, but on the modern peasant of the south-west counties.

Since then the appellation which I had thought to reserve to the horizons and landscapes of a partly real, partly dream-country, has become more and more popular as a practical provincial definition; and the dream-country has, by degrees, solidified into a utilitarian region which people can go to, take a house in, and write to the papers from. But I ask all good and idealistic readers to forget this, and to refuse steadfastly to believe that there are any inhabitants of a Victorian Wessex outside these volumes in which their lives and conversations are detailed.

Moreover, the village called Weatherbury, wherein the scenes of the present story of the series are for the most part laid, would perhaps be hardly discernible by the explorer, without help, in any existing place nowadays; though at the time, comparatively recent, at which the tale was written, a sufficient reality to meet the descriptions, both of backgrounds and personages, might have been traced easily enough. The church remains, by great good fortune, unrestored and intact* and a few of the old houses; but the ancient malt-house, which was formerly so characteristic of the parish, has been pulled down these twenty years; also most of the thatched and dormered cottages that were once lifeholds. The heroine's fine old Jacobean house would be found in the story to have taken a witch's ride of a mile or more from its actual position; though with that difference its features are described as they still show themselves to the sun and moonlight. The game of prisoner's-base, which not so long ago seemed to enjoy a perennial vitality in front of the worn-out stocks, may, so far as I can say, be entirely unknown to the rising generation of schoolboys there. The practice of divination by Bible and key, the regarding of valentines as things of serious import, the shearing-supper, the long smock-frocks, and the harvest-home, have, too, nearly disappeared in the wake of the old houses; and with them has gone, it is said, much of that love of fuddling to which the village at one time was notoriously prone. The change at the root of this has been the recent supplanting of the class of

---

*[Ed.] In the reprinting of this Preface in the Wessex Edition of 1912, Hardy here adds a footnote: 'This is no longer the case (1912).'

stationary cottagers, who carried on the local traditions and humours, by a population of more or less migratory labourers, which has led to a break of continuity in local history, more fatal than any other thing to the preservation of legend, folk-lore, close inter-social relations and eccentric individualities. For these the indispensable conditions of existence are attachment to the soil of one particular spot by generation after generation.

1895; 1902

The Woodlanders   (first published 1887)

Edition of 1895

In the present novel, as in one or two others of this series which involve the question of matrimonial divergence, the immortal puzzle – given the man and woman, how to find a basis for their sexual relation – is left where it stood; and it is tacitly assumed for the purposes of the story that no doubt of the depravity of the erratic heart who feels some second person to be better suited to his or her tastes than the one with whom he has contracted to live, enters the head of reader or writer for a moment. From the point of view of marriage as a distinct covenant or undertaking, decided on by two people fully cognizant of all its possible issues, and competent to carry them through, this assumption is, of course, logical. Yet no thinking person supposes that, on the broader ground of how to afford the greatest happiness to the units of human society during their brief transit through this sorry world, there is no more to be said on this covenant; and it is certainly not supposed by the writer of these pages. But, as Gibbon blandly remarks on the evidence for and against Christian miracles, 'the duty of an historian does not call upon him to interpose his private judgment in this nice and important controversy'.

The stretch of country visible from the heights adjoining the nook herein described under the name of Little Hintock, cannot be regarded as inferior to any inland scenery of the sort in the west of England, or perhaps anywhere in the kingdom. It is singular to find that a world-wide repute in some cases, and an absolute famelessness in others, attach to spots of equal beauty and equal accessibility. The neighbourhood of High-Stoy (I give, as elsewhere, the real names to natural features), Bubb-Down Hill, and the glades westward to Montacute; of Bulbarrow, Hambledon Hill, and the slopes eastward to Shaston, Windy Green, and Stour Head, teems with landscapes which, by a mere accident of iteration, might have been numbered among the scenic celebrities of the English shires.

September 1895

Wessex Edition of 1912

I have been honoured by so many inquiries for the true name and exact locality of the hamlet 'Little Hintock', in which the greater part of the action of this story goes on, that I may as well confess here once for all that I do not know myself where that hamlet is more precisely than as explained above and in the pages of the narrative. To oblige readers I once spent several hours on a bicycle with a friend in a serious attempt to discover the real spot; but the search ended in failure; though tourists assure me positively that they have found it without trouble, and that it answers in every particular to the description given in this volume. At all events, as stated elsewhere, the commanding heights called 'High-Stoy' and 'Bubb-Down Hill' overlook the landscape in which it is supposed to be hid.

In respect of the occupations of the characters, the adoption of iron utensils and implements in agriculture, and the discontinuance of thatched roofs for cottages, have almost extinguished the handicrafts classed formerly as 'copsework', and the type of men who engaged in them.

The Woodlanders was first published complete, in three volumes, in the March of 1887.

April 1912

2. EXTRACTS FROM *THE LIFE OF THOMAS HARDY*

On the Stinsford Choir ('Mellstock' in *Under the Greenwood Tree*)

. . . In this church [Stinsford] . . . the Hardys became well known as violinists, Thomas the Second, the poet and novelist's father aforesaid, after his early boyhood as chorister beginning as a youth with the 'counter' viol, and later taking on the tenor and treble.

They were considered among the best church-players in the neighbourhood, accident having helped their natural bent. This was the fact that in 1822, shortly after the death of the old vicar Mr Floyer, the Rev. Edward Murray, a connection of the Earl of Ilchester, who was the patron of the living, was presented to it. Mr Murray was an ardent musician and performer on the violin himself, and the two younger Hardys and sometimes their father used to practise two or three times a week with him in his study at Stinsford House, where he lived instead of at the Vicarage.

Thus it was that the Hardy instrumentalists, though never more than four, maintained an easy superiority over the larger bodies in parishes near. For while Puddletown west-gallery, for instance, could boast of eight players, and Maiden Newton of nine, these included wood-wind and leather – that is to say, clarionets and serpents – which were apt to be a little too sonorous, even strident, when zealously blown. But the few and well-practised violists of Stinsford were never unduly emphatic, according to tradition.

Elaborate Canticle services, such as the noted 'Jackson in F', and in 'E flat' – popular in the West of England, possibly because Jackson had been an Exeter man – Pope's Ode, and anthems with portentous repetitions and 'mountainous fugues', were carried through by the performers every Sunday, with what real success is not known, but to their own great satisfaction and the hearty approval of the musical vicar.

In their psalmody they adhered strictly to Tate-and-Brady – upon whom, in truth, the modern hymn-book has been no great improvement – such tunes as the 'Old Hundredth', 'New Sabbath',

'Devizes', 'Wilton', 'Lydia', and 'Cambridge New' being their
staple ones; while 'Barthélémon' and 'Tallis' were played to Ken's
Morning and Evening Hymns respectively every Sunday throughout
the year: a practice now obsolete, but a great stimulus to
congregational singing.

As if the superintendence of the Stinsford choir were not enough
distraction from business for Thomas Hardy the First, he would go
whenever opportunity served and assist other choirs by performing
with his violoncello in the galleries of their parish churches, mostly
to the high contentment of the congregations. Although Thomas
the Third had not come into the world soon enough to know his
grandfather in person, there is no doubt that the description by
Fairway in *The Return of the Native* of the bowing of Thomasin's
father, when lending his services to the choir of Kingsbere, is a
humorous exaggeration of the traditions concerning Thomas Hardy
the First's musical triumphs as locum-tenens.

In addition it may be mentioned that he had been a volunteer till
the end of the war, and lay in Weymouth with his company from
time to time, waiting for Bonaparte who never came.

Conducting the church choir all the year round involved carol-
playing and singing at Christmas, which Thomas Hardy the
Second loved as much as did his father. In addition to the ordinary
practice, the work of preparing and copying carols a month of
evenings before-hand was not light, and incidental expenses were
appreciable. The parish being a large and scattered one, it was the
custom of Thomas Hardy the First to assemble the rather
perfunctory rank-and-file of the choir at his house; and this
necessitated suppers, and suppers demanded (in those days) plenty
of liquor. This was especially the case on Christmas Eve itself,
when the rule was to go to the northern part of the parish and play
at every house before supper; then to return to Bockhampton and
sit over the meal till twelve o'clock, during which interval a good
deal was consumed at the Hardys' expense, the choir being mainly
poor men and hungry. They then started for the other parts of the
parish, and did not get home till all was finished at about six in the
morning, the performers themselves feeling 'no more than malkins'[1]
in church next day, as they used to declare. The practice was kept
up by Thomas Hardy the Second, much as described in *Under the
Greenwood Tree or The Mellstock Quire*, though its author, Thomas
Hardy the Third, invented the personages, incidents, manners,
etc., never having seen or heard the choir as such, they ending their

---

[1] *Malkin*, a damp rag for swabbing out an oven. [Hardy's note – Ed.]

office when he was about a year old. He was accustomed to say that on this account he had rather burlesqued them, the story not so adequately reflecting as he could have wished in later years the poetry and romance that coloured their time-honoured observances.

This preoccupation of the Hardys with the music of the parish church and less solemn assemblies did not, to say the least, assist their building business, and it was somewhat of a relief to Thomas Hardy the Second's young wife – though musical herself to a degree – when ecclesiastical changes after the death of Thomas Hardy the First, including the cession of the living by Murray, led to her husband's abandoning in 1841 or 1842 all connection with the choir. The First Thomas's death having been quite unexpected, inasmuch as he was playing in the church one Sunday, and brought in for burial on the next, there could be no such quiring over his grave as he had performed over the graves of so many, owing to the remaining players being chief mourners. And thus ended his devoted musical services to Stinsford Church, in which he had occupied the middle seat of the gallery with his bass-viol on Sundays for a period of thirty-five years – to no worldly profit; far the reverse, indeed. . . .   [pp. 9–13]

On 'Far from the Madding Crowd'

. . . in December 1872, Hardy had received at Bockhampton a letter from Leslie Stephen, the editor of the *Cornhill* – by that time well known as a man of letters, *Saturday* reviewer, and Alpine climber – asking for a serial story for his magazine. He had lately read *Under the Greenwood Tree*, and thought 'the descriptions admirable'. It was 'long since he had received more pleasure from a new writer', and it had occurred to him that such writing would probably please the readers of the *Cornhill Magazine* as much as it had pleased him.

Hardy had replied that he feared the date at which he could write a story for the *Cornhill* would be too late for Mr Stephen's purpose, since he already had on hand a succeeding novel (*i.e. A Pair of Blue Eyes*), which was arranged for; but that the next after should be at Mr Stephen's disposal. He had thought of making it a pastoral tale with the title of *Far from the Madding Crowd* – and that the chief characters would probably be a young woman-farmer, a shepherd, and a sergeant of cavalry. That was all he had done. Mr Stephen had rejoined that he was sorry he could not expect a story from Hardy at an earlier date; that he did not, however, mean to fix any particular time; that the idea of the story attracted him; also the proposed title; and that he would like Hardy to call and talk it over when he came to Town. There the matter had been left. Now Hardy set about the pastoral tale, the success of *A Pair of Blue Eyes* meanwhile surpassing his expectations, the influential *Saturday Review* pronouncing it to be the most artistically constructed of the novels of its time – a quality which, by the bye, would carry little recommendation in these days of loose constitution and indifference to organic homogeneity.

But Hardy did not call on Stephen just then.

It was, indeed, by the merest chance that he had ever got the *Cornhill* letter at all. The postal arrangements in Dorset were still so primitive at this date that the only delivery of letters at Hardy's father's house was by the hand of some friendly neighbour who had come from the next village, and Stephen's request for a story had been picked up in the mud of the lane by a labouring man, the school children to whom it had been entrusted having dropped it on the way.

While thus in the seclusion of Bockhampton, writing *Far from the Madding Crowd*, we find him on September 21, walking to Woodbury-Hill Fair, approximately described in the novel as 'Greenhill Fair'. On the 24th he was shocked at hearing of the tragic death of his friend Horace Moule, from whom he had parted cheerfully at Cambridge in June. The body was brought to be buried at Fordington, Dorchester, and Hardy attended the funeral. It was a matter of keen regret to him now, and for a long time after, that Moule and the woman to whom Hardy was warmly attached had never set eyes on each other; and that she could never make Moule's acquaintance, or be his friend.

On the 30th of September he sent to Leslie Stephen at his request as much of the MS. of *Far from the Madding Crowd* as was written – apparently between two and three monthly parts, though some of it only in rough outline – and a few days after a letter came from Stephen stating that the story suited him admirably as far as it had gone, and that though as a rule it was desirable to see the whole of a novel before definitely accepting it, under the circumstances he decided to accept it at once.

So Hardy went on writing *Far from the Madding Crowd* – sometimes indoors, sometimes out – when he would occasionally find himself without a scrap of paper at the very moment that he felt volumes. In such circumstances he would use large dead leaves, white chips left by the wood-cutters, or pieces of stone or slate that came to hand. He used to say that when he carried a pocket-book his mind was barren as the Sahara.

This autumn Hardy assisted at his father's cider-making – a proceeding he had always enjoyed from childhood – the apples being from huge old trees that have now long perished. It was the last time he ever took part in a work whose sweet smells and oozings in the crisp autumn air can never be forgotten by those who have had a hand in it.

Memorandum by T. H.:

'Met J. D., one of the old Mellstock fiddlers – who kept me talking interminably: a man who speaks neither truth nor lies, but a sort of Not Proven compound which is very relishable. Told me of Jack ——, who spent all the money he had – sixpence – at the Oak Inn, took his sixpence out of the till when the landlady's back was turned, and spent it over again; then stole it again, and again spent it, till he had had a real skinful. "Was too honest to take any money but his own", said J. D.' (Some of J. D.'s characteristics appear in 'the Tranter' of *Under the Greenwood Tree*.)

At the end of October an unexpected note from the *Cornhill* editor asked if, supposing he were to start *Far from the Madding Crowd* in the January number (which would be out the third week in December) instead of the spring, as intended, Hardy could keep in front of the printers with his copy. He learnt afterwards that what had happened was that the MS. of a novel which the editor had arranged to begin in his pages in January had been lost in the post, according, at any rate, to its author's account. Hardy thought January not too soon for him, and that he could keep the printers going. Terms were consequently arranged with the publishers and proofs of the first number sent forthwith, Hardy incidentally expressing with regard to any illustrations, in a letter of October 1873, 'a hope that the rustics, although *quaint*, may be made to appear intelligent, and not boorish at all'; adding in a later letter: 'In reference to the illustrations, I have sketched in my note-book during the past summer a few correct outlines of smockfrocks, gaiters, sheep-crooks, rick-"staddles", a sheep-washing pool, one of the old-fashioned malt-houses, and some other out-of-the-way things that might have to be shown. These I could send you if they would be of any use to the artist, but if he is a sensitive man and you think he would rather not be interfered with, I would not do so.'

No response had been made to this, and he was not quite clear whether, after all, Leslie Stephen had finally decided to begin so soon, when, returning from Cornwall on a fine December noontide (being New Year's Eve 1873–74), he opened on Plymouth Hoe a copy of the *Cornhill* that he had bought at the station, and there to his surprise saw his story placed at the beginning of the magazine, with a striking illustration, the artist being – also to his surprise – not a man but a woman, Miss Helen Paterson. He had only expected, from the undistinguished rank of the characters in the tale, that it would be put at the end, and possibly without a picture. Why this had come without warning to him was owing to the accident of his being away from his permanent address for several days, and nothing having been forwarded. It can be imagined how delighted Miss Gifford was to receive the first number of the story, whose nature he had kept from her to give her a pleasant surprise, and to find that her desire of a literary course for Hardy was in fair way of being justified.

In the first week of January 1874 the story was noticed in a marked degree by the *Spectator*, and a guess hazarded that it might be from the pen of George Eliot – why, the author could never understand, since, so far as he had read that great thinker – one of the greatest living, he thought, though not a born storyteller by any means – she had never touched the life of the fields: her country-people having seemed to him, too, more like small townsfolk than rustics; and as evidencing a woman's wit cast in country dialogue rather than real country humour, which he regarded as rather of the Shakespeare and Fielding sort. However, he conjectured, as a possible reason for the flattering guess, that he had latterly been reading Comte's *Positive Philosophy*, and writings of that school, some of whose expressions had thus passed into his vocabulary, expressions which were also common to George Eliot. Leslie Stephen wrote:

'I am glad to congratulate you on the reception of your first number. Besides the gentle *Spectator*, which thinks that you must be George Eliot because you know the names of the stars, several good judges have spoken to me warmly of the *Madding Crowd*. Moreover the *Spectator*, though flighty in its head, has really a good deal of critical feeling. I always like to be praised by it – and indeed by other people! . . . The story comes out very well, I think, and I have no criticism to make.'

Respecting the public interest in the opening of the story, in later days Miss Thackeray informed him, with some of her father's humour, that to inquiries with which she was beseiged on the sex of the author, and requests to be given an introduction to him or her, she would reply: '*It* lives in the country, and I could not very well introduce you to *it* in Town.' . . .

. . . Having attracted so much attention Hardy now again withdrew into retreat at Bockhampton to get ahead with the novel, which was in a lamentably unadvanced condition, writing to Stephen, when requesting that the proofs might be sent to the hermitage: 'I have decided to finish it here, which is within a walk of the district in which the incidents are supposed to occur. I find it a great advantage to be actually among the people described at the time of describing them.'

However, that he did not care much for a reputation as a novelist in lieu of being able to follow the pursuit of poetry – now for ever hindered, as it seemed – becomes obvious from a remark written to Mr Stephen about this time:

'The truth is that I am willing, and indeed anxious, to give up any points which may be desirable in a story when read as a whole, for the sake of others which shall please those who read it in numbers. Perhaps I may have higher aims some day, and be a great stickler for the proper artistic balance of the completed work, but for the present circumstances lead me to wish merely to be considered a good hand at a serial.' . . .

A peculiarity in the local descriptions running through all Hardy's writings may be instanced here – that he never uses the word 'Dorset', never names the county at all (except possibly in an explanatory footnote), but obliterates the names of the six counties, whose area he traverses in his scenes, under the general appellation of 'Wessex' – an old word that became quite popular after the date of *Far from the Madding Crowd*, where he first introduced it. So far did he carry this idea of the unity of Wessex that he used to say he had grown to forget the crossing of county boundaries within the ancient kingdom – in this respect being quite unlike the poet Barnes, who was 'Dorset' emphatically. . . .

[pp. 95–8, 99–100, 122–3]

Comments during composition of 'The Woodlanders'

1885 . . . '*November* 17–19. In a fit of depression, as if enveloped in a leaden cloud. Have gone back to my original plot for *The Woodlanders* after all. Am working from half-past ten A.M. to twelve P.M., to get my mind made up on the details.'

'*November* 21–22. Sick headache.'

'Tragedy. It may be put thus in brief: a tragedy exhibits a state of things in the life of an individual which unavoidably causes some natural aim or desire of his to end in a catastrophe when carried out.'

. . .

'*December* 9. "Everything looks so little – so ghastly little!" A local exclamation heard.'

'*December* 12. Experience *un*teaches – (what one at first thinks to be the rule in events).'

'*December* 21. The Hypocrisy of things. Nature is an arch-dissembler. A child is deceived completely; the older members of society more or less according to their penetration; though even they seldom get to realize that *nothing* is as it appears.'

'*December* 31. This evening, the end of the old year 1885 finds me sadder than many previous New Year's Eves have done. Whether building this house at Max Gate was a wise expenditure of energy is one doubt, which, if resolved in the negative, is depressing enough. And there are others. But:

'"This is the chief thing: Be not perturbed; for all things are according to the nature of the universal." ' [Marcus Aurelius.]

1886. '*January* 2 . . . Cold weather brings out upon the faces of people the written marks of their habits, vices, passions, and memories, as warmth brings out on paper a writing in sympathetic ink. The drunkard looks still more a drunkard when the splotches have their margins made distinct by frost, the hectic blush becomes a stain now, the cadaverous complexion reveals the bone under, the quality of handsomeness is reduced to its lowest terms.'

'*January* 3. My art is to intensify the expression of things, as is done by Crivelli, Bellini, etc., so that the heart and inner meaning is made vividly visible.'

'*Janurary* 6. Misapprehension. The shrinking soul thinks its weak place is going to be laid bare, and shows its thought by a suddenly clipped manner. The other shrinking soul thinks the clipped manner of the first to be the result of its own weakness in some way, not of its strength, and shows its fear also by its constrained air! So they withdraw from each other and misunderstand.'

'*March* 4. Novel-writing as an art cannot go backward. Having reached the analytic stage it must transcend it by going still further in the same direction. Why not by rendering as visible essences, spectres, etc., the abstract thoughts of the analytic school?'

This notion was approximately carried out, not in a novel, but through the much more appropriate medium of poetry, in the supernatural framework of *The Dynasts* as also in smaller poems. And a further note of the same date enlarges the same idea:

'The human race to be shown as one great network or tissue which quivers in every part when one point is shaken, like a spider's web if touched. Abstract realisms to be in the form of Spirits, Spectral figures, etc.

'The Realities to be the true realities of life, hitherto called abstractions. The old material realities to be placed behind the former, as shadowy accessories.' ...   [pp. 176, 177]

On the ending of 'The Woodlanders'

... About this time [July 1889] Hardy was asked by a writer of some experience in adapting novels for the theatre – Mr J. T. Grein – if he would grant permission for *The Woodlanders* to be so adapted. In his reply he says:

'You have probably observed that the ending of the story – hinted rather than stated – is that the heroine is doomed to an unhappy life with an inconstant husband. I could not accentuate this strongly in the book, by reason of the conventions of the libraries, etc. Since the story was written, however, truth to character is not considered quite such a crime in literature as it was formerly; and it is therefore a question for you whether you will accent this ending, or prefer to obscure it.'

It appears that nothing arose out of the dramatization, it becoming obvious that no English manager at this date would venture to defy the formalities to such an extent as was required by the novel, in which some of the situations were approximately of the kind afterwards introduced to English playgoers by translations from Ibsen. ...   [pp. 220–1]

SOURCE: excerpts from Florence Emily Hardy, *The Life of Thomas Hardy, 1840–1928* (London, 1928, 1930; reissued in one volume, 1962); in fact, written by Hardy himself.

PART TWO

Reviews and Early Criticism

Reviews and Early Criticism

Horace Moule   (1872)

On *Under the Greenwood Tree*

This novel is the best prose idyl that we have seen for a long while past. Deserting the more conventional, and far less agreeable, field of imaginative creation which he worked in his earlier book, called *Desperate Remedies*, the author has produced a series of rural pictures full of life and genuine colouring, and drawn with a distinct minuteness reminding one at times of some of the scenes in *Hermann und Dorothea*. Anyone who knows tolerably well the remoter parts of the South-Western counties of England will be able to judge for himself of the power and truthfulness shown in these studies of the better class of rustics, men whose isolated lives have not impaired a shrewd common sense and insight, together with a complete independence, set off by native humour, which is excellently represented in these two volumes.

Reuben Dewy, the 'tranter' or irregular carrier, is the principal character in the book, and is the most fully worked-out type of the class we have been mentioning. At the very outset of events, during the rounds made by the Christmas 'waits' of Mellstock parish church, Dick Dewy, the son and partner of Reuben, falls in love with Fancy Day, daughter of a neighbouring keeper well to do in the world, and newly appointed schoolmistress of the parish. The 'course of true love' in this simple village couple, interrupted only by the gawky attentions of Mr Shiner,[1] a wealthy farmer and churchwarden, and by a curious episode with the vicar towards the end, forms the unpretending thread of the story. But the subsidiary scenes, such as the description of the carol-singers' rounds, the village-party at the tranter's, the interview of the choir with the vicar, and the bee-taking at the keeper Geoffrey Day's, are worked in with as much care as if the writer had been constructing a sensation plot of the received model; and each one of these scenes contributes its share to a really pleasant and entertaining whole.

Under the Greenwood Tree is filled with touches showing the close sympathy with which the writer has watched the life, not only of his fellow-men in the country hamlets, but of woods and fields and all the outward forms of nature. But the staple of the book is made up of personal sketches, the foremost figure, as we have said, being that of the 'tranter' Dewy, a man 'full of human nature', fond of broaching his cider with his village friends about him, straightforward and outspoken, yet inclined from good nature towards compromise, not however to the excessive degree that his duties as publican imposed upon Mr Snell in *Silas Marner*. Grouped around the tranter are several figures, all distinctive and good in their way, the chief of whom are old William Dewy, the grandfather, and the leader in all things musical, Mr Penny the bootmaker, and Thomas Leaf, who sang treble in the choir at a preternaturally late date, and whose upper G could not be dispensed with, though he was otherwise 'deficient', and awkward in his movements, 'apparently on account of having grown so fast that before he had had time to grow used to his height he was higher'. . . .

It is strong praise of any book to say that, besides being a novel of great humour and general merit, it would make no bad manual for any one who, from duty or from choice, is desirous to learn something of the inner life of a rural parish. Yet *Under the Greenwood Tree* fairly deserves the amount of praise. It is a book that might well lie on the table of any well-ordered country house, and that might also be borne in mind by the readers during kindly rounds undertaken among the cottages. There are, to be sure, weak points in the writing. The love passages of Dick and Fancy incline here and there to be unnecessarily prolonged, and it is needful throughout to recollect that they are being faithfully drawn as *rustic* lovers. There is also one definite fault in the dialogues, though it makes its appearance only at wide intervals. We mean an occasional tendency of the country folk, not so much to think with something of subtle distinction (for cottagers can do that much more completely than the well-dressed world are apt to suppose), but to express themselves in the language of the author's manner of thought, rather than in their own. The tranter, for example, should not be allowed to call the widow Leaf (in an otherwise very amusing passage) an 'imaginative woman on the subject of children'; nor should old William speak of barrel-organs and harmoniums, even though he has wound himself up for a great effort, as 'miserable machines for such a divine thing as music'.

There is nothing better in the whole book than the pictures of Geoffrey Day and his house in the greenwood. Geoffrey was a man of few words. His neighbours were fully alive to this 'Silent', they would say: 'ah, he is silent! That man's silence is wonderful to listen to. Every moment of it is brimming over with sound understanding.' His trapper Enoch was almost as silent as himself. This man was admitted to take his dinner at the keeper's table, and would come in behind his master, at the carefully considered interval of three minutes. 'Four minutes had been found to express indifference to indoor arrangements, and simultaneousness had implied too great an anxiety about meals.' . . .

The double sets of furniture, one being destined for Fancy whenever she should marry, and the two eight-day clocks, 'which were severally two and a half minutes and three minutes striking the hour of twelve', and which bore respectively the names of two rival clockmakers, long since departed, Thomas Wood and Ezekiel Sparrowgrass² – these and innumerable other touches combine to make up the picture of an interior entirely justifying the author's mention of the Dutch school upon his title-page. The bee-taking we must leave alone, though it is a thoroughly amusing and well-drawn scene; and the same may be said of the passage about Elizabeth Endorfield, the witch, or, in more modified terms, the 'deep body, who was as long-headed as she was high'. We will take leave of Geoffrey with one brief and characteristic touch, which will come home to any one who has observed the ways of dogs. Having been out with his trapper, he had been made unusually pensive by that person's account of the pining state into which Fancy had been thrown by her father's temporary refusal of Dick's offer, and his preference for Mr Shiner. Upon this 'the keeper resumed his gun, tucked it under his arm, and went on without whistling to the dogs, who however followed, with a bearing meant to convey that they did not expect any such attentions when their master was reflecting'. It is needless to say that their master soon relented, and that all ends happily. The portraiture of Fancy herself conveys a kind of satire on the average character of a girl with good looks, capable of sound and honest affection, but inordinately moved by admiration. Serious mischief threatens for a moment, just towards the close, on the side of the Vicar; but this episode, whether wisely introduced or not, is too brief to signify much in the working out of the story.

Regarded as a whole, we repeat our opinion that the book is one of unusual merit in its own special line, full of humour and keen observation, and with the genuine air of the country breathing throughout it. . . .

SOURCE: extracts from article in *Saturday Review*, XXXIV (28 September 1872).

NOTES

1. Our revision. The name was spelled as 'Shinar' in the first edition, and so given in Moule's review.

2. The name was revised by Hardy to 'Ezekiel Saunders' after the first edition.

Henry James (1874)

On *Far from the Madding Crowd*

Mr Hardy's novel came into the world under brilliant auspices – such as the declaration by the London *Spectator* that either George Eliot had written it or George Eliot had found her match. One could make out in a manner what the *Spectator* meant. To guess, one has only to open *Far from the Madding Crowd* at random: 'Mr Jan Coggan, who had passed the cup to Henery, was a crimson man with a spacious countenance and a private glimmer in his eye, whose name had appeared on the marriage register of Weatherbury and neighbouring parishes as best-man and chief witness in countless unions of the previous twenty years; he also very frequently filled the post of head godfather in baptisms of the subtly-jovial kind.' That is a very fair imitation of George Eliot's humorous manner. Here is a specimen of her serious one: 'He fancied he had felt himself in the penumbra of a very deep sadness when touching that slight and fragile creature. But wisdom lies in moderating mere impressions, and Gabriel endeavoured to think little of this.' . . .

. . . The author has evidently read to good purpose the low-life chapters in George Eliot's novels; he has caught very happily her trick of seeming to humour benignantly her queer people and look down at them from the heights of analytic omniscience. But we have quoted the episode because it seems to us an excellent example of the cleverness which is only cleverness, of the difference between original and imitative talent – the disparity, which it is almost unpardonable not to perceive, between first-rate talent and those inferior grades which range from second-rate downward, and as to which confusion is a more venial offence. Mr Hardy puts his figures through a variety of comical movements; he fills their mouths with quaint turns of speech; he baptizes them with odd names ('Joseph Poorgrass' for a bashful, easily-snubbed Dissenter is excellent); he pulls the wires, in short, and produces a vast deal of sound and commotion; and his novel, at a cursory glance, has a rather promising air of life and warmth. But by critics who prefer a grain of substance to a pound of shadow it will, we think, be pronounced a decidedly delusive performance; it has a fatal lack of magic. We have found it hard to read, but its shortcomings are easier to summarize than to encounter in order. Mr Hardy's novel is very long, but his subject is very short and simple, and the work has been distended to its rather formidable dimensions by the infusion of a large amount of conversational and descriptive padding and the use of an ingeniously verbose and redundant style. It is inordinately diffuse, and, as a piece of narrative, singularly inartistic. The author has little sense of proportion, and almost none of composition. We learn about Bathsheba and Gabriel, Farmer Boldwood and Sergeant Troy, what we can rather than what we should; for Mr Hardy's inexhaustible faculty for spinning smart dialogue makes him forget that dialogue in a story is after all but episode, and that a novelist is after all but a historian, thoroughly possessed of certain facts, and bound in some way or other to impart them. To tell a story almost exclusively by reporting people's talks is the most difficult art in the world, and really leads, logically, to a severe economy in the use of rejoinder and repartee, and not to a lavish expenditure of them. *Far from the Madding Crowd* gives us an uncomfortable sense of being a simple 'tale', pulled and stretched to make the conventional three volumes; and the author, in his long-sustained appeal to one's attention, reminds us of a person fishing with an enormous net, of which the meshes should be thrice too wide.

We are happily not subject, in this (as to minor matters) much-emancipated land, to the tyranny of the three volumes; but we confess that we are nevertheless being rapidly urged to a conviction that (since it is in the nature of fashions to revolve and recur) the day has come round again for some of the antique restrictions as to literary form. The three unities, in Aristotle's day, were inexorably imposed on Greek tragedy: why shouldn't we have something of the same sort for English fiction in the day of Mr Hardy? Almost all novels are greatly too long, and the being too long becomes with each elapsing year a more serious offence. Mr Hardy begins with a detailed description of his hero's smile, and proceeds thence to give a voluminous account of his large silver watch. Gabriel Oak's smile and his watch were doubtless respectable and important phenomena; but everything is relative, and daily becoming more so; and we confess that, as a hint of the pace at which the author proposed to proceed, his treatment of these facts produced upon us a deterring and depressing effect. If novels were the only books written, novels written on this scale would be all very well; but as they compete, in the esteem of sensible people, with a great many other books, and a great many other objects of interest of all kinds, we are inclined to think that, in the long run, they will be defeated in the struggle for existence unless they lighten their baggage very considerably and do battle in a more scientific equipment. Therefore, we really imagine that a few arbitrary rules – a kind of depleting process – might have a wholesome effect. It might be enjoined, for instance, that no 'tale' should exceed fifty pages and no novel two hundred; that a plot should have but such and such a number of ramifications; that no ramification should have more than a certain number of persons; that no person should utter more than a given number of words; and that no description of an inanimate object, should consist of more than a fixed number of lines. We should not incline to advocate this oppressive legislation as a comfortable or ideal finality for the romancer's art, but we think it might be excellent as a transitory discipline or drill. Necessity is the mother of invention, and writers with a powerful tendency to expatiation might in this temporary strait-jacket be induced to transfer their attention rather more severely from quantity to quality. The use of the strait-jacket would have cut down Mr Hardy's novel to half its actual length and, as he is a clever man, have made the abbreviated work very ingeniously pregnant. We should have had a more occasional taste of all the barn-yard worthies – Joseph Poorgrass, Laban Tall, Matthew Moon, and the rest – and the vagaries of Miss Bathsheba would have had a more sensible consistency. Our restrictions would have been generous, however, and we should not have proscribed such a fine passage as this:

Then there came a third flash. Manoeuvres of the most extraordinary kind were going on in the vast firmamental hollows overhead. The lightning now was the colour of silver, and gleamed in the heavens like a mailed army. Rumbles became rattles. Gabriel, from his elevated position, could see over the landscape for at least half a dozen miles in front. Every hedge, bush, and tree was distinct as in a line engraving. In a paddock in the same direction was a herd of heifers, and the forms of these were visible at this moment in the act of galloping about in the wildest and maddest confusion, flinging their heels and tails high into the air, their heads to earth. A poplar in the immediate foreground was like an ink-stroke on burnished tin. Then the picture vanished, leaving a darkness so intense that Gabriel worked entirely by feeling with his hands.

Mr Hardy describes nature with a great deal of felicity, and is evidently very much at home among rural phenomena. The most genuine thing in his book, to our sense, is a certain aroma of the meadows and lanes – a natural relish for harvesting and sheep-washings. He has laid his scene in an agricultural county, and his characters are children of the soil – unsophisticated country-folk. Bathsheba Everdene is a rural heiress, left alone in the world, in possession of a substantial farm. Gabriel Oak is her shepherd, Farmer Boldwood is her neighbour, and Sergeant Troy is a loose young soldier who comes a-courting her. They are all in love with her, and the young lady is a flirt, and encourages them all. Finally she marries the Sergeant, who has just seduced her maid-servant. The maid-servant dies in the workhouse, the Sergeant repents, leaves his wife, and is given up for drowned. But he reappears and is shot by Farmer Boldwood, who delivers himself up to justice. Bathsheba then marries Gabriel Oak, who has loved and waited in silence, and is, in our opinion, much too good for her. The chief purpose of the book is, we suppose, to represent Gabriel's dumb, devoted passion, his biding his time, his rendering unsuspected services to the woman who has scorned him, his integrity and simplicity and sturdy patience. In all this the tale is very fairly successful, and Gabriel has a certain vividness of expression. But we cannot say that we either understand or like Bathsheba. She is a young lady of the inconsequential, wilful, mettlesome type which has lately become so much the fashion for heroines, and of which Mr Charles Reade is in a manner the inventor – the type which aims at giving one a very intimate sense of a young lady's *womanishness*. But Mr Hardy's embodiment of it seems to us to lack reality; he puts her through the Charles Reade paces, but she remains alternately vague and coarse, and seems always artificial. This is Mr Hardy's trouble: he rarely gets beyond ambitious artifice – the mechanical simulation of heat and depth and wisdom that are absent. Farmer Boldwood is a shadow, and Sergeant Troy an elaborate stage-figure. Everything human in the book strikes us as factitious and insubstantial; the only things we believe in are the sheep and the dogs. But, as we say, Mr Hardy has gone astray very cleverly, and his superficial novel is a really curious imitation of something better.

SOURCE: extracts from review article in *Nation* (New York, 24 December 1874); reprinted in A. Mordell (ed.), *Literary Reviews and Essays by Henry James* (1957).

Anonymous   (1875)

On *Far from the Madding Crowd*

Mr Hardy still lingers in the pleasant byways of pastoral and agricultural life which he made familiar to his readers in his former novels, *Under the Greenwood Tree* and *A Pair of Blue Eyes*. Indeed the first of these can hardly be called a novel. It was rather a series of rustic sketches – Dutch paintings of English country scenes after the manner of *Silas Marner*. But, like its successor, *A Pair of Blue Eyes*, it brought with it a genuine fresh flavour of the country, and of a part of the country that has not yet become hackneyed. There was promise, too, in both these books of something really good being produced in future works. And that promise, though not quite fulfilled, is given again in *Far from the Madding Crowd*. It is nearer fulfilment than it was, though much nearer in the first half of the first volume than in the remainder of the book, where the characters both of the heroine and of the hero fall off. But there is still a good deal wanting, and Mr Hardy has much to learn, or perhaps we ought to say, to unlearn, before he can be placed in the first order of modern English novelists. He takes trouble, and is not in a hurry to work off his sketches. They are imaginative, drawn from the inside, and highly finished. They show power also of probing and analysing the deeper shades of character, and showing how characters are affected, and how destinies are influenced for good or evil, by the circumstances which act upon them. But Mr Hardy disfigures his pages by bad writing, by clumsy and inelegant metaphors, and by mannerism and affectation. What, for instance, could be worse as a piece of composition than the following?

His tone was so utterly removed from all she had expected as a beginning. It was lowness and quiet accented: an emphasis of deep meanings, their form, at the same time, being scarcely expressed. Silence has sometimes a remarkable power of showing itself as the disembodied soul of feeling wandering without its carcase, and it is then more impressive than speech.

The grammar in this passage is faulty, the metaphor is far-fetched and awkward, the thought poor, and the expression of it affected. Again, how could a man of good taste – and good taste Mr Hardy certainly has – permit this hideous metaphor to appear? – 'It' ('the element of folly') 'was introduced as lymph on the dart of Eros, and eventually permeated and coloured her whole constitution'. A quack doctor before the days of Public Vaccinators might have written such a sentence as a taking advertisement. But a man of refinement, and not without a sense of humour, might surely have put the not unprecedented fact that a girl fell in love with a soldier in simpler and less professional language. Why, again, should he talk of Bathsheba's beauty 'belonging rather to the redeemed-demonian than to the blemished-angelic school', or of 'a little slip of humanity for alarming potentialities of exploit', or of 'the spherical completeness of his existence heretofore slowly spreading into an abnormal distortion in the particular direction of an ideal passion'? Eccentricities of style are not characteristic of genius, nor of original thinking. If Mr Hardy is not possessed of genius, he is possessed of something quite good enough for the ordinary purposes of novel-writing to make him independent of anything like counterfeit originality or far-fetched modes of thought. If he has the self-control to throw aside his tendency to strain after metaphorical effects, and if he will cultivate simplicity of diction as effectually as he selects simple and natural subjects to write about, he may mellow into a considerable novelist. But if he suffers this tendency to grow into a habit – and there is quite as much of it in this as in his previous novels – he will very speedily lose the not inconsiderable reputation which he has justly gained.

Mr Hardy, whether by force of circumstances or by fortunate selection, has in this story hit upon a new vein of rich metal for his fictitious scenes. The English Bœotian has never been so idealised before. Ordinary men's notions of the farm-labourer of the Southern counties have all been blurred and confused. It has been the habit of an ignorant and unwisely philanthropic age to look upon him as an untaught, unreflecting, badly paid, and badly fed animal, ground down by hard and avaricious farmers, and very little, if at all, raised by intelligence above the brutes and beasts to whom he ministers. These notions are ruthlessly overturned by Mr Hardy's novel. Under his hand Bœotians became Athenians in acuteness, Germans in capacity for philosophic speculation, and Parisians in polish. Walter Scott has left many sketches and some highly finished portraits of the humbler class of Scotch peasants, and has brought out the national shrewdness and humour, and the moral and intellectual 'pawkiness' for which that class of Scotch society is justly celebrated. But he had good material to work on and two out of every three of his characters were in all probability drawn from life. George Eliot in her early books, and even in *Felix Holt*, has drawn specimens of the illiterate class who talk theology like the Bench of Bishops – except that they are all Dissenters – and politics like the young Radicals who sit, or used to sit, below the gangway. But the reader felt that the author had seen these rustic theologians and politicians and heard their conversations. Shakespeare also has his metaphysical clowns ready by force of mother-wit to discuss generalities on most subjects. But neither his clowns, nor George Eliot's rustics, nor Scott's peasants, rise to anything like the flights of abstract reasoning with which Mr Hardy credits his cider-drinking boors. Humorous many of his descriptions of them certainly are; as, for instance, the following account of the various ways in which the news of Bathsheba's sheep breaking fence on Sunday and 'blasting' themselves with young clover affected the farm servants individually:

Joseph's countenance was drawn into lines and puckers by his concern. Fray's forehead was wrinkled both perpendicularly and crosswise, after the pattern of a portcullis, expressive of a double despair. Laban Tall's lips were thin, and his face was rigid. Matthew's jaws sank, and his eyes turned whichever way the strongest muscle happened to pull them.

'Yes', said Joseph, 'and I was sitting at home, looking for Ephesians, and says I to myself, " 'Tis nothing but Corinthians and Thessalonians in this danged Testament", when who should come in but Henery there: "Joseph", he said, "the sheep have blasted themselves –".'

No objection could be taken to the treatment of these choruses of agricultural labourers if it were confined to such descriptions. But when we find one of these labourers – 'a cherry-faced' shepherd lad, 'with a small circular orifice by way of a mouth' – discourse on ecclesiastical politics in this style –

'There's two religions going on in the nation now, High Church and High Chapel. And thinks I, I'll play fair; so I went to High Church in the morning and High Chapel in the afternoon . . . Well at High Church they pray singing, and believe in all the colours of the rainbow; and at High Chapel they pray preaching, and believe in drab and whitewash only.'

– we feel either that we have misjudged the unenfranchised agricultural classes, or that Mr Hardy has put his own thoughts and words into their mouths. And this suspicion necessarily shakes our confidence in the truthfulness of many of the idyllic incidents of rustic life which are so plentifully narrated throughout these volumes. The descriptions of the farming operations, for instance, the sheepshearing, and the haymaking, and the sheep-washing, with the tender episode attached to it, and the lambing in the cold winter months among the snow, are graphically given. There is a vivid reality about the description of the fire in the farmsteading, the terrible thunderstorm that ruined love-lorn Farmer Boldwood's stacks, though it failed to awaken the drunken revellers in Bathsheba's barn, and the midnight pursuit of Bathsheba when she stole away to Bath. Then there is that most unconventional picture in 'the hollow amid the ferns.' Here Sergeant Troy with startling dexterity performs a rape of a lock from the shoulder of his mistress with a cut of a heavy cavalry sabre – or, as Mr Hardy more finely puts it, with 'a circumambient gleam accompanied by a keen sibilation that was almost a whistle' – and in the next moment transfixes with the same instrument a caterpillar on her breast, or, to use the gallant Sergeant's words, 'gave point to her bosom where the caterpillar was, and instead of running her through, checked the extension a thousandth of an inch short of her surface'. Doubting the authenticity of the conversations, we are led to question the truthfulness of such scenes as these. Are they a faithful rendering of real events taking place from time to time in the South-Western counties, or are they not imaginary creations with possibly some small groundwork of reality?

These are difficulties which suggest themselves to the most cursory reader. But perhaps it does not very much matter (except to the student of the political capabilities of the agricultural labourer) whether either the conversations or the descriptions are true or false. They are in keeping with the general character of the novel to this extent, that they are worked up with unusual skill and care. Each scene is a study in itself, and, within its own limits, effective. And they all fit into the story like pieces of an elaborate puzzle, making, when they are so fitted in, an effective whole. Mr Hardy's art consists principally in the way in which he pieces his scenes one with the other. He determines, for instance, that the moral discipline through which his heroine has to pass to render her a fitting helpmate to Gabriel Oak shall culminate in the scene where she sees her husband weeping over the coffin of her rival and kissing her dead lips. But how is this crisis to be brought about in a natural and ordinary way? Fanny Robin dies in the workhouse, and Joseph Poorgrass is sent for her coffin so that she may have a decent burial in the parish churchyard by Bathsheba's house. Joseph arrives late on an autumn afternoon. Driving homewards, with his burden covered over with evergreens, a thick sea fog – the first of the autumn fogs – rolls up quite naturally, overshadowing the whole country, and wetting Joseph to the skin. By the roadside, not two miles from the churchyard where the parson is waiting for him, stands the 'Buck's Head Inn'. Wet and miserable, Joseph cannot pass the familiar door. Two of his boon companions – 'owners of the two most appreciative throats in the neighbourhood' – are in the warm kitchen sitting face to face over a three-legged circular table like 'the setting sun and the full moon shining *vis-à-vis*

across the globe'. They drink and talk as only Mr Hardy's rustics
can talk, especially with such a topic as death for a text, and
Joseph joins them – his sense of duty urging him to leave, but the
talk and the drink prevailing on him to stay. Oak comes in upon
them, and, finding Joseph helpless, leaves him in the inn, and
drives the cart to the churchyard. The parson is still there, though
the night is closing in. It is not too late. But 'Have you the
Registrar's certificate?' No, Joseph had omitted to give it, and
Joseph was two miles off, at the 'Buck's Head', helplessly drunk.
The funeral had to be put off, and the coffin is taken for the night
to Bathsheba's house. Thus Bathsheba learned the secret of poor
Fanny's death, and saw revealed to her Troy's selfish perfidy to
Fanny, and felt the weight of his cruelty to herself. And this, the
most dramatic incident in the book, is brought about by what? By
Joseph Poorgrass's innocently and naturally going into the 'Buck's
Head' to warm himself at the kitchen fire. In this careful fitting in
of the pieces of his puzzle, and in the use of trifling circumstances
either to work up to the *dénouement* or to prepare the mind for the
incidents which are to follow, Mr Hardy shows his skill. The book
is prodigal of incidents apparently irreconcilable with each other.
But by delicate contrivances of the kind indicated they are made to
cohere, and to form a connected and not altogether incredible
story.

It is impossible to give the roughest outline of the plot, nor can
we even attempt to analyse the characters. 'Bathsheba and her
Lovers' the novel might have been called (except that its own title
is very much better), and the interest of the story consists in
contrasting the three lovers in their respective attitudes towards the
heroine. She is a rustic beauty fond of admiration, loving her
independence, without much heart but with a brave spirit, a sharp
hand at a bargain, an arrant flirt over-flowing with vanity, but
modest withal. 'As a girl, had she been put into a low dress, she
would have run and thrust her head into a bush; yet she was not a
shy girl by any means. It was merely her instinct to draw the line
dividing the seen from the unseen higher than they do in towns.'
'She has her faults', says Oak to the toll-keeper, after his first
meeting with her, 'and the greatest of them is – well, what it is
always – vanity.' 'I want somebody to tame me', she says herself;
'I'm too independent.' Oak is not the man to perform so difficult
an achievement. He has too many Christian characteristics and too
limited a power of utterance to succeed with Bathsheba. He finds
difficulty in 'mapping out his mind upon his tongue'. He wishes she
knew his impressions, but 'he would as soon have thought of

carrying an odour in a net as attempting to convey the intangibilities of his feeling in the coarse meshes of language.' He serves her like a faithful dog for many weary years, suffering patiently more than the usual share of ill-treatment, until, after various vicissitudes in her existence and in that of her two more favoured lovers, he finally reaps the reward of his dumb devotion.

The main stream of the narrative, though sparkling with fun, and sunshine, and green fields, is deeply tragic, culminating in murder, madness, and something very like what Jan Coggan (one of the rustics) calls 'committing the seventh'. But inside the main stream and eddying, as it were, beneath it, there runs a sad episode, the episode of Fanny Robin. She appears only three times; once when she meets Oak on the night of the fire when she is running away from home; a second time, wandering all alone by the riverside in the dark winter night, and attempting to attract Troy's attention by feebly throwing little fragments of snow at his barrack-room window 'till the wall must have become pimpled with the adhering lumps of snow'; and a third time struggling faintly and with faltering steps to the workhouse, when her exhausted nature could scarce support the weight of the wretched burden it had to bear. The author has put out his whole force in the description of these last two incidents. The first is original. The second may have been suggested by the well-known chapter in *Adam Bede* entitled 'The Journey in Despair'. But, whether so suggested or not, it stands comparison not unfairly even with that most painful narrative of the shipwreck of a girl's life. And the power and taste which Mr Hardy shows in these scenes and in others, some of which we have noticed indirectly, justify the belief that, if he will only throw aside his mannerism and eccentricity, and devote himself zealously to the cultivation of his art, he may rise to a high position among English novelists.

SOURCE: unsigned review article in *Saturday Review* xxxix (9 January 1875), pp. 57–8.

Anonymous   (1887)

On *The Woodlanders*

In *The Woodlanders* Mr Hardy returns to that region of Wessex in which his early successes were made. Without attempting too rashly to conjecture the exact scene of the story, we can plainly enough gather from indications which the author gives that it lies near the centre of the county of Dorset, not far from the hilly and orchard-covered confines of the beautiful Vale of Blackmore. This district inspired the most characteristic pieces of the late Mr Barnes; and it is sequestered, picturesque, and individual enough to be well worthy of the devotion of a poet or a novelist. Mr Hardy has treated other parts of his native county before, but we have not found ourselves in exactly the company we meet with in *The Woodlanders* since he published *Under the Greenwood Tree*.

The opening pages of *The Woodlanders* give a very impressive notion of the solitude that reigns over vast tracts in this region of orchards. The villages are few and far apart, and they are apt to lie just off the desolate high-road, up cosy lanes, as though to escape the notice of those who walk and drive along the highway. It is in the concentration of a woodland village, where all persons are known to one another, and all are thrown upon the emotional resources of each other, that great dramas may be silently enacted, in the simplicity of an almost primitive form of society. Mr Hardy, as he has so often proved, enjoys nothing so much as to observe the effect of bringing the unsophisticated elements of village life into contact with the world and outer fashion. It is his peculiarity that, while others have so freely chronicled the comic elements of the result, he has been mainly drawn to the tragic ones. The tone of his best novels, as will have been observed, is almost always what the old playwrights knew as tragi-comical, the solemn problems of life being presented in his pages tempered by the humours of what is often little else than a chorus of peasants. In *The Woodlanders* we find the natural order of development in a cider-village disturbed by two figures whose place should be rather in London or Paris than in a remote Dorsetshire community. These two personages set all the woodland music in a discord, and what would else be comedy comes in their hands to a tragic issue.

In the tiny village of Little Hintock the principal native inhabitant is a timber merchant of the name of Melbury, whose one daughter,

Grace, has been educated, as the saying runs, 'above her station'. She is absent when the story opens, but is expected home very shortly. By an old vague agreement Grace Melbury is half-betrothed to Giles Winterborne, a fine young fellow engaged in the apple trade. This man is the hero of the story. Several of the villagers, and Winterborne in particular, keep the tenure of their houses upon lifehold, and are at the mercy of the lady of the manor. This is a very eccentric personage, widow of a rich man much older than herself, who married her off the stage, and who has died, leaving her quite young. Mrs Charmond is seldom at Hintock House, and when she appears she is not much approved of. Her manners are thus discussed by some spar-makers at work:

'My brother-in-law told me, and I have no reason to doubt it', said Creedle, 'that she'd sit down to her dinner with a frock hardly higher than her elbows. "Oh, you wicked woman!" he said to himself when he first saw her; "you go to your church, and sit, and kneel, as if your knee-joints were greased with very saint's anointment, and tell off your hear-us-good Lords as pat as a business man counting money; and yet you can eat your victuals such a figure as that!" Whether she's a reformed character by this time I can't say; but I don't care who the man is, that's how she went on when my brother-in-law lived there.'

The other disturbing element is a Dr Fitzpiers, a young physician of great, though superficial, abilities and dangerous good looks, who settles at Little Hintock, to be in the midst of a country practice. Another leading character is Marty South, a taciturn, lonely girl, who lives by making spars, and who nourishes a dumb and hopeless love for Giles Winterborne. These are the principal characters which unite to form the impassioned drama of this romance.

It is in no carping spirit, but rather to ensure that justice should be done to Mr Hardy, that we venture to encourage the reader to go carefully through the early chapters of the first volume of *The Woodlanders*. They will probably feel, with ourselves, that after the very felicitous opening scene with Marty South in her cottage, the narrative becomes not a little stiff and laboured for several chapters. We do not remember any previous book in which Mr Hardy has been so unfortunate as he is here in making Melbury get out of bed and walk in his garden at two o'clock in the morning in order that his wife may follow him, and may be told certain incidents in his early life in tones loud enough to be heard by Marty South, who also happens, providentially, to be out in her garden at that unearthly hour. This, or we are much mistaken, is forced indeed. But Mr Hardy soon warms to his work, throws off what may perhaps be signs of fatigue, and, by the time he is half-way through the first volume, has completely recovered his tone. The second volume is, in our opinion, one of the best that he has ever written, and the third is little inferior to it. It is a pity that the beginning of the book should have the air of being written in defiance of Minerva.

While we are finding fault, we may as well have our quarrel out with Mr Hardy. We are not of those who call in question the wit and ingenuity of the conversation which he puts into the mouths of his countryfolk. The objection to such talk as unnatural is made by those who do not know the Wessex yeoman and journeyman, by those who, when they meet an inhabitant, talk over his head with their London jargon, or strike him into suspicious and sarcastic silence by their fashionable airs. But, although we know the Dorsetshire man too well not to be aware that Mr Hardy holds the secret of his speech, and perfectly well understands what he is doing in reproducing his idiom, we yet think that the novelist is a little inconsistent in his standard of conversation. It appears to us that he vacillates between giving an exact facsimile of the village talk and doing what many French novelists think it proper to do – that is to say, putting pure town talk into the lips of their peasants. We will give an instance of what we conceive to be confusion in this matter from the amusing passage at the beginning of volume II, where Grammer Oliver talks to Grace about the bargain she had made to sell her brain for dissection after death to Dr Fitzpiers. Most of this conversation is in the broadest Dorset, with its delightful appeal to the girl to 'save a poor old woman's skellington from a heathen's chopper'; but it ends thus:

Ay, one can joke when one is well, even in old age; *but in sickness one's gaiety falters*; and that which seemed small looks large, and the grim far-off seems near.

This, surely, strikes a thoroughly false note, especially the words which we have italicised, than which nothing less in keeping with poor old Grammer's habits of mind or speech could well be conceived. Occasional lapses of this kind, and a habit of using strained and over-technical words for simple things, seem to us to be the snares against which Mr Hardy needs to guard himself.

We are giving, however, but a poor idea of the richness and humanity of the book. Mr Hardy has not often drawn a more sympathetic character than that of the undemonstrative, patient, and self-denying Giles Winterborne. The picture of him when Grace first compares him wittingly with the shallow and flashy

Edred Fitzpiers, when she sees Giles in the sunset light, following his apple-mill, and looking like the very genius of the orchards, is in a high degree subtle and original. Not less admirable in their own way are the passages in which Grace and Mrs Charmond lose their way in the wood; that in which Fitzpiers, dead asleep from fatigue, is carried through the moonlight upright in his saddle; or the final scene in which Giles dies in the hut in the copse. Mr Hardy has never written a novel in which the landscape takes a more important place than it does in *The Woodlanders*; it does not intrude itself, but at every point the novelist introduces some touch which brings up a picture before our eyes, and we see the warm-coloured figures of his vivid drama moving against a background of rich orchard-country, with the light violet mist floating over it, and vaulted by a low sky, which is constellated with what are not stars, but every variety of pale green and light golden and dark red apples. We may instance the description of the sudden coming of winter as a particularly favourable instance of the sympathetic treatment of landscape, not as an outside adornment, but as an essential part of the scheme of the story. The humorous element in *The Woodlanders* is not very prominent. We have already casually mentioned the two principal comedians – the old Creedle, and Grammer Oliver, the ancient caretaker. In closing we may express a hope that Mr Hardy, whose characters are wont to be so essentially persons of flesh and blood, will not be led astray by the desire to idealise. Giles Winterborne is perhaps, a little too consciously treated as the incarnation of a phase of village civilisation, and not quite enough as an individual. . . .

SOURCE: extract from unsigned article reviewing newly published novels, in *Saturday Review*, LXIII (2 April 1887), pp. 484–5.

J. M. Barrie (1889)

On Hardy's Wessex and its Folk

. . . There are clever novelists in plenty to give us the sentimental aspect of country life, and others can show its crueller side. Some paint its sunsets, some never get beyond its pig-troughs or its

alehouses; many can be sarcastic about its dulness. But Mr Hardy
is the only man among them who can scour the village and miss
nothing; he knows the common as Mr [Richard] Jefferies knew it;
but he knows the inhabitants, as well as the common. Among
English novelists of today he is the only realist to be considered, so
far as life in country parts is concerned. The professional realists of
these times, who wear a giant's robe and stumble in it, see only the
seamy side of life, reproducing it with merciless detail, holding the
mirror up to the unnatural instead of to nature, and photographing
by the light of a policeman's lantern. The difference between them
and the man whose name they borrow is that they only see the
crack in the cup, while he sees the cup with the crack in it. There
are novelists of society whose realism is as genuine as Mr Hardy's,
but they are not so fortunate in their subject. The face of society
has changed but little since Thackeray reflected it, and his portraits
swallow theirs. With country life it is different. The closing years of
the nineteenth century see the end of many things in country parts,
of the peasantry who never go beyond their own parish, of quaint
manners and customs, of local modes of speech and ways of looking
at existence. Railways and machinery of various sorts create new
trades and professions, and kill old ones. The rustics of Warren's
malthouse, who went to the Casterbridge fair with sheep-crooks in
their hands and straw woven round their hats, are already to be
seen tailor-made twice a year in Oxford Street. Thus, the shepherds
and thatchers and farmers and villagers, who were, will soon be no
more, and if their likeness is not taken now it will be lost for ever.
Mr Hardy has given much of his life to showing who these rustics
were and how they lived, and his contemporaries have two reasons
for believing his pictures true. One is that Billy Smallbury,
Poorgrass, Grandfather William, and the others are still to be met
with, though their days are numbered. Posterity will not have them
to measure the rustics of Mr Hardy by, but it will have the other
and lasting test. The truth lives on in literature, because it is felt to
be true, and one knows that whoever reads of Dick Dewy in 1989
will feel as sure of him as we are of the Vicar of Wakefield.
Frequently it is said good-naturedly of novelists that they provide
material from which history can be written. One may venture to
say that such good history as the courtship of Fancy Day will
never be boiled down or written up into anything better. With
Bathsheba's story and Henchard's, it will keep as it is, and not
turn sour.

There must be many persons who find it difficult to realise that
there is no town called Casterbridge in the map. Mr Hardy has

given England a town. Unfortunately, he has not limited himself to
the country of which Casterbridge is the centre. Rich as English
literature is by his Wessex tales, it would have been richer had he
not sometimes wandered abroad and astray for his chief characters.
Never a careless writer, he has thrown away skill on books that
have no value and little momentary interest. He is only on firm
ground in the country, and not even then when he brings Society
figures into it. Some writers have created great characters
representative of a class with which they had little personal
acquaintance, but Mr Hardy has no such art. London society and
London professional life must be known to him, at least superficially,
but they are strange to the Wessex he has by heart, and in
attempting to draw them he fails absolutely. Even a man of letters
is not in his ken, for Elfride's lover, Knight, who is meant to be a
very admirable man, is simply the most insufferable prig in fiction.
The Hand of Ethelberta is a 'comedy in chapters', hardly less doleful
than most modern comedies in acts, and it is a disappointment of a
double kind. It is not a comedy, and its London life is preposterous.
A Laodicean and *Two on a Tower* are not comedies, but they may be
classed among Society novels. They are both dull books: here and
there, nasty as well, and the besom of oblivion will soon pass over them.
The tranter's dance, Bob Loveday's escape from the pressgang,
Henchard or Bathsheba Everdene in the market-place – any one of
these scenes outweighs all Mr Hardy's Society stories.

  Silas Marner is a great novel, but when the wealth of rural life
given us by Mr Hardy is taken into account, it must be conceded
that he has enriched the fiction which deals with heaths and
villages much more than George Eliot. Mr Jefferies, it is true, has
done as much for the natural scenery, for the hedges and ditches,
and wild and garden flowers, and woods and glades and commons,
but he has not done more. Mr Hardy's passionate love of Nature is
sunk into him: he not only knows the land of Wessex with the life
that grows out of it, he has not only seen it in every weather, but he
has felt its moods; they have been communicated to him until he
has shared Nature's joys and struggles, and become one of its
poets. Only a poet could have put Egdon Heath so wonderfully
into *The Return of the Native*, only a poet could have described the
thunderstorm of *Far from the Madding Crowd*. Yet, being a true
novelist, the scenery is with Mr Hardy only a fine setting. Not the
heath, but those who cross it, are his subjects. His first book,
Desperate Remedies, is only a study in other people's methods. With
Under the Greenwood Tree, which made way with the public as slowly
as *Lorna Doone*, the Wessex series began, and perhaps since

Goldsmith's death there has been no such idyll of country life. It is
not Mr Hardy's greatest book, but it is his most perfect; from the
moment Dick Dewy appears, singing of 'daffodowndillies', till he
and Fancy, newly married, listen to the nightingale, the story glides
on like a Wessex stream. It is Mr Hardy's one novel in which there
is nothing to jar. A tranter and his son, a schoolmistress, a
gamekeeper and a village choir are the simple company of whom an
artist's magic make us one. Here, and in *Far from the Madding
Crowd*, which first awakened the public to the new novelist, the
rustics are at their best. They are never again quite so fresh and
natural when they meet to drink cider. In the following books one
has now and again a suspicion that they are introduced as a
puppet-show between the more serious acts. They took the public
so well in the earlier stories that they must be offered again and
again, as Mr Sothern had to go on playing Dundreary. Characters
at first, they become rather characteristics, only those eccentricities
being given prominence that are calculated to raise the readiest
laugh. There are times when they are only a funny chorus, playing
somewhat obviously for applause. The most unlettered villager
may have natural wit or humour, but 'rustics' are not usually
amusing by intention, and in Mr Hardy's earlier novels they are
unconscious humorists, as where Fancy's stepmother will not have
Dick Dewy eat his dinner with her second-best knives and forks lest
people should think she has nothing better. Hundreds of touches
equally true to life are to be found in the rustic pictures of the early
novels, and there are even many in the later ones. But there is now a
tendency to spoil the rustics by putting clever sayings into their
mouths. 'Why should death deprive life of fourpence?' asks a toper,
taking possession of the four penny pieces set apart for keeping down
the eyelids of a dead woman. A drunken hag is on trial, and, on a
constable's repeating certain remarks of hers, she argues, 'I was not
capable enough to hear what I said, and what's said out of my hearing
isn't evidence.' The same woman would see Henchard humiliated
because 'I do like to see the trimming pulled off such Christmas
candles.' A pretty wife is 'an uncommon picture for a man's best
parlour', a woman gets married 'by the grace of God and a ready
young man'. Any one of these remarks will pass, but we get them in
sheaves. Rustics do not fling such smart things about promiscuously.
Sometimes, too, the author goes to the other extreme, making his
rustics hardly human in their ignorance. 'Oh, and what d'ye think I
found out, Mrs Yeobright? The parson wears a suit of clothes under
his surplice! I could see his black sleeve when he held up his arm.' A
clever City man could evolve rustics capable of providing this sort of

amusement to other City men. It is not the realism that gives Mr Hardy's rural figures a chance of living on.

English fiction is so much wealthier in heroines than in heroes that the ladies who have immortality will survive as widows. To create an attractive young man is the hardest thing in the trade: when he is meant to be a fine fellow he is nine times in ten a prig; at the best he has only the making in him of a nice lady. Scott admitted his failures here, and Pickwick is worth all Dickens's other heroes. Mr Hardy's heroes, however, by whom is meant the men that fall in love with his Bathshebas and Anne Garlands, will accompany his young ladies into the next century, a fortunate arrangement, for these exasperating and adorable women are not for travelling alone. Somerset, Swithin and the other men of the Society novels will be happily lost, but Gabriel Oak, Troy, Bob and John Loveday, Henchard (triumphing at last over the Scotsman, who speaks a fearsome tongue of his own) have still, one feels, a career before them. These are Mr Hardy's greatest 'rustics', for every one of them is country born and bred. The village or farm chorus is delightful, but its quaintness is comparatively only a knack the author has. Having the manners and ways of the most homespun country folk at his finger ends, so to speak, he can play upon them as easily as Bathsheba thrummed her much-discussed piano, but it is another matter to catch a rustic young and make a man of him as Mr Hardy does with Gabriel Oak. *Far from the Madding Crowd* is a great novel, and it gets some of its greatness from Gabriel and Troy. Oak is the hero whom novelists try to draw eternally, the good fellow with a head as well as a heart, and where nearly all are unsuccessful Mr Hardy triumphs. John Ridd is the prominent yeoman of romance, Gabriel Oak of realistic fiction. A manlier Englishman was never drawn. Gabriel is the true growth of Wessex soil, and, with the brothers Loveday, forms one of a strong trio. John Loveday, the gallant soldier who bravely leaves his sweetheart, 'to blow his trumpet till silenced for ever upon one of the bloody battlefields of Spain', and the more fickle but not less gallant Bob, are part of England's greatness. Yet the chivalrous trumpet-major is not the soldier of whom Mr Hardy's readers will think first. The trumpet blows to introduce gay, witty Sergeant Troy, whom Bathsheba marries because he says he must have her or another. The whole incident of Troy's wooing is incomparable. Grant that women are Bathshebas, and it is obvious that he is not to be resisted. The lady-farmer is not the only person whom he carries off her feet. His brilliant audacity casts a glamour over the readers as well, and they race after the sergeant, unable to reflect, captivated, until the knot is tied. Mr Hardy does not introduce Troy to preach a moral. The moral is there, and an awful tragedy beats it into Bathsheba's heart, but such things are, such men are, and that is sufficient for the author, who is always an artist, here a supreme one. He does not draw a male flirt to show that the species are contemptible, but because there are male flirts; nor are the two terrible scenes, Fanny's death and Bathsheba opening the coffin, introduced to warn womenkind against the Troys. Bathsheba's mistake and its results are part of the tragedy of life which this author feels so keenly, so oppressively one might say. Never until Troy was shown at work had we learned from fiction how such a being may mesmerise a bewitching and clever woman into his arms. Many writers say their Troys do it, but Mr Hardy shows it being done. There is the devil's fascination in the wonderful scene in the hollow where Troy goes through his sword exercise, with Bathsheba for an audience:

In an instant the atmosphere was transformed to Bathsheba's eyes. Beams of light, caught from the low sun's rays, above, around, in front of her, well-nigh shut out earth and heaven – all emitted in the marvellous evolutions of Troy's reflecting blade, which seemed everywhere at once, and yet nowhere specially. These circling gleams were accompanied by a keen rush that was almost a whistling – also springing from all sides of her at once. In short, she was enclosed in a firmament of light, and of sharp hisses, resembling a sky-full of meteors close at hand. . . .

SOURCE: extract from article, 'Thomas Hardy: The Historian of Wessex', in *Contemporary Review*, LVI (1889).

Joseph Warren Beach   (1922)

On *Far from the Madding Crowd*

. . . One would like to know whether, in designing this novel, the author started with a plot and added a setting, or started with a setting and got himself a plot to suit it. My impression is that he started with the setting. He conceived the idea of a pastoral idyll, in which he should bring together the greatest possible number of country scenes and occupations such as, taken together, would amount to a reconstruction of his ideal 'Wessex', or – more specifically – of that particular department of Wessex known as 'Weatherbury'. Mr Hardy tells us in the Preface that it was first in this book that he 'ventured to adopt the word "Wessex" from the pages of early English history, and give it a fictitious significance as the existing name of the district once included in that extinct kingdom. The series of novels I projected being mainly of the kind called local, they seemed to require a territorial definition of some sort to lend unity to their scene.' He discusses at some length the peculiarities of 'the village called Weatherbury', which, owing to the disappearance of many of the customs and architectural features following the growth of migratory labor, 'would perhaps be hardly discernable by the explorer, without help, in any existing place nowadays'.

We are made to feel that the book is primarily a reconstruction of a 'realistic dream-country', and that the plot – which, as we know, was procured from a purveyor of such wares – was introduced as a necessary means of giving coherence to the dream. In any case, it is evidently a composition of pastoral elements very consciously designed. This appears, for one thing, in the classical and biblical allusions, which seem to occur more frequently in this book than elsewhere, as if the author had been reading up his subject in the prescribed poetic manuals. The renewed activity of the vegetable world in early spring makes him think of the dryads 'waking for the season'. The ballad sung by Jacob Smallbury at the shearers' feast was 'as inclusive and interminable as that with which the worthy toper, old Silenus, amused on a similar occasion the swains Chromis and Mnasylus, and other jolly dogs of his day'. Gabriel calling his lost sheep makes the valleys and hills resound 'as when the sailors invoked the lost Hylas on the Mysian shore'; and at the grindstone, sharpening his shears, Gabriel 'stood somewhat as Eros is represented when in the act of sharpening his arrows'.

Some of these allusions seem a little forced, and as if introduced consciously for decoration. More natural and in keeping are the biblical allusions. These are heard not merely from the pious mouth of Joseph Poorgrass, for whom they make the chief trait in his humorous characterisation, but also from those of other serious persons such as Farmer Boldwood. Very effective is the author's comparison of Gabriel Oak to Moses on the occasion when Bathsheba sent him off and bade him never let her see his face any more. ' "Very well, Miss Everdene – so it shall be." And he took his shears and went away from her in placid dignity, as Moses left the presence of Pharaoh.'

The very names are chosen largely for their combination of biblical and rustic associations, from the archangelic Gabriel Oak and Bathsheba Everdene, recalling the lady for whom King David sinned, down to Joseph Poorgrass, Jacob Smallbury, Matthew Moon and Laban Tall. If there is a third range of association to which appeal is made, besides the Bible and the English land itself, it is the imaginative demesne of *As You Like It* and *A Midsummer-Night's Dream.*

But more convincing than literary allusion and the association of names are the actual character and behavior of the people of the story; and these are almost exclusively of the true agricultural, or more specifically pastoral stamp. The nearest approach to the modern industrial order is Bathsheba paying off her men 'pen in hand, with a canvas moneybag beside her'. And the key to the whole composition is given in the scenes of Gabriel playing his flute in his shepherd's hut as the Grecian shepherds sounded their oaten pipes, and watching the stars and reckoning time from the top of Norcombe Hill as certain other shepherds watched by night in scriptural story. It is a question whether Gabriel or Bathsheba should be regarded as the leading character. As Bathsheba is undoubtedly the central actor in the drama, so Oak is the central feature of the pictorial composition, the poem, to which the drama was attached. We are most interested in the emotional history of Bathsheba, but Oak is the indispensable and characteristic figure in those rural scenes which form so large a part of the design. We see him waking in his hut to take up the new-born lamb revived by the warmth of his fire, or standing sorrowful on the brow of the hill beneath which lie the mangled carcasses of his flock. We see him presiding at the sheep-washing by the pool in the meadows, or at the sheep-shearing in the great barn, or lancing the stricken beasts with his own sure merciful hand to save their lives. And when it was not the sheep, it was the grain which solicited his anxious care. It was he who saved the wheatricks from fire and from rain; it was the trained eye of the watcher in the pastures that read the signs of the approaching storm. It was he who by long-proved competence in affairs, and by tender and dogged faithfulness of heart, amply earned at last the heart and hand of the wayward Bathsheba.

All three of the serious main characters, all but the soldier-villain himself, are conceived in the large grave manner of Scripture pastorals. By their comely dignity, by their respect for one another and for themselves, by their direct and deliberate manner of speech and action, they remind us of characters in the Old Testament – in the story of Joseph or of Ruth, of King David or of Queen Esther. There is none of the small change of the modern drawing-room. Their language is worthy of the open air in which they move and the wide horizons on which they rest their eyes. They 'deal boldly', like Wordsworth's pastoral poet, 'with substantial things'. Thus it is that Gabriel delivers, in precise and measured terms, his judgement upon the behavior of Miss Everdene toward Farmer Boldwood. Thus it is that Farmer Boldwood puts away Bathsheba's offer of pity, and wants to know what has become of her seeming promise of love.

'Your dear love, Bathsheba, is such a vast thing beside your pity, that the loss of your pity as well as your love is no great addition to my sorrow, nor does the gain of your pity make it sensibly less. Oh sweet – how dearly you spoke to me behind the spear-bed at the washing-pool, and in the barn at the shearing, and that dearest last time in the evening at your home! Where are your pleasant words all gone – your earnest hope to be able to love me? Where is your firm conviction that you would get to care for me very much?'

It is with the same high gravity that Bathsheba makes her defence to Boldwood, as she had formerly made her defence to Gabriel against similar reproaches.

She checked emotion, looked him quietly and clearly in the face, and said in her low, firm voice, 'Mr Boldwood, I promised you nothing. Would you have had me a woman of clay when you paid me that furthest, highest compliment a man can pay a woman – telling her he loves her? I was bound to show some feeling, if I would not be a graceless shrew. Yet each of those pleasures was just for the day – the day just for the pleasure. How was I to know that what is a pastime to all other men was death to you? Have reason, do, and think more kindly of me!'

M. René Bazin remarks of one of his peasant characters, 'She expressed herself well, with a certain studied refinement which denoted the habit of reading'. Something of that sort is true of all the characters of Hardy, especially the main characters in the more serious novels. But it is not the habit of reading that is responsible for this adequacy and propriety of self-expression. It is a certain simple elevation of mind, a freedom from sophistication, and a directness in dealing with solid realities. It is the mutual respect of the speakers born of an instinctive regard for the human soul. This the author shares with his creatures. Whatever may be said of Hardy's irony, his pessimism, his want of religious faith, there can be no question of the dignity with which he invests the human soul itself. The manner of speech of Bathsheba and Gabriel and

Boldwood is the manner of speech of Eustacia Vye and Wildeve and Clym and Mrs Yeobright; of Henchard and Farfrae and Lucetta; of Tess and Angel Clare; even of Jude and Sue. At first it may strike the reader as somewhat awkward and unnatural, somewhat formal and precise, like the expression of foreigners who speak with care a language learned from books. The reader has been used – in books and in daily experience – to a more trifling and more trivial style, the common style of the tea table or the railway train. He must accustom his ear again to the broad simple accents of scriptural speech. He is at first more ready to believe that people talk like the witty fencers of [Meredith's] *The Egoist* and [Henry James's] *The Awkward Age*, or in the broken sentences and slangy 'patter' of the characters of Messrs Wells, Walpole & Co. But in time one comes to love these squared and grounded sentences, as one loves the large deliberate movements of those who speak them; and one yields with delight to the thought of people as strong and simple as those in Genesis or the *Iliad*, 'in the early ages of the world'.

This style first appears in all its beauty in *Far from the Madding Crowd*. There had not been earlier any sufficient occasion to draw it out. The slight story of *Under the Greenwood Tree*, a story of boy and girl love, had not depth enough to call for speech of any force or dignity. Neither had the somewhat labored and childish exchanges of Smith and Elfride in *A Pair of Blue Eyes*, nor the shallow literary encounters of Elfride and Knight. But the characters in the later story are given weight and consistency by the obvious importance of the things with which they deal, and the whole action impresses by virtue of the material stakes involved.

Bathsheba is the first of a series of independent Shakespearean women capable of taking strong hold upon life and meeting men upon something like an equal footing. And it is the Weatherbury composition that promotes the development and display of this superb character; such character first shows itself upon the use of the Wessex setting in connection with a real story. The discovery of Bathsheba in the rôle of a personage capable of giving employment to the shepherd, her discharge of the dishonest bailiff and her payment of the laborers in person, her appearance in the corn market to do business with men, and at the head of the table at the harvest festival as patron of the feast – all these are incidents in building up a personality of unusual impressiveness. We are prepared for her display of Roman heroism after the shooting of Troy, when she took command of the situation with such matronly coolness, instead of fainting and giving up the guidance to others.

She proved then, as Hardy says, that 'she was of the stuff of which great men's mothers are made.'

It is true that, after all necessary steps were taken in the case of the murdered husband, Bathsheba did give way to fainting fits, and went to bed; just as after laboring with Gabriel in the storm till the grain was practically secured she had consented to give over, being weary. It is true that, with all her pride and candor, her fairness and moral responsibility, she became the victim of a woman's vanity, helpless against the assaults of gallant flattery; and that, without the heart of a coquette, she managed to play the rôle of one. These are weaknesses which detract less from her charm than they add to her lifelikeness. They are the debt she paid to nature. They are what she has in common with Elfride and with the heroine of *Under the Greenwood Tree*. They are the source of all her trouble and the mainspring of the plot; and they serve to set in higher relief her more heroic qualities. It is the strong and the weak in her nature taken together that make her so very real. And yet it is her strength that gives her her special interest; and it is her position of Weatherbury farmer that accounts for the appearance of such a character in English fiction.

It is not necessary to labor this point in connection with Oak and Boldwood. Both of these have much of that generous helpfulness of nature toward the loved one which Hardy is so fond of representing in men of country breeding – witness the self-effacing love of Diggory Venn in *The Return of the Native* and of Giles Winterborne in *The Woodlanders*. The most affecting instance of the tenderness of Oak and Boldwood was their chivalrous conspiracy to keep from Troy's wife a knowledge of the story of Fanny Robin. Such gentleness is particularly natural to the shepherd, with his humane and motherly regard for silly beasts. When he found his sheep all dead at the foot of the fatal cliff, his first feeling 'was one of pity for the untimely fate of these gentle ewes and their unborn lambs'; it was only in the second place that he remembered the sheep were not insured, and that he had lost in one night his labor of ten years. Is it any wonder that such a man should have watched so long over his lady's interests as if they were his own, that he should have cared more for her happiness than for his own success with her?

The feeling of the characters for one another, as well as their personal quality, is developed by their rural occupations so as to give especial reality to the story. Mr Hardy remarks, when he has at last brought about the engagement of Bathsheba and Gabriel:

Theirs was that substantial affection which arises (if any arises at all) when the two who are thrown together begin first by knowing the rougher sides of each other's character, and not the best till further on, the romance growing up in the interstices of a mass of hard prosaic reality. This goodfellowship – *camaraderie* – usually occurring through similarity of pursuits, is unfortunately seldom superadded to love between the sexes, because men and women associate, not in their labours, but in their pleasures merely. Where, however, happy circumstance permits its development, the compounded feeling proves itself to be the only love which is strong as death – that love which many waters cannot quench, nor the floods drown, beside which the passion usually called by the name is evanescent as steam.

Whether Mr Hardy succeeded in convincing us of the existence of a love between Bathsheba and Gabriel worthy of such romantic phrasing is a matter of doubt. It is always very hard – as Meredith found in *Diana* – to satisfy the reader of romance with the wise second or third love of a woman who has imprudently dispensed her youthful passion. But however we may feel about the *love* to which the good-fellowship was added, we are made to believe fully in the good-fellowship, the *camaraderie*, which has grown up through the similarity of pursuits of Bathsheba and Gabriel. We are made to realise it in ways much more convincing, because so much more directly appealing to the senses, than in the case of Diana and Redworth. To have saved the shepherd's life was a good beginning. And this was well followed up by her recognising in the one who played so manly a part at the burning of the straw stack the same who had proposed marriage to her not long before, and being practically compelled, by the general opinion of his merits, to offer him employment. The various incidents of farm life give body and color to their relation, which is not rendered less intimate and binding by the little quarrels arising from his well-deserved reproofs. The scene which more than any other brings them close is that in which they work together to save the wheat-ricks from the storm while the lightning flashes and her drunken husband sleeps with his men in the barn.

Never was growing friendship displayed under more picturesque aspects. It is a wonder the makers of 'movies' have not discovered the possibilities of these pictures as they have those of *Tess*. All the while our hero was showing himself the best man in ways equally well approved, in the long run, by romance and real life.

And Bathsheba was playing a rôle not the less convincing for being partly politic. When, after his dismissal, she could not get him to help her with the swollen sheep by oral command, she wrote him a polite note, at the end of which she added, out of 'strategy,' the more tender appeal, 'Do not desert me, Gabriel!' So she played upon his sentiments. And when he had finished his surgery:

> When the love-led man had ceased from his labours, Bathsheba came and looked him in the face.
>
> 'Gabriel, will you stay on with me?' she said, smiling winningly, and not troubling to bring her lips quite together again at the end, because there was going to be another smile soon.
>
> 'I will', said Gabriel.
>
> And she smiled on him again.

It is true she needed him in a business way. But we cannot suppose that this incident and her strategic smiles left her entirely without a more personal regard for the man who was her moral support as well as her man of affairs. And after the death of Troy and the incarceration of mad Boldwood, it was by no means solely the threatened loss of her superintendent that made her so desolate at the thought of losing Gabriel. But he could not have played better cards if he had done it deliberately than to go about his own· business at Weatherbury and make his plans for emigration. The rest followed naturally; and if it was not *la grande passion* which led her to the altar, it was at least the affectionate regard and the feeling of absolute security with which a woman who has proved the perils and betrayals of love looks to the man of tried strength and fidelity.

To one who has read the book there is a smack of irony in the title. But the emotional strife which makes up this drama is not the 'ignoble strife' which the poet had in mind; and it may well be that, in choosing his title, the author had no thought of an ironic bearing. He intended to compose an idyll of pastoral and agricultural life as he had composed a sylvan idyll in *The Greenwood Tree*; and he was moved solely by the sentiment proper to the lovely peaceful life remote from the insane huddle of the market. But meanwhile, in *A Pair of Blue Eyes* he had achieved the construction of an exciting plot of deeply human interest; and he doubtless felt the need of introducing in his pastoral setting a much more gripping action than he had done in the sylvan one. He had probably been impressed with the possibilities of the country for moving drama mentioned later in *The Woodlanders*. And so he proceeded to secure his plot in the way we have seen, and to adjust it to the circumstances and personal types of Weatherbury life.

It may be that some of the later scenes are of a violence for which we are not prepared; and certainly there is an artificiality in the contrivance of some of the situations which displays the ingenuity rather than the humane art of the craftsman. But if the plot is not at every point made consistent with the original design of the piece, it owes to this original design its general plausibility, its *vraisemblance*, its local color and life. The setting, we may suppose, came before the plot in the author's plan; and it is the setting which 'made' the plot. So that we have the emergence of a really convincing and characteristic story simultaneously with the emergence of what we call Wessex. What we call Wessex is an indispensable element in the formula for a first-rate novel by Hardy.

What we call Wessex is a composite of many things, a harmony of many traits, physical and moral, human and non-human. It is, in the first place, a physical background of landscapes and interiors, with enveloping conditions of climate and atmosphere. It is next an economic order, a social order, with its well-marked types and classes of men, an order practically extinct since the time that Mr Hardy began to write of it, since the railways came to interrupt the continuity of tradition and break the molds. And then it is the manners and customs that have crystallised about this order, suiting themselves to these ways of maintaining life, the modes under which men and women have expressed the joy of life and found consolation for its sorrows, their style of etiquette and philosophy and humor. And finally there is the sharpness of vision by which the author has penetrated its meanings, the art with which he has composed its divers aspects, and the love with which he has brooded over all, the deep poetic sentiment by virtue of which he can hardly speak of the more signal beauties of his subject without falling into musical cadence.

Quite different in feeling are the descriptions of nature in *A Pair of Blue Eyes* and *Far from the Madding Crowd*. Mr Hardy, in the Preface of 1895, characterises the scene of the earlier story as 'a region of dream and mystery', to which the various features of the seaside lend 'an atmosphere like the twilight of a night vision'. But in the book he did not succeed overwell in creating such an atmosphere. And if he had done so, it would still not satisfy the demands of our imagination nourished on the more substantial reality of his settings in later books, where the characters are so part and parcel of the landscape and product of the soil. Egdon Heath, in *The [Return of the] Native*, is truly enough 'a region of dream and mystery', with an 'atmosphere like the twilight of a night vision'. And Clym, the 'native', gathering furze, the reddleman camped by night in the sandpit under the hill, and the 'anxious wanderers' in the rainy midnight of November, belong to this scene in a way quite different from that in which Elfride and the parson belong to the vicarage of Endelstow. In *A Pair of Blue Eyes* we have landscapes, and charming ones; we have sufficient indications of direction and the lay of the land. But we have not that sense of the fundamental topography, the underlying anatomy of the landscape, which is so prominent in *The Native*, *The Woodlanders* and *Tess*; and which is first impressed on the reader in *Far from the Madding Crowd*.

The city-dweller knows the country by glimpses on summer afternoons when the weather is fine. It is in winter and by night, in storm and wind, that the country yields up its intimacies; then alone it reveals itself to those who actually live in its bosom, to those who must meet the elements in person, and cannot take shelter in the securities of the walled town. One cannot account for the beauty and the convincing air of nature that invests the action of Hardy's stories until one realises how almost exclusively it takes place out of doors, and how largely by night, under black or starry skies, and with the utmost freedom of ventilation. If he would give us an impression of the life of the shepherd, he begins with the bleak hillside where his hut is perched, and the wind beating about the corners and playing its various tunes upon the trees, the grass, and the fallen leaves.

The thin grasses, more or less coating the hill, were touched by the wind in breezes of differing powers, and almost of differing natures – one rubbing the blades heavily, another raking them piercingly, another brushing them like a soft broom. The instinctive act of human kind was to stand and listen, and learn how the trees on the right and the trees on the left wailed or chaunted to each other in the regular antiphonies of a cathedral choir, how hedges and other shapes to leeward then caught the note, lowering it to the tenderest sob, and how the hurrying gust then plunged into the south, to be heard no more.

It is with senses refreshed and gratified that we accompany Gabriel Oak in his night journey to Weatherbury, reckoning the hour no more by the sun or by the hands of a clock, but by the angle of Charles's Wain to the Pole star, judging the distance of the receding wagon not by sight but by hearing, as the 'crunching jangle of the waggon dies upon the ear', and informing ourselves through the soles of our feet that it is plowed land we have leaped upon, the other side of the gate. We are making across the field with Gabriel toward the great fire, which appears about half a mile away; and as we get nearer, we see his weary face 'painted over with a rich orange glow, and the whole front of his smock-frock and gaiters covered with a dancing shadow pattern of thorn-twigs – the light reaching him through a leafless intervening hedge – and the metallic curve of his sheep-crook silver-bright in the same abounding rays'.

Perhaps the most living scene of drama in the book is that where Gabriel and Bathsheba thatch the wheatricks amid the incessant flashes of the storm. The fearful crash and the sulphurous smell in the air when a tree is struck by lightning serve to impress us with the courage of Bathsheba, and make natural the emotional state in which she confides to Gabriel the circumstances of her marriage. And since we are dealing here with a man professionally weatherwise, we are privileged to read with him the complicated signs of coming storm as notified by toads and slugs and by his sheep. 'Apparently there was to be a thunder-storm, and afterwards a cold continuous rain. The creeping things seemed to know all about the later rain, but little of the interpolated thunder-storm; whilst the sheep knew all about the thunder-storm and nothing of the later rain.'

Such precision in the noting of natural phenomena at times and seasons strange to the dweller in towns might perhaps be cultivated deliberately by a painter of rural life determined to give to his human narrative as fresh and true an air as the notebooks of Richard Jefferies or Mr Hudson. But only the lift of the heart, only the rhythmical pulsation of deep emotion, could give to his phrases that poetic cast – worthy of Mr Hudson himself – which one feels in so many passages of description.

It was now early spring – the time of going to grass with the sheep, when they have the first feed of the meadows, before these are laid up for mowing. . . . The vegetable world begins to move and swell and the saps to rise, till in the completest silence of lone gardens and trackless plantations, where everything seems helpless and still after the bond and slavery of frost. . . .

Only the instinct to prolong the sensation of beauty could lead him into cadences so delicately turned. The phrases go in pairs as in the prose of Sir Thomas Browne or other relishers of words that balance and reinforce one another.

It is again with sentiment like that of the doctor of Norwich that the Dorchester story-teller describes 'the panoramic glide of the stars past earthly objects'.

The poetry of motion is a phrase much in use, and to enjoy the epic form of that gratification it is necessary to stand on a hill at a small hour of the night, and, having first expanded with a sense of difference from the mass of civilized mankind, who are horizontal and disregardful of all such proceedings at this time, long and quietly watch your stately progress through the stars. After such a nocturnal reconnoitre among these astral clusters, aloft from the customary haunts of thought and vision, some men may feel raised to a capability for eternity at once.

So stood Gabriel Oak, and told the time of night by certain starry indications. And then, because he was a man conscious of a charm in the life he led,

He stood still after looking at the sky as a useful instrument, and regarded it in an appreciative spirit, as a work of art superlatively beautiful. For a moment he seemed impressed with the speaking loneliness of the scene, or rather with the complete abstraction from all its compass of the sights and sounds of man. Human shapes, interferences, troubles, and joys were all as if they were not, and there seemed to be on the shaded hemisphere of the globe no sentient being save himself; he could fancy them all gone round to the sunny side.

Such passages occupy very little space in *Far from the Madding Crowd*, and they are seldom detachable. Readers who feel the impulse to skip them in order to get on with the story might almost as well not give their time to the reading of Hardy. For they make a difference out of all proportion to their length and prominence. They are largely what give color and fragrancy and the freshness of earth to novels which more than any others in English suggest the beauties of painting or of poetry. And they count for much in the sense of reality which one has so strong in the greater novels of Hardy. One never feels here that vagueness and thinness – that impalpability – which attaches to the place and action in so many excellent works of fiction. We know by the evidence of all our senses that we are dealing here with 'substantial things'.

But this is only the physical background of the story. There is another background of equal importance, to which much greater attention is paid by the author – the social background, made up of the numerous minor characters from the Wessex peasantry. These humble characters are almost invariably treated in a light and playful manner, and they constitute the 'comic relief' in the generally somber stories. It is mainly on these rustic humors that the author relies to make palpable the old order of things, which counts for so much in making his stories lifelike as well as picturesque. It is they that furnish the rich subsoil of custom and belief in which the main action is so securely rooted. Like the deep bed of rotting leaves in an ancient forest, they give forth an acrid woodsy perfume that stirs more than anything else the sense of the successive generations of life. Over them broods the author's humor, that composite of tenderness, amusement, and reverence which plays about the moss-grown, tenacious institutions doomed in the end to yield to a new order.

Mr Hardy had already made one charming study of such types in *The Greenwood Tree*. This is largely taken up with the quaint west-gallery fiddlers of the Mellstock choir, their round of Christmas carols, and the vain attempt to prevent their supersession by a more up-to-date organist or harmonium-player. These ancient amateurs are well satisfied of their own competence, and they cannot find words strong enough to express their abhorrence of the intrusive new instruments. They know what is seemly in the service of the Lord; and they are deeply shocked when, for the first time in the history of the church, the singing from the girls' side takes on a fulness and independence as great as that of the choir itself. Heretofore 'the girls, like the rest of the congregation, had always been humble and respectful followers of the gallery, singing at sixes and sevens if without gallery leaders, never interfering with the ordinances of these practised artists – having no will, union, power, or proclivity except it was given them from the established choir enthroned above them'. As one of the gallery puts it, ''Tis the gallery have got to sing, all the world knows'. But now they have received clear notice of their obsoleteness.

It is natural that the converse of such people should be largely of a reminiscential sort, like that of Justice Shallow, and full of anecdotes retailed with full Shakespearean gusto. Slight experiences of a humorous or surprising nature are treasured with all the fondness of men whose lives are not rich in excitement or variety; and friends never tire of hearing how Tranter Dewy was taken in in the purchase of a cider cask, or how the shoemaker once identified a drowned man by the mere sight of the family foot.

The social obscurity of these people does not prevent them from showing a decided proficiency in the art of conversation, which means even more to them than to people with greater resources for amusement. The author often calls attention to the instinct with which they determine how far to carry a given topic, as where the shoemaker, who had been showing his last, 'seemed to perceive that the sum-total of interest the object had excited was greater than he had anticipated, and warranted the last's being taken up again and exhibited'. And what is lacking in the actual substance of the words spoken is amply made up in the range and subtlety of tone, gesture, facial expression, all noted by the author with loving care. The taking in of Tranter Dewy by a sharp salesman is occasion for a great variety of vocal expression.

'Ah, who can believe sellers!' said old Michael Mail in a *carefully-cautious voice*, by way of tiding-over this critical point of affairs.

'No one at all', said Joseph Bowman, in *the tone of a man fully agreeing with everybody.*

'Ay', said Mail, in *the tone of a man who did not agree with everybody as a rule, though he did now*, 'I know'd a auctioneering fellow once. . . .'

and so on to an anecdote.

All resources of manner are drawn upon by these simple people in the interest of decency, politeness, and mutual consideration. They have learned very well how to subordinate the mere appetites of the body to the more elegant demands of social intercourse. While Mr Penny was explaining the interesting points of a certain last, 'his left hand wandered towards the cider-cup, as if the hand had no connection with the person speaking'. He felt that one need not call attention crudely to the act of refreshing the inner man. When Mrs Dewy at the Christmas party mentioned the subject of supper, 'that portion of the company who loved eating and drinking put on a look to signify that till that moment they had quite forgotten that it was customary to expect suppers on these occasions; going even further than this politeness of feature, and starting irrelevant subjects, the exceeding flatness and forced tone of which rather betrayed their object.' Delicate subjects are carefully avoided by these peaceable and sensitive natures, and there is always someone ready with a remark like Michael Mail, in 'a carefully cautious voice, by way of tiding-over' any 'critical point of affairs'. When Mrs Dewy mentions the awkward circumstance that 'Reuben always was such a hot man,' Mr Penny knows how to imply 'the correct species of sympathy that such an affliction required, by trying to smile and to look grieved at the same time.' Mr Dewy is the mildest and most full of resources for social conciliation of anyone in Mellstock parish. When he, as leader of the delegation to the vicar, wishes to broach the ticklish subject of the church music, 'what I have been thinking,' he says, and implies 'by this use of the past tense that he was hardly so discourteous as to be positively thinking it then'.

Nothing speaks more eloquently of the delicacy and good-nature of these simple folk than their attitude toward Thomas Leaf, the parish fool. Leaf made frequent candid acknowledgment of the fact that he 'never had no head'; and 'they all assented to this, not with any sense of humiliating Leaf by disparaging him after an open confession, but because it was an accepted thing that Leaf didn't in the least mind having no head, that deficiency of his being an unimpassioned matter of parish history'. And since his family was in general the most melancholy in their experience, and since Leaf sang a very high treble and they didn't know 'what they should do without en for upper G', they consented, on the tranter's motion, to let him come along with them to the famous interview with Parson Maybold. On that occasion he was treated by everyone with the same tender consideration, and the same combination of pity and satisfaction taken in his peculiar defect. Quite similar was the treatment of other fools in later novels – of the bashful Joseph Poorgrass in *The Madding Crowd*, and the half-witted Christian Cantle in *The Native*. By virtue of its humaneness, the community spirit managed to turn a social liability into a social asset.

It is on the whole a very attractive picture of Wessex humanity that Mr Hardy gives us in these rustic sketches: meekly submissive to what they take for the decrees of fate, backward and without initiative, naïve, and of limited vision; but mild and innocent, abounding in social refinements, and full of the milk of human kindness. It is a picture bearing the stamp of truth, and done with great delicacy and sympathetic feeling, in a manner suggesting that of Addison, of Goldsmith, or of Shakespeare.

The rustic humors were practically the whole subject of this 'rural painting of the Dutch school', hero and heroine being so much less substantial figures than those of the 'background' itself. The background figures themselves were not deeply conceived; and there was no such opportunity as in *The Madding Crowd* to use them for deepening the harmonies of a richer orchestration.

In *The Madding Crowd* there is a serious main plot, in connection with which the rustic humors find their significant employment. They make a true chorus to the doings of the great ones, applying to an action outside their own scope and capacity the general social philosophy in relation to which it must be viewed. They make up the audience before whom Bathsheba Everdene plays her part. They are also actually made use of in carrying forward the story. It is in conversations among them that many circumstances of the action transpire. In one case they are made the unconscious instruments in provoking the central catastrophe. For it was Joseph Poorgrass's love of comfort and the cup that delayed the arrival of Fanny's coffin so that it was determined to leave it for the night in Bathsheba's sitting-room. He is thus as great an instrument of tragedy as Christian Cantle in *The Return of the Native*, whose indulgence in the folly of the dice box results in such fatal bitterness and misunderstanding.

Hardy had up to this time produced no humorous passage so

rich in ironic overtones as this scene in the Buck's Head Inn, where Joseph, intrusted with the transference of Fanny's body from the Casterbridge poorhouse to Weatherbury church, takes comfort in a mug of ale with his pals, while the flower-laden coffin waits in the rain. It was but solemn conviviality in which they indulged, displaying their wisdom chiefly on the subject of religion. But the judgment of Gabriel is none the less severe, when he finds his messenger drunk in the company of drunkards he 'does his wicked deeds in such confoundedly holy ways'. However, the topers are by now too well armed against all ills to be much troubled by Gabriel's reproaches. Mark Clark expresses his convivial philosophy in a song celebrating the advantage of today over tomorrow as a time for feasting. And Jan Coggan, more profound, more cynical, and more to the point, makes their measured defence, speaking, toper-like "with the precision of a machine".'

'Nobody can hurt a dead woman. All that could be done for her is done – she's beyond us: and why should a man put himself in a tearing hurry for lifeless clay that can neither feel nor see, and don't know what you do with her at all? If she'd been alive, I would have been the first to help her. If she now wanted victuals and drink, I'd pay for it, money down. But she's dead and no speed of ours will bring her back to life. . . . Drink, shepherd, and be friends, for tomorrow we may be like her.'

But we are not left with a drunkard's view of the matter. Gabriel and Bathsheba are tender enough in their concern for even the lifeless body of Fanny; and the parson at least knows how to take his cue. 'Perhaps Mrs Troy is right in feeling that we cannot treat a dead fellow-creature too thoughtfully. We must remember that though she may have erred grievously in leaving her home, she is still our sister; and it is to be believed that God's uncovenanted mercies are extended towards her, and that she is a member of the flock of Christ.' 'The parson's words spread out into the heavy air with a sad yet unperturbed cadence.' It is just such a cadence that the rustics have generally a perfect command of. Especially the topers of the Buck's Head have the whole range of sanctimonious expression, and know how to use a pious tone in reference to their own frailties. Even their capacity for liquor 'is a talent the Lord has mercifully bestowed upon us, and we ought not to neglect it'.

Hardy, like a true humorist, knows how to give us, by infinite fine touches, a sense of the droll puppet-like speech and movement of the humble upon earth, copies as they are of the great ones, but sufficiently reduced in stature so that we, the great ones, may laugh at them without too vivid a consciousness of kinship. They are, however, but copies of their masters, with the same aspirations and pretensions, caught in the same machinery of circumstance, enveloped by the same atmosphere of dim brightness in the midst of a wide obscurity. It is a characteristic feature in the Wessex composition that the denizens of these secluded valleys should discuss with simple wonder the ways of 'strange cities' – how, in Bath, for a present example, the people 'never need to light their fires except as a luxury, for the water springs up out of the earth ready boiled for use'. It is pleasantly characteristic of more than Wessex humanity, the way Joseph Poorgrass comes to the defense of his simple-minded friend for some rather incoherent statement with his own naïve philosophical reflections: 'Let en alone. The boy's maning that the sky and the earth in the kingdom of Bath is not altogether different from ours here. 'Tis for our good to gain knowledge of strange cities, and as such the boy's words should be suffered, so to speak it.'

Not the least happy trait of human nature, in its littleness and imperfection, is the disposition to take a complacent view of one's circumstances, even when they reflect no particular credit upon one, and especially to make the most of one's defects. The blushful timidity of Joseph Poorgrass arouses so much interest in the countrymen gathered at Warren's malthouse that it comes to fill him 'with a mild complacency'. Later we find him actually regarding his extreme modesty in the presence of women as a sort of superior gift to which he was born, and an occasion for hiding his light – rather ostentatiously – under a bushel. It may be that the point is a bit labored for effect. Certainly more delicious in its humorous truthfulness is the maltster's childish pride in his extreme old age – that being the most remarkable fact about him. It is his son Jacob – himself a man of the considerable age of sixty-five, who, to put his father in good humor, suggests that he should favor the newly arrived shepherd with 'the pedigree of his life'. This the maltster proceeds to do, after clearing his throat and elongating his gaze, 'in the slow speech justifiable when the importance of a subject is so generally felt that any mannerism must be tolerated.' After he has given the items of his career – how long he lived in each of the places where he has labored – another old gentleman 'given to mental arithmetic' calculates the number of years as one hundred and seventeen.

'Well, then, that's my age', said the maltster, emphatically.

'Oh, no father!' said Jacob. 'Your turnip-hoeing were in the summer and your malting in the winter of the same years, and ye don't ought to count both halves, father.'

'Chok' it all! I lived through the summer, didn't I? That's my question. I suppose ye'll say next I be no age at all to speak of?'

'Sure we shan't', said Gabriel, soothingly.

'Ye be a very old aged person, malter', attested Jan Coggan, also soothingly. 'We all know that, and ye must have a wonderful talented constitution to be able to live so long, mustn't he, neighbours?'

'True, true, ye must, malter, wonderful', said the meeting unanimously.

The maltster, being now pacified, was even generous enough to voluntarily disparage in a slight degree the virtue of having lived a great many years, by mentioning that the cup they were drinking out of was three years older than he.

The same polite consideration that is shown toward Joseph and the maltster appears in the attitude of all the rustics toward one another. It implies the self-respect and the respect for one's fellow-mortal exhibited by the more heroic characters. It implies a regard for the human soul itself irrespective of social position, material possessions, intellectual attainments, and such-like irrelevant circumstances which, if we are to believe our Wordsworth and our Hardy, characterise English humanity

> Far from the madding crowd's ignoble strife.

The very farm hands approach one another with a high and simple dignity worthy of patriarchs and shepherd-kings 'in the early ages of the world'.

This spiritual culture and philosophy have their roots, we realise, in an old and well-established tradition. These humble folk are deeply conscious of a historical background. The frequenters of Warren's malthouse are well acquainted with the antecedents of their patroness of Weatherbury Farm, and can give you anecdotes from her father's domestic life. When Gabriel Oak drops in for a chat, the aged maltster can swear that he recognised by his looks the grandson of 'Gabriel Oak over at Norcombe'; and when the new shepherd shows himself politely disregardful of a little 'clean dirt' in meat and drink, it is seen that 'he's his grandfer's own grandson – his grandfer were just such a nice unparticular man!'

By such means the entire picture is given that mellow consistency which we prize so highly in certain of the old masters – not that caused by the fading and toning down of colors, but that which comes of a sentiment for objects harmonised themselves by the composing brush of time. The architectural backgrounds are always such as to make us feel the age and ripeness of this society. The author dwells with tender awe upon the long use and the nobility of design of the great shearing-barn, resembling a church in its ground plan, 'wealthy in material', with its 'dusky, filmed, chestnut roof, braced and tied in by huge collars, curves, and diagonals'. It was four centuries old. 'Standing before this abraded pile, the eye regarded its present usage, the mind dwelt upon its past history, with a satisfied sense of functional continuity throughout – a feeling almost of gratitude, and quite of pride, at the permanence of the idea which had heaped it up.'

Hardy has studied well the less sublime among the Dutch masters, and his own pictures have often a suggestion of the manner of Terburg or Gerard Douw. But still more one is reminded, by interiors and night scenes out of doors, in *The Native* and *The Madding Crowd*, of the deep and eloquent chiaroscuro of Rembrandt. Hardy loves to note the effects of a small point of bright light, with its rays soon dissipated in the surrounding gloom. He loves to show the gigantic shadows of human figures about a fire, or the 'wheeling rays' from a passing lantern cast on the ceiling of a room. The old men were sitting about in the dark corners of the malthouse. The room 'was lighted only by the ruddy glow from the kiln mouth, which shone over the floor with the streaming horizontality of the setting sun, and threw upward the shadows of all facial irregularities in those assembled round'. Out of the prevailing darkness would come the slow, deliberate accents of the speakers, as half-guessed incidents of ancient history emerge from the soundless obscurity of lost ages. The topers of the Buck's Head were sinking into the double dimness of the misty day and the evening twilight, symbolic of human weakness and ignorance. As the comfort of the strong drink stole over them, their consciousness of mortal sorrows and obligations itself grew dim. 'The longer Joseph Poorgrass remained, the less his spirit was troubled by the duties which devolved upon him this afternoon. The minutes glided by uncounted, until the evening shades began perceptibly to deepen, and the eyes of the three were but sparkling points on the surface of darkness.'

Such scenes and the sentiment associated with them give to the whole composition a depth of imaginative appeal which would not derive from the main action taken by itself. It is the depth of poetic feeling, the depth we recognise as that of life itself. All is in perfect keeping. And so by the magic of harmonic enrichment, the story of *Far from the Madding Crowd* takes on a degree of truth and beauty which for the first time we are willing to acknowledge as entirely worthy of the genius of Thomas Hardy.

SOURCE: extract from *The Technique of Thomas Hardy* (New York, 1922), pp. 50–79.

Virginia Woolf   (1928)

On Hardy's Achievement

... That [Hardy] was a poet should have been obvious; that he was a novelist might still be held uncertain. But the year after, when *Under the Greenwood Tree* appeared, it was clear that much of the effort of 'feeling for a method' had been overcome. Something of the stubborn originality of the earlier book was lost. The second is accomplished, charming, idyllic compared with the first. The writer, it seems, may well develop into one of our English landscape painters, whose pictures are all of cottage gardens and old peasant women, who lingers to collect and preserve from oblivion the old-fashioned ways and words which are rapidly falling into disuse. And yet what kindly lover of antiquity, what naturalist with a microscope in his pocket, what scholar solicitous for the changing shapes of language, ever heard the cry of a small bird killed in the next wood by an owl with such intensity? The cry 'passed into the silence without mingling with it'. Again we hear, very far away, like the sound of a gun out at sea on a calm summer's morning, a strange and ominous echo. But as we read these early books there is a sense of waste. There is a feeling that Hardy's genius was obstinate and perverse; first one gift would have its way with him and then another. They would not consent to run together easily in harness. Such indeed was likely to be the fate of a writer who was at once poet and realist, a faithful son of field and down, yet tormented by the doubts and despondencies bred of book-learning; a lover of old ways and plain countrymen, yet doomed to see the faith and flesh of his forefathers turn to thin and spectral transparencies before his eyes.

To this contradiction Nature had added another element likely to disorder a symmetrical development. Some writers are born conscious of everything; others are unconscious of many things. Some, like Henry James and Flaubert, are able not merely to make the best use of the spoil their gifts bring in, but control their genius in the act of creation; they are aware of all the possibilities of every situation, and are never taken by surprise. The unconscious writers, on the other hand, like Dickens and Scott, seem suddenly and without their own consent to be lifted up and swept onwards. The wave sinks and they cannot say what has happened or why. Among them – it is the source of his strength and of his weakness – we must place Hardy. His own word, 'moments of vision', exactly describes those passages of astonishing beauty and force which are to be found in every book that he wrote. With a sudden quickening of power which we cannot foretell, nor he, it seems, control, a single scene breaks off from the rest. We see, as if it existed alone and for all time, the wagon with Fanny's dead body inside travelling along the road under the dripping trees; we see the bloated sheep struggling among the clover; we see Troy flashing his sword round Bathsheba where she stands motionless, cutting the lock off her head and spitting the caterpillar on her breast. Vivid to the eye, but not to the eye alone, for every sense participates, such scenes dawn upon us and their splendour remains. But the power goes as it comes. The moment of vision is succeeded by long stretches of plain daylight, nor can we believe that any craft or skill could have caught the wild power and turned it to a better use. The novels therefore are full of inequalities; they are lumpish and dull and inexpressive; but they are never arid; there is always about them a little blur of unconsciousness, that halo of freshness and margin of the unexpressed which often produce the most profound sense of satisfaction. It is as if Hardy himself were not quite aware of what he did, as if his consciousness held more than he could produce, and he left it for his readers to make out his full meaning and to supplement it from their own experience.

For these reasons Hardy's genius was uncertain in development, uneven in accomplishment, but, when the moment came, magnificent in achievement. The moment came, completely and fully in *Far from the Madding Crowd*. The subject was right; the method was right; the poet and the countryman, the sensual man, the sombre reflective man, the man of learning, all enlisted to produce a book which, however fashions may chop and change, must hold its place among the great English novels. There is, in the first place, that sense of the physical world which Hardy more than any novelist can bring before us; the sense that the little prospect of man's existence is ringed by a landscape which, while it exists apart, yet confers a deep and solemn beauty upon his drama. The dark downland, marked by the barrows of the dead and the huts of shepherds, rises against the sky, smooth as a wave of the sea, but solid and eternal; rolling away to the infinite distance, but sheltering in its folds quiet villages whose smoke rises in frail columns by day, whose lamps burn in the immense darkness by night. Gabriel Oak tending his sheep up there on the back of the world is the eternal shepherd; the stars are ancient beacons; and for ages he has watched beside his sheep.

But down in the valley the earth is full of warmth and life; the farms are busy, the barns stored, the fields loud with the lowing of cattle and the bleating of sheep. Nature is prolific, splendid, and lustful; not yet malignant and still the Great Mother of labouring men. And now for the first time Hardy gives full play to his humour, where it is freest and most rich, upon the lips of country men. Jan Coggan and Henry Fray and Joseph Poorgrass gather in the malthouse when the day's work is over and give vent to that half-shrewd, half-poetic humour which has been brewing in their brains and finding expression over their beer since the pilgrims tramped the Pilgrims' Way; which Shakespeare and Scott and George Eliot all loved to overhear, but none loved better or heard with greater understanding than Hardy. But it is not the part of the peasants in the Wessex novels to stand out as individuals. They compose a pool of common wisdom, of common humour, a fund of perpetual life. They comment upon the actions of the hero and heroine, but while Troy or Oak or Fanny or Bathsheba come in and out and pass away, Jan Coggan and Henry Fray and Joseph Poorgrass remain. They drink by night and they plough the fields by day. They are eternal. We meet them over and over again in the novels, and they always have something typical about them, more of the character that marks a race than of the features which belong to an individual. The peasants are the great sanctuary of sanity, the country the last stronghold of happiness. When they disappear, there is no hope for the race. . . .

SOURCE: extract from essay, 'The Novels of Thomas Hardy', written in January 1928, *The Common Reader*, vol. II (1932); reproduced in *Collected Essays*, vol. I (London, 1966), pp. 257–60.

PART THREE

Modern Studies on Individual Novels

1. *Under the Greenwood Tree*
2. *Far from the Madding Crowd*
3. *The Woodlanders*

1. *UNDER THE GREENWOOD TREE*

John F. Danby 'The Individual and the Universal' (1959)

Under the Greenwood Tree was published in 1872. In 1912 Hardy wrote:

In re-reading the narrative after a long interval there occurs the inevitable reflection that the realities of which it was spun were material for another kind of study of this little group of church musicians than is found in the chapters here penned so lightly, even so farcically and flippantly at times. But circumstances would have rendered any aim at a deeper, more essential, more transcendent handling inadvisable at the date of writing.

Makers are notoriously bad judges of their own creations. Hardy himself obviously preferred the longer, 'deeper, more essential, more transcendent' novels he subsequently wrote. *Under the Greenwood Tree* is shorter than *Jude the Obscure*. It is also less pretentious. It is, however, not less deep and not less transcendent. Already in 1872 it says as much as Hardy will ever be able to say, and maybe in a form more satisfactory than any he later devised. It has no obvious design on depth or transcendence, but achieves profundity nevertheless. It is as simple and as satisfying and as deep as 'Paying Calls' – a lyric which Hardy, no doubt, would have rated very low as compared with *The Dynasts*:

> I went by foot-path and by stile
>   Beyond where bustle ends,
> Strayed here awhile, and there awhile,
>   And called upon some friends.
>
> On some of them I had not seen
>   For years past did I call,
> And then on others who had been
>   The oldest friends of all.
>
> It was the time of midsummer,
>   When they had used to roam,
> But now, though quiet was the air,
>   I found them all at home.

> I talked to one and other of them,
> By mound and stone and tree,
> Of things we had done in days long gone
> But they spoke not to me.

All Hardy is present in the lyric, as he is in *Under the Greenwood Tree*. In neither the poem nor the novel is 'philosophy' forced upon us. In both it is implied. The 'philosophy' is the story-world as the poet-and-novelist constructs it. To appreciate the one we must enter the other, enter it carefully in company with the story-teller, taking things in the order in which he offers them to us.

Wuthering Heights is timeless and placeless compared with *Under the Greenwood Tree*. The problem it is interested in is a problem that concerns persons as such – persons considered in themselves and in isolation from everything else, persons reduced to the single primary personal need for 'an existence of yours beyond you'. *Wuthering Heights* is a heroic assertion of the human conceived of as the purely personal. Cathy and Heathcliff would continue to exist if all the rest of mankind and their containing universe were destroyed, provided they continued to exist for each other. There is, therefore, no organised society in *Wuthering Heights*. Liverpool, where Heathcliff was picked up, might as well be a Javan jungle. London, the home of some of the people in the novel, might just as well be Kamchatka. There is no village, no community into which the characters fit – nothing but the hillside and those elemental forces which constitute the real surroundings of Thrushcross Grange.

Under the Greenwood Tree is in abrupt contrast with *Wuthering Heights* in both these respects. No novel in English has a stronger sense of the linkage of people into families, and of families into communities, and of communities into the wider fellowship still of the succeeding generations of men. And instead of asserting the individual and the personal to the utmost, as Emily Brontë does, Hardy makes a carefully diminished claim. To do so most emphatically, he chooses that sphere where the personal and the individual seem most unassailable – the sphere of Romantic Love where Emily Brontë found her strongest argument for an imperishable and inextinguishable value in personality as such.

Under the Greenwood Tree is a love-story, but the private romance of Dick Dewy and Fancy Day is framed within the story of Mellstock Quire. 'The name of the story', Hardy tells us, 'was originally intended to be, more appropriately, *The Mellstock Quire*.' Two strands are intertwined in the novel. The main apparent emphasis is on the love-story, but Hardy's original title reflects what he thought (rightly) to be the more important theme. For, as we shall see, the importance of the love-story, in Hardy's view, like the importance of the lovers to each other, is that really it is unimportant: or not really important in the way those immediately concerned in it think it is. The life of the individual and the feelings that seem to dominate one's private world are epiphenomenal only. The explicit pessimism of the later Hardy is already implicit in his first work. The need for an existence of yours beyond you is pathetically ineluctable, and the assurance that such exists pathetically fallacious.

I want, then, merely to indicate how Hardy's view of life expresses itself through the narrative he writes and the narrative procedure he adopts, following the writer as he assembles the bits of his world, carefully grouping and composing, floating in this detail and that, with the patient and expert attention to *minutiae* we might expect in 'A Rural Painting of the Dutch School'. Novels such as *Under the Greenwood Tree* require to be read with the same concentration as poems.

The story begins in Mellstock Lane, which connects 'one of the hamlets of Mellstock parish with Upper Mellstock and Lewgate'. 'A man' is walking up the lane. He is heard singing:

> 'With the rose and the lily
> And the daffadowndilly
> The lads and the lasses a-sheep-shearing go'.

The 'man', who is shortly hailed by a fellow countryman also walking in the lane, is Dick Dewy – the 'hero' of the story. First merely a voice singing an age-old song, then a name on the lips of a friendly neighbour, he now detaches himself from the darkness and is visible against the night-sky. We see him only in outline:

his profile appearing on the light background like the portrait of a gentleman in black cardboard. It assumed the form of a low-crowned hat, an ordinary-shaped nose, an ordinary chin, an ordinary neck, and ordinary shoulders. What he consisted of further down was invisible from lack of sky low enough to picture him on.

This is one of those imaginative moments which constantly recur in Hardy's work. Less obtrusively 'essential' and 'transcendent' than, say, the description of Egdon Heath, this introduction is nevertheless as powerfully symbolic – this instance of age-old Man in general, this moving part of a particular countryside, this ordinary person, one half silhouetted against the night-sky, the other invisible and as it were buried waist-deep in the earth. Dick is joined by the rest of the group: Michael Mail, Robert Penny the Shoemaker, Elias Spinks, Joseph Bowman, Thomas Leaf. They go on together to Dick's home. As they

go their silhouettes suggest 'some processional design on Greek or
Etruscan pottery'. They remain, however, 'the chief portion of
Mellstock Quire'.

This method of introducing us to the hero is repeated with the
heroine later. We see her through the shoemaker's eyes, and the
eyes of his tradition and trade. The shoemaker is carrying one of
her shoes in his pocket, and the last on which her father's shoes are
made. The last is the same he used for her father's father, with only
minor modifications to allow for the individual differences of the
son, and with still less important additions from time to time (a
lump of leather to allow for the bunion he's had ever since being a
boy, another piece for where a horse trod on his foot) to cover the
slight changes introduced by one's vagarious biography. The
shoemaker's eye can tell that the dainty woman's shoe in his pocket
bears a family resemblance to the shoe of the father, as the father's
does to the grandfather's.

Hardy's aim all through the novel is to put the individual (for
whom such heroic claims are sometimes made, and who seems so
important to himself) in his 'proper' place. He likes to dwell on the
various and endless vistas in which particular man is set. Thus we
have seen the Mellstock Quire in the perspective of its own more
ancient countryside, and outlined against the same sky that framed
Greek and Etruscan. When they arrive inside Dick's home we are
to see them as vital parts of the continuing generation of men –
vital, but also deciduous. Dick Dewy is the eldest of a family of five.
His father is tapping a cider-barrel. Mrs Dewy welcomes each
guest and enters into the easy intimacies of the village. Suddenly
the casual words, so naturally introduced, develop their characteristic
overtones:

'Here, Mr Penny', resumed Mrs Dewy, 'you sit in this chair. And how's
your daughter, Mrs Brownjohn?'

'Well, I suppose I must say pretty fair.' He adjusted his spectacles a
quarter of an inch to the right. 'But she'll be worse before she's better, 'a
b'lieve.'

'Indeed – poor soul! And how many will that make in all, four or five?'

'Five; they've buried three. Yes, five; and she not much more than a
maid yet. She do know the multiplication table unmistakable well. –
However, 'twas to be, and none can gainsay it.'

Mrs Dewy resigned Mr Penny. 'Wonder where your grandfather James
is?' she inquired of one of the children. 'He said he'd drop in tonight.'

'Out in fuel-house with grandfather William', said Jimmy.

Dick Dewy is the eldest of five in a community where others
(scarcely older than himself) also know the table of increase and

multiply, as he, no doubt, will learn it soon. Then, casually, Hardy's eye travels past Dick and his father and mother to the two grandfathers 'out in fuel-house' splitting logs for the yule fire. The bright-lit room is suddenly set among the great shadowy darknesses of the generations past and generations to come.

The first four or five chapters of *Under the Greenwood Tree* are all-important for telling us what the book is really about, and a superb example of Hardy's technique at its best. They do not exist merely to provide atmosphere, or to arrange an externally correct stage for the drama about to begin. Hardy's story begins with the first sentence of the book. Man in time, and the transactions of Time with men, are his story. Time is his chief character as it is later in *Jude*. The first chapters exist to set up the real framework of all the stories Hardy believes can ever be told. The vast perspectives of time that have been before the here-and-now of the narrative, the equally vast spaces that will succeed when the story is finished, are essential inward parts of Hardy's deepest feeling about the human fates he is describing. There is nothing unutterably special in one's private romance. The individual love-story of Dick Dewy and Fancy Day is like the foliage on the trees, and they themselves are merely trees in a larger forest. The significance of their story is that it has all happened before, wherever there have been men and maids, and will continue to happen in roughly similar ways so long as

> The lads and the lasses a-sheep-shearing go.

If, Hardy suggests, there is any comfort to be extracted from our contemplation of lonely man – this creature who has struggled half out of the dark earth only to outline himself in blackness against a pale night-sky – it is not to be sought in the individual heart as such. There is no safety or permanence or assurance in the joys or fears, the hopes or the despairs, which make up any private story. The only possibility of solace is to be sought in Time itself – which brings griefs but which also bears them away, which replaces keen feelings with steady and settled habits, which allows the individual to become merely a part of the good-neighbourly village, with its assured and settled ways, its well-known and established grooves worn smooth by generations of use and acceptance, found to be best for men. Time levels the greatest tragedies with the most minor annoyances, and past laughter mellows into a regretful smile.

Hardy doesn't sermonise in *Under the Greenwood Tree* as we have done here, and as Hardy himself will do later (at the time when he sees in his first novel material for a study far different from the light, flippant, and even farcical thing it is). Explicit sermonising is unnecessary when such swifter and completer means of expression are open to him as the following:

'Reuben, don't make such a mess o' tapping that barrel as is mostly made in this house', Mrs Dewy cried from the fireplace. 'I'd tap a hundred without wasting more than you do in one. Such a squizzling and squirting job as 'tis in your hands! There, he always was such a clumsy man indoors.'

'Ay, ay; I know you'd tap a hundred beautiful, Ann – I know you would; two hundred, perhaps. But I can't promise. This is a' old cask, and the wood's rotted away about the tap-hole. The husbird of a fellow Sam Lawson – that ever I should call'n such, now he's dead and gone, poor heart! – took me in completely upon the feat of buying this cask. "Reub", says he – 'a always used to call me plain Reub, poor old heart! – "Reub", he says, says he, "that there cask, Reub, is as good as new. 'Tis a wine-hogshead; the best port-wine in the commonwealth have been in that there cask; and you shall have 'en for ten shillens, Reub" – 'a said,' says he – ' "he's worth twenty, ay, five-and-twenty, if he's worth one; and an iron hoop or two put round 'en among the wood ones will make 'en worth thirty shillens of any man's money, if –" '

'I think I should have used the eyes that Providence gave me to use afore I paid any ten shillens for a jimcrack wine-barrel; a saint is sinner enough not to be cheated. But 'tis like all your family was, so easy to be deceived.'

'That's as true as gospel of this member', said Reuben.

Mrs Dewy began a smile at the answer, then altering her lips and refolding them so that it was not a smile, commenced smoothing little Bessy's hair.

This is another passage that looks forward and looks back. It looks back to Sam Lawson, 'dead and gone', and to an incident in Reuben Dewy's past which is quickly recognised by his neighbours as typical, is seized upon and generally applied. It levels, too. All deceits, in retrospect, are reduced to the scale of a bad bargain over a cider-barrel; past villanies also are mellowed in memory to forgivable idiosyncracies. Sam Lawson is no sooner reviled for the 'husbird' he was, than he is remembered with regret for the vanished neighbour he somehow still is, 'now he's dead and gone, poor heart'. In the over-all wisdom of the countryside, which sees its established ways as supervening authoritatively on even the most ambitious and approvable of human efforts, the levelling goes even further: 'a saint is sinner enough not to be cheated.' It also looks forward. To be deceived is a family fate among the Dewys. Mrs Dewy's ambiguous smile seems to cast back a fleeting glance to the beguiling days of her courtship and Reuben's. A failing so generally recognised and so universally understood, however, is not a thing over which to take up a tragic stance. It has all moved on to this resting stage of habitual and comfortable acceptance, this mutual knowledge and the taking of ups and downs for granted. Dick Dewy can hear the conversation. It is not to be expected that he should understand it yet. He has not yet qualified for the wisdom it embodies. He has not yet fallen in love, been himself deceived maybe, suffered certainly, and in due time got over his suffering. He has not yet grown up. The story of *Under the Greenwood Tree* will be the story of his growing pains, of his becoming more nearly what his father and mother and all their neighbours have become. Whether or not he has fulfilled the family fate will still be an open question at the end of the novel. That his wife, looking back on the courtship after forty years, will be able to smile at him is certainly not.

At the end of chapter VIII occurs one of the most striking passages in the book. It projects Dick's individual and romantic love-affair against the habit of marriage as a general human thing. The Dewys have had their party, and Dick has met Fancy Day in the flesh for the first time. He has helped himself to potatoes from the same tureen, he has danced with her, he has all but kissed her, he has fallen abyssmally in love with her. Now the house is left to Dick and his father and mother: the guests have gone, and Mr Shiner is seeing Fancy home:

'All was over; and Dick surveyed the chair she had last occupied, looking now like a setting from which the gem has been torn. There stood her glass, and the romantic teaspoonful of elder wine at the bottom that she couldn't drink by trying ever so hard, in obedience to the mighty arguments of the tranter (his hand coming down on her shoulder the while like a Nasmyth hammer); but the drinker was there no longer. There were the nine or ten pretty little crumbs she had left on her plate; but the eater was no more seen.

There seemed a disagreeable closeness of relationship between himself and the members of his family, now that they were left alone again face to face. His father seemed quite offensive for appearing to be in just as high spirits as when the guests were there; and as for grandfather James (who had not yet left), he was quite fiendish in being rather glad they were gone.

'Really', said the tranter, in a tone of placid satisfaction, 'I've had so little time to attend to myself all the evenen, that I mean to enjoy a quiet meal now! A slice of this here ham – neither too fat nor too lean – so; and then a drop of this vinegar and pickles – there, that's it – and I shall be as fresh as a lark again! And to tell the truth, my sonny, my inside has been as dry as a lime-basket all night.'

'I like a party very well once in a while', said Mrs Dewy, leaving off the adorned tones she had been bound to use throughout the evening, and returning to the natural marriage voice; 'but, Lord, 'tis such a sight of heavy work next day! What with the dirty plates, and knives and forks, and dust and smother, and bits kicked off your furniture, and I don't know what all, why a body could a'most wish there were no such things as Christmases . . . Ah-h dear!' she yawned, till the clock in the corner had ticked several beats. She cast her eyes round upon the displaced, dust-laden furniture, and sank down overpowered at the sight.

'Well, I be getting all right by degrees, thank the Lord for 't!' said the tranter cheerfully through a mangled mass of ham and bread, without lifting his eyes from his plate, and chopping away with his knife and fork as if he were felling trees. 'Ann, you may as well go on to bed at once, and not bide there making such sleepy faces; you look as long-favoured as a fiddle, upon my life, Ann. There, you must be wearied out, 'tis true. I'll do the doors and draw up the clock; and you go on, or you'll be as white as a sheet tomorrow."

'Ay; I don't know whether I shan't or no.' The matron passed her hand across her eyes to brush away the film of sleep till she got upstairs.

Dick wondered how it was that when people were married they could be so blind to romance; and was quite certain that if he ever took to wife that dear impossible Fancy, he and she would never be so dreadfully practical and undemonstrative of the Passion as his father and mother were. The most extraordinary thing was, that all the fathers and mothers he knew were just as undemonstrative as his own.

Dick looking at his parents is looking at what he and Fancy, with only insignificant differences, will eventually become. It is the comedy of human romance, tragic only to those who never find safe harbourage in 'the village'. Hardy's eye rests – or seems to rest – on the stable forms of the village's way of life.

The resting-stage is only an apparent one, however. But it is a resting-stage, and that is why he could be content with the mellow comedy of *Under the Greenwood Tree*. But in 1912 Hardy realised even more clearly than in 1872 that the possibilities of such a comic resolution of the human plight, the transformation of private pains into public habits of wisdom, were gone for good. The comic resolution required the assumption that the village of Mellstock Quire would always be there. And already it was vanishing. *Under the Greenwood Tree* dramatises the first shocks to its structure: the new parson who is not content to be good but is bent also, unfortunately, on being 'religious good'; the new Church organ, the symbol of an invasion that will sweep away the age-old pattern; Fancy Day herself, the new school-teacher, unconscious harbinger of standards and institutions different from any the village has known. The bases for comedy have already been attacked. The world Fancy and Dick will grow up in will be very different from that within which their courtship has been conducted. The resting-stage of 'the village' Hardy knows is only temporary, already part of a dream. Yet his later novels make no advance into the new time that is being born. Hardy prefers to go back to the social setting of early nineteenth-century Wessex. Only, at the same time, his knowledge that 'the village' is a dead one is accentuated: the dream is an anxious one. 'Paying Calls' is an allegory of Hardy's innermost life.

The great novels, we said, should be read as we read poems. In poems the ending is often in the beginning – once we have come to the end and we can know that that is so. This is true of *Wuthering Heights*, with its nightmare that can be either prologue or epilogue to the story. It is also true of *Under the Greenwood Tree*. This is the opening paragraph: it could well be a final comment on the deciduous generations in their endless and multifarious perspectives of Nature and Time. It could also be a fitting summary of Hardy's art – an art that never generalises except through the particular, and that never sees the particular without remembering also the universal:

To dwellers in a wood almost every species of tree has its voice as well as its feature. At the passing of the breeze the fir-trees sob and moan no less distinctly than they rock; the holly whistles as it battles with itself; the ash hisses amid its quiverings; the beech rustles while its flat boughs rise and fall. And winter, which modifies the note of such trees as shed their leaves, does not destroy its individuality.

Source: essay, 'Under the Greenwood Tree', in *Critical Quarterly*, I, no. 1 (Spring 1959), pp. 5–13.

Michael Millgate   'Elements of Several Literary Modes'   (1971)

. . . When submitting the manuscript to Macmillan Hardy had referred to it as *Under the Greenwood Tree*, but its first page must still have shown, as it does now, the deletion of 'The Mellstock Quire'. These words did not appear on the first edition title-page, but

Hardy later brought them back as an alternative title, implying in the 1912 Preface that he would have restored them to their original position had it not seemed 'undesirable to displace . . . the title by which the book first became known'. It is difficult to share this preference for an inertly descriptive title, however appropriate to a genre painting 'of the Dutch school', over one so richly suggestive – . . .

Clearly, the final title was not – as *Early Life* implies – picked out casually from *The Golden Treasury* in order to satisfy a contemporary fashion for 'titles from poetry'. The phrase of course comes from the song in *As You Like It* [II v], a play which seems to have had a special fascination for Hardy. His poem, 'To an Impersonator of Rosalind', shows that he was much impressed by the performance of Mrs Scott-Siddons in that role in 1867 (see also the later 'The Two Rosalinds'), and the 'neat figure' and 'freedom of gesture' with which Mrs Scott-Siddons is credited in contemporary accounts may conceivably have contributed something to the emphasis in *Under the Greenwood Tree* on Fancy Day's ease and grace of movement: 'Flexibility was her first characteristic, by which she appeared to enjoy the most easeful rest when she was in gliding motion.' Fancy, indeed, has a good deal about her of the Shakespearean comic heroine, not least the quickness of wit she displays in her exchange with Farmer Shiner in the chapter of the honey-taking, and her early treatment of Dick suggests a less sophisticated version of Rosalind's teasing of the devoted Orlando – apparently a high-point of Mrs Scott-Siddons's performance.

The main function of the *As You Like It* allusion in the title of *Under the Greenwood Tree* is anticipated, interestingly enough, by an allusion to the same song in *Desperate Remedies*. Cytherea, just entering into service at Miss Aldeclyffe's, gazes out of the window as she reflects on her unhappy situation:

The petty, vulgar details of servitude that she had just passed through, her dependence upon the whims of a strange woman, the necessity of quenching all individuality of character in herself, and relinquishing her own peculiar tastes to help on the wheel of this alien establishment, made her sick and sad, and she almost longed to pursue some free, out-of-doors employment, sleep under trees or a hut, and know no enemy but winter and cold weather, like shepherds and cowkeepers, and birds and animals – ay, like the sheep she saw there under her window.

The sheep are used in the following paragraphs to establish a narrative link, but their introduction here (as in the opening scene of *The Trumpet-Major*) helps to establish a specifically pastoral pattern of reference. The Shakespearan allusion fits into that pattern, and it again does so throughout *Under the Greenwood Tree*, where it is worked into the very fabric of the book – in terms, for instance, of the actual greenwood tree which provides the centre-piece for the wedding celebrations at the end of the novel, and of the final scene of all, with its reference, in the nightingale's 'come hither', to the same song from *As You Like It*. As Fancy promises Dick that she will have no secrets from him 'from to-day':

> From a neighbouring thicket was suddenly heard to issue in a loud, musical, and liquid voice –
> 'Tippiwit! swe-e-et! ki-ki-ki! Come hither, come hither, come hither!'
> 'O 'tis the nightingale', murmured she, and thought of a secret she would never tell.

Fancy's secret, unlike that of the nightingale, is of her own guilt, not of another's: in Arcadian Mellstock, clearly, as in the Forest of Arden, the ways of women may present a hazard at least as threatening as that of 'winter and rough weather'.

It would be too much to suggest that Hardy attempted or even contemplated any detailed pattern of correspondences between his novel and Shakespeare's play. Consciously and unconsciously, however, *As You Like It* was a lively presence in his imagination, prompting by its structural incorporation of music, song and dance his own adoption of comparable techniques, encouraging and sustaining him in his choice of a pastoral theme and treatment, in the composition of a story with the patterned simplicity of a country dance and the time-honoured familiarity of a ballad. Because it is so simple, so familiar and so highly patterned, it is hard not to think of *Under the Greenwood Tree* as a kind of parable carrying with it the sort of mild moral always implicit in the simplest of pastorals – a moral, here, of individual transience and racial permanence:

> Yonder a maid and her wight
>   Come whispering by:
> War's annals will cloud into night
>   Ere their story die.

Hardy seems to have conceived of *Under the Greenwood Tree* as a kind of woodland pastoral, moving in time with the procession of the seasons (an idea Hardy may have taken from Elizabethan pastorals, from Thomson or from William Barnes) and in isolation from the world of great events. The characters are mostly musicians; their festivals and important occasions are musically celebrated.

On the first page of the book Dick Dewy sings a song about sheep-shearing; in the final chapter the extended description of his marriage-day culminates in the dancing under the greenwood tree. The image of the dance, so persistent throughout Hardy's work, is here especially pervasive, closely related as it is to the theme of choosing and exchanging partners. Dick's situation, for instance, is beautifully defined in terms of the dance of 'Triumph, or Follow my Lover' during the tranter's party: in this dance, 'according to the interesting rule laid down', partners change from time and time, so that although Dick is initially successful in securing Fancy as his 'prize' he has still to endure the sight of her coming down the room with Farmer Shiner 'like two persons tripping down a lane to be married' – just such a lane, it might be added, as the actual wedding party walks down in the chapter called 'The Knot There's No Untying'.

If the characters tend to range themselves dynastically, 'two and two: every man hitched up to his woman', they also tend in general conversation to bear an independent part as in a musical performance: each has his or her 'note', and each – even Thomas Leaf – has his turn to sound it. The practical question of the church music is central to the story, and Parson Maybold's infatuation with Fancy reaches its height on the day of her first appearance as church organist. Music, indeed, is of such importance throughout the novel that responsiveness to it becomes – as so often with Shakespeare and the Elizabethan poets – a criterion of moral evaluation. We learn much of Fancy Day, Farmer Shiner and Parson Maybold as – by one of Hardy's happiest devices – we are introduced to them in turn as the choir makes its rounds on Christmas Eve. Later in the novel it is Fancy's sensitivity to music which prevents her being regarded as the choir's enemy, while the essential coarseness of Farmer Shiner is confirmed by his singing unsuitable ballads in Fancy's presence. It is true that Dick criticises the rhymes of the ballad rather than its statements, but Hardy must have expected some at least of his readers to know that Shiner's ballad was, as he himself later remarked to a correspondent, 'a coarsely humorous one' with a first stanza somewhat as follows:

> King Arthur he had three sons,
> Big rogues as ever did swing,
> He had three sons of wh——s
> And he kicked them all three out-of-doors
> Because they could not sing.

Of the musicians themselves it is William Dewy, the most devoted to music, who displays the greatest magnanimity, and it is with his point of view that Hardy's own position seems to be most closely identified, insofar as he can be said to have taken a position at all within the world of the novel. Harmony becomes a dominant concept, and in the speech of these country people who make their own music images of harmony recur with a marvellous inevitability:

> Mrs Dewy came up, talking to one person and looking at another, 'Happy, yes', she said. ''Tis always so when a couple is so exactly in tune with one another as Dick and she.'
> 'When they be'n't too poor to have time to sing', said grandfather James.

Grandfather James, not a musician, is the melancholy Jaques of this greenwood – the correspondence of names may not be accidental, although James was also a Hardy family name – and his 'inharmonious' note of cold realism is consistently disruptive of the idyllic surface. *As You Like It* is full of songs of youth and love which find their echo in *Under the Greenwood Tree*, but it also contains 'Blow, blow, thou winter wind' as well as the disquisition of Jaques on the seven ages of man, and these anti-pastoral themes are also heard in Hardy's novel: the book is, as it were, framed between grandfather William and grandfather James. Much is made of the sequence, the conflict, and ultimately the succession of the generations. The recurrent dances effectively divide the group into the children, the young, the middle-aged, and the old, while the retrospective tendency of the conversation and the very antiquity of the customs being observed all promote a constant awareness that those who are old were once young and those now in the energy of youth will soon become old in their turn. Dick Dewy becomes dimly aware of such truths as he argues with his father about Fancy Day across the gap of a generation, as he notes the curious similarities in the behaviour of all long-married couples or listens to their talk of their own courtships. And these are among the truths symbolised in the greenwood tree itself.

Under the Greenwood Tree is to some extent an ironic title, and fairly radical patterns of irony can be traced within the book itself – although 'irony' may not always be quite the right term for that perpetual re-adjustment of the human balance which is what really seems to be going on. Each gain in the book has its counter-balancing loss, each happiness its sadness, each despair its triumph; there *are* enemies under the greenwood tree, nonetheless the 'winter wind' does blow some people some good. Grandfather James's disenchanted comments have their due impact, but many of

Hardy's effects are achieved in less explicit ways. In Part the Fifth, in particular, there is to the wedding of Dick and Fancy a quiet but audible undertone of foreboding, not so much of a troubled marriage ahead (though that suspicion is not entirely absent) as of the consequences which the passage of time will bring in its train. Dick, his romantic feelings already giving way to practical good sense, arrives late because he has paused to hive a swarm of bees: as grandfather James observes, 'marrying a woman is a thing you can do at any moment; but a swarm o' bees won't come for the asking'. Fancy, six hours a wife, tries to look matronly, but there are plenty of pointers to suggest that she will be a matron all too soon: Nat Callcombe says the married couple have so much food and furniture 'that anybody would think they were going to take hold the big end of married life first, and begin wi' a grown-up family'. The furniture removed to Dick's house has sadly depleted the keeper's cottage, and we have a sense of the Day household itself having been broken up. Enoch has left (as appears is an oddly disturbing episode at the end of the penultimate chapter), and Mrs Day, retreating even further from reality, has gone upstairs to dust the second-best china. Life, it seems, has moved on and away from the keeper's cottage, and it may not be irrelevant to note that Dick's bees have swarmed while Mrs Day's have not.

The importance given to bees – they are persistently associated with crucial events in Dick's courtship of Fancy – exemplifies Hardy's extraordinary success in this novel in evoking large patterns in terms of trivial details, rooting the symbolic in the domestic and everyday. Whatever suggestions the bees may prompt – from thoughts of the fourth book of the *Georgics* and of the seasonal cycle to images of female domination – their presence in the book depends upon the importance of honey in the rural economy at a period when sugar was an imported luxury, expensive and heavily taxed. Similarly grounded in the realities of Dorset life in the first half of the nineteenth century, before that exodus of rural craftsmen which Hardy laments in 'The Dorsetshire Labourer' and elsewhere, is the early episode in which Mr Penny dramatically places before his fascinated audience the boot belonging to Miss Fancy Day:

'Now, neighbours, though no common eye can see it', the shoemaker went on, 'a man in the trade can see the likeness between this boot and that last, although that is so deformed as hardly to recall one of God's creatures, and this is one of as pretty a pair as you'd get for ten-and-sixpence in Casterbridge. To you, nothing; but 'tis father's voot and daughter's voot to me, as plain as houses.'

The scene itself is superbly realised, with the glances of the men 'converged like wheel-spokes upon the boot in the centre of them': the heroine is auspiciously and (since Fancy is to prove quick-footed enough) appropriately heralded; one of the major themes of the novel, the inevitable procession of the generations, is stated early and in the most concrete of terms. Fancy's boot may lack the allusive potential of the greenwood tree in Part the Fifth, but it is a beautifully calculated embodiment of the book's abstract themes.

In praising the controlled composition of *Under the Greenwood Tree* – and it is the most nearly flawless of Hardy's novels – it is essential not to undervalue its immense page-by-page vitality and toughness of texture. The strength here comes primarily from the humour, all-pervasive though elusive of definition; from the dialogue, an unmistakably rural speech that avoids mere quaintness and dialectal eccentricity while achieving distinctiveness through a reassuring sufficiency of localisms; and from the discriminating use of 'placing' detail in the evocation of setting and scene, as in the descriptions of the living-rooms of the Day and Dewy households. Hardy's intimate and affectionate familiarity with his material is fundamental to the success, and to the assurance, of *Under the Greenwood Tree*. The detailed descriptions of the various members of the Mellstock Quire, the account of Mr Penny at his work, the long passages of country conversation – these are by no means essential to the 'story', the contest for the hand of Fancy Day, but they are the very stuff of the book.

As Hardy originally conceived of the book it may have been even more of a series of sketches and impressions – a kind of 'Scenes from Rural Life' – than it is at present. The manuscript preserves indications of more numerous chapter divisions: the chapter called 'Honey-taking, and Afterwards', for example, seems at one time to have been three separate chapters, 'Honey-taking', 'Emptying the hives' and 'Dick pleads his cause'. The novel remains unusually rich in visual impressions, and the relevance of the sub-title, 'A Rural Painting of the Dutch School', seems to extend beyond these to the deliberate delineation of customs, beliefs, attitudes, the whole fabric of rural life. The slight tale in its restricted setting is filled with figures, highly individualised as to both personality and social role, each of whom finds his place in the tightly-organised overall structure in terms not so much of plot as of what might in a painting be called composition: each has his position in the design, and whether that position be dominant or subordinate the figure itself appears in sharp focus.

The society presented in the novel is, in pastoral fashion, both remote and remarkably homogeneous: there is scarcely a murmur of the world outside, and Hardy may deliberately have excluded the inhabitants of the local manor-house in the interests of limiting the greenwood world to those who truly belong there. Yet he insists, with a mild exploitation of pastoral for purposes of satire, that even Mellstock folk display a passionate preoccupation with questions of economic and social status, an intense concern for niceties of behaviour and of domestic arrangement. Here as elsewhere Hardy anticipates Lawrence in stressing the perpetual conflict between the women's striving towards gentility and the unregenerate 'animality' of the menfolk, and if vanity and social ambition are dangerous flaws in the personality of Fancy Day, her stepmother's obsession with 'appearances' has reached a point not far short of madness:

> The table had been spread for the mixed midday meal of dinner and tea which was common among frugal countryfolk. 'The parishioners about here', continued Mrs Day, not looking at any living being, but snatching up the brown delf tea-things, 'are the laziest, gossipest, poachest, jailest set of any ever I came among. And they'll talk about my teapot and tea-things next, I suppose!' She vanished with the teapot, cups, and saucers, and reappeared with a tea-service in white china, and a packet wrapped in brown paper. This was removed, together with folds of tissue-paper underneath; and a brilliant silver teapot appeared.

The second Mrs Day is, however, only sustaining a tradition firmly established by the first. It is a crucial element in Fancy's power to disturb both men and customs that she is of higher educational and social standing than anyone in Mellstock apart from Parson Maybold: her father's wealth is much discussed, her mother was a governess, and she herself has been given an education unusually good for a young woman in the first half of the nineteenth century. The disruptive side-effects of Fancy's education are evident enough: that she becomes entangled in disagreements among the vicar, the church-warden and the choir is not simply because she is pretty but because she has been taught to play the organ, and if she is not herself an active innovator she is inevitably associated with the pressures making for social change. Hardy also emphasises that she, like her father, belongs not to Mellstock itself but to a neighbouring parish. Yet the disappearance of the choir and of the traditions and values which it embodied cannot be laid at Fancy's door. Choirs in other parishes have already disappeared, and the Mellstock choir has its internal weaknesses, among them the quiet cynicism of Reuben Dewy and the incipient defection of Dick. It is the chief pillar of the choir's strength, William Dewy himself, who is most indulgent towards Parson Maybold's innovation and most insistent that disbandment be accepted in a dignified and charitable manner. As for Fancy's specifically sexual role, it is notable that in the revisions which he made to the novel of 1896 and 1912 Hardy deliberately raised the social and economic status of Geoffrey Day – it is only in the 1912 edition that Day can contrast his earlier position as keeper with a situation in which he has 'a dozen other irons in the fire as steward here for my lord' – and, at the same time, significantly increased the dialect element in the speech of Dick Dewy. The effect of these changes is to place Fancy, in socio-economic terms, further away from Dick and closer to Maybold, to re-emphasise her social location somewhere between the two men, and to increase both the credibility of Maybold's proposal and the reality of his threat. Farmer Shiner's vulgarity (Hardy seems originally to have conceived of him as a publican) soon disqualifies him as a likely victor in the contest for Fancy's hand, but he too is a richer man than Dick and easily gains the support of Fancy's father.

Hardy once said that he was not interested in manners, and it may indeed have been that he did not feel particularly concerned with the manners of those urban middle and upper classes which had most often been made the subjects of nineteenth-century fiction. He had nonetheless a profound appreciation of the behavioural standards and social discriminations current among the country people he had known in his childhood and youth, and his fascination with these was sufficient to make *Under the Greenwood Tree* something very like a novel of rural manners. The book has already been referred to as pastoral, idyll and potential parable; to define it also as a novel of rural manners may seem a little excessive. In fact, *Under the Greenwood Tree* cannot be precisely fitted into any terminological pigeonhole. While it displays elements of several literary modes it does not fully exemplify any one of them, and nothing in the book is more impressive than Hardy's refusal to allow it to become wholly predictable along the lines of a single formal precedent. Although the temptation in the final scenes to avoid reminders of Fancy's moment of weakness must have been a strong one, Hardy's chosen ending is far from conventional felicity, except in the sense that the book itself has by this time established its own conventions in terms of which the marriage of Dick and Fancy can be recognised as being reasonably fortunate – as marriages go. By the end of the novel something real if scarcely tangible has been lost, something detectable in the contrast between the air of unease and restraint which hangs over the dance under

the greenwood tree and the comfortable enjoyment which marked
the party at the tranter's in the opening pages. For all the
celebration of vanished woodland days and ways it is necessary to
acknowledge that if *Under the Greenwood Tree* is an idyll it is one in
which, at the end, many things are less than idyllic.

SOURCE: extract from ch. 3 of *Thomas Hardy: His Career as a Novelist*
(London, 1971), pp. 44–54.

Norman Page   Hardy's Dutch Painting
(1976)

Although it shows him already in possession of some of the devices
of story-telling and description which were to become characteristic,
Desperate Remedies, Hardy's first novel, is in most respects a blind
alley, after which he found himself compelled to resume the quest
for a form of fiction more consonant with his talents and his
experience. The book which followed, *Under the Greenwood Tree*, is,
very consciously, an exercise in a totally different genre. It rejects
as a model the sensation fiction of Wilkie Collins, which Hardy had
taken up against the grain of his natural inclinations and in
consequence of a misunderstanding of the advice given by
Macmillan's reader, George Meredith; and puts in its place the
rustic-nostalgic, sentimental-ironic vein of the early George Eliot.
(Soon afterwards, indeed, the anonymously-published *Far from the
Madding Crowd* was to be attributed to the latter author.) When
Hardy gave his new novel the subtitle 'A Rural Painting of the
Dutch School', he was perhaps recalling a passage in Eliot's *Adam
Bede* – the passage which begins:

It is for this rare, precious quality of truthfulness that I delight in many
Dutch paintings, which lofty-minded people despise. I find a source of
delicious sympathy in these faithful pictures of a monotonous homely
existence, which has been the fate of so many more among my fellow-
mortals than a life of pomp or of absolute indigence, of tragic suffering or
of world-stirring actions . . .   [ch. 17]

and which goes on to include a reference to 'that village wedding
. . . where an awkward bridegroom opens the dance . . . while

elderly and middle-aged friends look on' – a scene which, with
some modifications, forms the closing chapter of Hardy's novel. He
may well also have been recalling the opening pages of *Scenes of
Clerical Life*, with its account of 'improvements' affecting both the
physical fabric of the village church and the mode of worship
practised therein, and its 'regret that dear, old, brown, crumbling,
picturesque inefficiency is everywhere giving place to spick-and-
span new-painted, new-varnished efficiency, which will yield endless
diagrams, plans, elevations, and sections, but alas! no picture'.
Hardy, whose work as an architectural assistant had been mainly
concerned with ecclesiastical rebuilding, must have felt the force of
these sentiments; and George Eliot's lament for the passing of the
village choir may have provided one of the central motifs for his
novel, the original title of which was 'The Mellstock Quire'.

The pictorial allusions in these passages, reinforced by references
to the kind of Dutch and Flemish canvases with which Hardy had
become familiar during his regular frequentation of the National
Gallery, must also have struck him with unusual force. Moreover,
remembering his exceptional sensitiveness to criticism, we may
surmise that he was consciously or unconsciously recalling in his
subtitle the comment made in the anonymous and largely hostile
review of *Desperate Remedies* in the *Spectator* (22 April, 1871), in which
the reviewer found himself 'irresistibly reminded of the paintings of
Wilkie, and still more, perhaps, of those of Teniers . . .' This was
the review which (as he confessed half a century later in the *Life*)
caused Hardy such acute and unforgettable anguish. The fact that
he had taken this particular passage to heart is attested by his
quoting it in a letter to Macmillan's dated 7 August 1871, in which
he offered them the manuscript of *Under the Greenwood Tree*.

Whatever the origins of the subtitle, however – and one further
suggestion will be offered shortly – critics have been apt to take it
at its face value and to obey Hardy's apparent directions to judge
the novel by the standards of realistic art. Its earliest critics,
including Hardy's close friend Horace Moule, who reviewed it in
the *Saturday Review* [see Part Two, above – Ed.], were able to fault it
for failing to live up to the standards of realism, notably in some of
the dialogue. This is to ignore, however, the main title as finally
determined, with its Shakespearean allusion and its associations
with pastoral romance. In *As You Like It* the Forest of Arden is seen
primarily (though not exclusively) as offering an idyllic escape from
responsibility and from the corrupt world of the court. To take the
hint of the main title in conjunction with that of the subtitle is to
understand Hardy as offering simultaneously both romance and

realism, and as demanding from his readers a correspondingly
flexible approach. The point is worth stressing because he continued
to make similar demands in his later novels. What can be
specifically argued with respect to *Under the Greenwood Tree* is that,
whilst the pictorial mode of presentation is widely used, the parallel
with realistic painting put forward by the subtitle does not provide
an adequate analogy to the kind of narrative and descriptive art
which is in question.

It is perfectly true, of course, that there are many 'Dutch'
pictures of scene and character. Grandfather James is introduced,
as he steps forward from the crowd gathered in the tranter's
cottage, with the significant expression that 'his stooping figure
formed a well-illuminated picture as he passed towards the fireplace'; and the description that follows involves a patient
enumeration of visual details in which emphasis is placed on shape,
colour and texture [p. 23: this and other references are to the 1966
edition of the novel (London: Macmillan)]. Various garments and
types of material are specified: for Hardy, it seems, as for the
portrait painter, man is, initially at least, largely what he wears. A
later instance is the description of the gamekeeper's cottage, with
its precise account of the 'large nail, used solely and constantly as a
peg for Geoffrey's hat; the nail was arched by a rainbow-shaped
stain, imprinted by the brim of the said hat when it was hung there
dripping wet' [p. 98]. Such descriptions enact verbally the mental
responses of one who examines with close attention a realistic
painting, whether of the 'Dutch school' or a Victorian Academy
picture, in their use of visual signs to stimulate the imaginative
reconstruction of a way of life. A static *object*, that is (in this case
the stain), suggests a *story*, or at least the notion of human action in
a social environment. As already suggested, such appeals are not
restricted to classic art but are legion in the paintings of Victorian
England; and there is an interesting parallel between one specific
painting and a major element in Hardy's novel. Anyone who has
read *Under the Greenwood Tree* is likely to recall its humorous and
affectionate account of the Mellstock choir on encountering the
painting titled 'A Village Choir' by Thomas Webster. This was
exhibited in the Royal Academy in 1847, and ten years later came
into the possession of the Victoria and Albert Museum, London,
as part of the Sheepshanks gift. There is no direct evidence that
Hardy knew Webster's painting, but it would be surprising if he
overlooked it in the course of his regular visits to the London
galleries in the eighteen-sixties, especially in view of his strong

family associations with church music. If he saw it, it might naturally have occurred to him as he worked on a novel which draws on this area of his early experiences; and the tone of finely-observed rustic comedy is common to both painting and novel.

But there are at least two elements in the novel which seemed to demand a different response from that appropriate to realistic art, and to suggest a relationship to different schools of painting. One is the use in many scenes of dramatic chiaroscuro effects. The story opens in starlight and closes in moonlight; nocturnal lighting effects, natural and man-made, produce shadows and silhouettes which are often referred to in preference to solid forms, and show familiar objects in unexpected guises. The other is the presentation of the heroine, Fancy Day, in the fifth chapter: to the members of the choir, standing in the outer darkness, she appears at a lighted upper window, 'framed as in a picture by the window-architrave' [p. 35], holding a candle in one hand, the other 'being extended to the side of the window'. She is wrapped in a white robe, her 'bright eyes' look 'into the gray world outside with an uncertain expression', and she exhibits a 'twining confusion of marvellously rich hair'. The whole passage not only reads like a description of a painting; it strongly recalls the kind of Pre-Raphaelite type of female beauty that Hardy might have encountered not only on the canvases of the Pre-Raphaelite Brotherhood but also in Dante Gabriel Rossetti's poem 'The Blessed Damozel'. As in Hardy's description of Fancy Day, the opening lines of the poem focus attention in turn on the subject's 'eyes', 'robe' and 'hair'. This type of beauty was to remain a favourite of Hardy's; in his fiction he was to develop the type more fully and insistently in such later characters as Eustacia Vye in *The Return of the Native* and Avice III of *The Well-Beloved*. Fancy's status as a living work of art receives its meed of recognition in the limited aesthetic vocabulary of the rustic viewers:

'How pretty!' exclaimed Dick Dewy.
'If she'd been rale wexwork she couldn't ha' been comelier', said Michael Mail.

We need go no further than the opening chapter of the novel to find an insistence on visual effects which pervades the entire book and, indeed, much of Hardy's most successful work. The Mellstock villagers, silhouetted against the night sky, resemble 'some processional design on Greek or Etruscan pottery' (Hardy was no doubt recalling the British Museum collections); the profile of one

of their number is 'like the portrait of a gentleman in black
cardboard' [pp. 12–13]. In the community to which the characters
belong, the familiar has not lost its power to interest and delight.
Conversations follow well-trodden paths [p. 51], and similarly the
eye rests gratefully on the restricted world of objects with
associations strengthened by time and use. Even the children are
fascinated by appearances: Bessy inspects her plaid frock, 'to notice
the original unfaded pattern of the material' [p. 16]: and this habit
of affectionate contemplation of the commonplace is shared by the
narrator, who notes the wood-smoke rising from a chimney 'like a
blue feather in a lady's hat' [p. 97]. At moments of emotion,
perception is heightened: Dick not only watches Fancy Day in
church but also notes 'the appearance of the layer of dust upon the
capitals of the piers' and 'that the holly-bough in the chancel
archway was hung a little out of the centre' [p. 46].

Two factors in Hardy's life may be adduced to help to account
for the intense and loving perceptiveness of *Under the Greenwood
Tree* – apart, that is, from his natural gift for visualisation, sharpened
by training and practice. The novel was written at Bockhampton,
in the cottage of his parents, in the early summer of 1871. For
Hardy this was a homecoming; and the contrast between the dusty
and noisy streets of London, where his health had deteriorated, and
the fresh greenness of the surroundings that had been familiar from
his earliest memories, had its effect on the world of the novel.
Furthermore, he was in love – he had met Emma Lavinia Gifford
in the previous year, and visited her in Cornwall in May and
October of 1871 – and was finding the world a source of unusual
delight. Thus he was able to see the familiar with new eyes, and to
make fresh discoveries about the world of visible beauty in the
company of one he loved. The result was a novel which has been
described both as 'unusually rich in visual impressions' and as 'the
most nearly flawless of Hardy's novels'.[1]

Its 'Dutch' quality, then – celebrating commonplace objects
endeared by long familiarity and observed with loving and minute
particularity – is a major aspect of the novel to which the subtitle
rightly draws attention. At the same time, the label is not sufficient
to account for all the visual responses stimulated by the book, its
heroine, for instance, belonging to a different pictorial tradition.
Here and later, Hardy's debts and analogues, pictorial as well as
literary, are more wide-ranging and complex than might be
supposed. Alastair Smart's contention that, while Hardy was deeply
indebted to the classical schools of painting, he was 'not . . . much
in sympathy with his own times, least of all with what we now

regard as typically Victorian art' cannot be accepted without qualification.[2]

SOURCE: essay in *Thomas Hardy Year Book* no. 5 (Guernsey, 1976), pp. 39–42.

NOTES

[Abbreviated and renumbered from the original – Ed.]

1. M. Millgate, *Thomas Hardy: His Career as a Novelist* (London, 1971), pp. 51, 50. [See preceding excerpt – Ed.]
2. A. Smart, 'Pictorial Imagery in the Novels of Thomas Hardy', *Review of English Studies*, n.s. 12 (1961), p. 276.

Peter J. Casagrande   'Man's Goodnesse': A Comedy of Forgiveness   (1982)

Rightly regarded as the most nearly perfect of the early novels, *Under the Greenwood Tree* (1872) is also Hardy's most complete exhibition of the human powers of redemption that reside in the community and the family. It is frequently argued that *Greenwood Tree* was salvaged from the wreckage of 'The Poor Man and the Lady', and it indeed seems probable that some of the rustic scenes originated there. But *Greenwood Tree* is too well constructed, too subtle in its irony and use of allusion, to be derivative in any important sense. Hardy not only changed from a first-person to a third-person narrative; he also turned from social satire to pastoral comedy. More important, he made Fancy Day's return to her native Mellstock after a lengthy absence the central, unifying event in his narrative. In 'The Poor Man' at least in those elements of it said to be preserved in *An Indiscretion in the Life of an Heiress*, Egbert's return to Tollamore is placed late in the story (like Springrove's return to Carriford in *Desperate Remedies*), and is subordinated to the love story and the social criticism. But Fancy's return occurs early and the effects of her return shape the entire narrative. The painfulness of homecoming is at the heart of *Greenwood Tree*, making it the prototype of *The Return of the Native* and *The Woodlanders*.

If *Greenwood Tree* derives in an important sense from 'The Poor Man', it is because it fuses two elements from it – the motif of return and the search for regeneration – into a story of regeneration through return. Because she finds love and forgiveness among those she has left and returned to, Fancy Day accomplishes what Geraldine Allenville could not.

Fancy's homecoming kindles a series of conflicts, and all of them are settled harmoniously. She encourages the attentions of Dick Dewy, is opposed by her father, feigns illness at the advice of a witch, and is indulged by her doting parent. But Fancy is not easily satisfied. She next flirts with Farmer Shiner and is forgiven by Dick; she accepts Maybold's offer of marriage while betrothed to Dick, then turns back to Dick, and Maybold, though shattered, forgives her. Finally, the venerable members of the Mellstock Quire, not without bitter complaint, withdraw in a peaceful, dignified way to make room for the barrel organ that Maybold, Shiner, and especially Fancy introduce. As one critic has said, the novel raises communal values above personal and individual ones. Its strength is its profound 'sense of the linkage of people into families, and of families into communities, and of communities into the wider fellowship still of the succeeding generations of men'. There are other examples of a unique capacity for reconciliation in Mellstock. The foolish Thomas Leaf is not mocked, confined or banished; he is made a welcome part of the community and its activities, and in the end seems not so foolish. The marriages of the Dewys and the Days are stable because the tranter and the keeper, with patient affection, tolerate their wives' eccentricities.

Because tolerance, good humour and love are alive in Mellstock, Fancy can be both an agent of disruption and a source of orderly change. As teacher, as musician and as wife, she presides, in a distinctly amusing way, over the 'fall' of a traditional order. And this, it seems, is why she is ushered into the novel on Christmas Eve by an 'ancient body of minstrels' singing an 'ancient and time-worn hymn, embodying a quaint Christianity':

> Remember Adam's fall,
>   O thou Man
> Remember Adam's fall
>   From Heaven to Hell
> Remember Adam's fall;
> How he hath condemned all
> In Hell Perpetual
> There to dwell.

> Remember God's goodnesse,
>   Oh thou Man
> Remember God's goodnesse,
>   His promise made.
> Remember God's goodnesse
> He sent his Son sinlesse
> Our ails for to redress;
>   Be not afraid!
>
> In Bethlehem He was born
>   O thou Man
> In Bethlehem He was born
>   For mankind's sake.
> In Bethlehem He was born,
> Christmas-day in the morn;
> Our Saviour thought no scorn
>   Our faults to take.
>
> Give thanks to God alway
>   O thou Man:
> Give thanks to God alway,
>   With heart-most joy.
> Give thanks to God alway
> On this our joyful day:
> Let all men sing and say
>   Holy, holy!   [I: ch. 4]

Sung by the Quire to bring Fancy to her window, the hymn recounts the cardinal events of the Christian story – the fall, the condemnation, God's mercy, and man's redemption through Christ. In the manuscript version of the novel (in the Dorset County Museum), Hardy used only the first two lines of the hymn; he added the remainder, with its account of the Atonement, later, possibly in 1912. In so doing he inserted an explicit account of the traditional scheme of redemption that it is one of his purposes in the novel to set gently aside as a remnant of 'a quaint Christianity'. In this traditional view, sinful men are wholly in the land of a wise and merciful God whose son carries out His loving design for them. In the 'modern' view set forth in the novel, an analogous and wholly human scheme of redemption is presented. In this view, men are in the hands of men, and (even worse) of women. *Greenwood Tree* is the story of a pastoral Eden's invasion by new ways in the person of the fascinating homecomer who charms all the men she meets. In the Christmas Eve scene mentioned above, for example, the Adamic Dick Dewy is stunned by Fancy's beauty

and is a lost soul forever after. It might even be said that the 'fall'
of Dick and the traditional order of Mellstock is a 'fortunate' one,
the forgiveness and forbearance inspired by Fancy's actions being
the secular equivalent of the Divine mercy inspired by Eve's.
Though the comic elements of the novel invite this optimistic view
of evil and disruption, it is impossible to go very far with it. For the
thematic structure of *Greenwood Tree* is essentially that of *Desperate
Remedies* and 'The Poor Man', and of such a poem as 'The Ruined
Maid'. Innocence is lost (Cytherea's, Geraldine's, Dick's and
Mellstock's, 'Melia's); reconciliation and atonement come about
through wholly human means: Egbert forgives, Dick forgives,
Cytherea forgives, Mellstock is tolerant and patient, 'Melia laughs
ironically. But at this point of reconciliation, in every case, we are
brought up short. The movement toward redemption is blocked by
an evil beyond the reach of intelligence, of love or of laughter. Thus
Squire Allenville's refusal to forgive Geraldine, Manston's inexpiable
guilt, and Fancy's incurable capriciousness are discords that,
finally, cannot be harmonised. In sum, the 'fortune fall' of Mellstock
is qualified by Hardy's use of irony to show that things in Mellstock
are neither so placid nor so happy as they seem.

This bucolic world is no paradise; in it pain always accompanies
forgiveness. There is, for example, something besides paternal love
in Reuben Dewy's 'smile of miserable satire' at learning that Dick
loves Fancy [II: ch. 3]. Dewy knows well the price of harmony in a
marriage in which the man is the woman's social inferior. When
the girls' chorus, led by Fancy, drowns out the playing of the
Quire, Mr Spinks's laughing acknowledgement ('We useless ones
had better march out of church, fiddles and all') contains a
'horrible bitterness of irony', a 'ghastliness' understood only by
other members of Quire [II: ch. 6]. When Dick asks the money-
minded Keeper Day for Fancy's hand in marriage, he is leaning on
the top rail of Day's pig-pen, contemplating a 'whitish shadowy
shape . . . moving about and grunting'. Dick's anguish at Day's
blunt refusal is anticipated by the shriek of 'some small bird that
was being killed by an owl in an adjoining wood' [IV: ch. 2]. Then
there is Enoch, Mr Day's trapper, who entertains political views
'very damaging to the theory of master and man' in the view of
Day (II: ch. 6). Enoch scoffs at the trust in Providence among the
"twas to be' school of thinkers on the subject of marriage [II: ch. 6].
He cynically reminds Day that the keeper's sole motive in killing
thousands of honey bees is purely and simply monetary: "Tis the
money. . . . For without money man is a shadder! [IV: ch. 4]. But
cynics are punished in Mellstock, and so Enoch is placed in the

stocks, then banished, allegedly for drunkenness. The closing episode of the story is not simply the communal ritual of marriage – symbol of harmony and regeneration – under the spreading greenwood tree. It is that *and* Enoch, bearer of the name of the son of Cain, working alone in a distant turnip field, excluded from the festivity because he sees, like the wise fool Leaf, that chance, money and greed play a part – perhaps as great a part as intelligence and love – in human affairs. His cynicism, it should be noted, is matched by a cynicism about the nature of women exhibited throughout the novel, which ends ominously, with a secret that Fancy will not tell Dick. It is incautious to acknowledge the insistent realism of *Greenwood Tree* and yet to urge that it is a pastoral novel that 'perceives rural life in lyrical tones', maintains a 'nostalgic quality', and depicts 'stylised and charming' rustics in a 'peaceful and idyllic' love story. In *Greenwood Tree* the elements of disorder, implacable and immune to human means of remedy, are simply kept beneath the surface, though they threaten to break through at every turn.

If we ask several questions – What if Fancy's reforms had been openly opposed?, What if Keeper Day has persisted in his opposition to Dick?, What if Dick and Maybold had refused to forgive Fancy for whimsies? – we find ourselves in the world of Hardy's next novel and on the brink of tragedy, which for Hardy unfolds when men and women find the defects in nature and in themselves that lie beyond their limited powers of remedy. Hardy knew 'the tragedy that underlies Comedy if you only scratch it deeply enough' [*Life*, p. 439]. In *A Pair of Blue Eyes* (1873) he penetrated to the tragic substrata of comedy: Stephen Smith (unlike Fancy Day) cannot go home again, and Henry Knight (unlike Parson Maybold) cannot forgive a capricious and erring sweetheart.

Source: extract from ch. 2 of *Unity in Hardy's Novels* (London and Basingstoke, 1982), pp. 81–5.

2. *FAR FROM THE MADDING CROWD*

Roy Morrell   A Novel as an Introduction to
Hardy's Novels   (1965)

Far from the Madding Crowd is more typical of Hardy than a casual reading and a simplifying memory might indicate. The end, for example, is emphatically not a romantic happy-ever-after affair. We need not take Joseph Poorgrass's final 'it might have been worse' at quite its long-face value; and we can see the title of the final chapter ('A Foggy Night and Morning') as perhaps Hardy's way of touching wood: there is, indeed, a suppressed and sober, but none the less noticeable, elation about the tone of the end; but the fact remains that Gabriel is no Prince Charming for a girl of three-or four-and-twenty. Ahead of Gabriel and Bathsheba is no romance, but a reality that Hardy represents as more valuable, a reality of hard and good work on the two farms:

> He accompanied her up the hill, explaining to her the details of his forthcoming tenure of the other farm. They spoke very little of their mutual feelings; pretty phrases and warm expressions being probably unnecessary between such tried friends. Theirs was that substantial affection which arises (if any rises at all) when the two who are thrown together begin first by knowing the rougher sides of each other's character, and not the best till further on, the romance growing up in the interstices of a mass of hard prosaic reality . . .   [ch. LVI]

The trend of thought should by this time be familiar enough; but the passage also illustrates Hardy's 'hard prosaic' – sometimes awkward – way of thinking and writing, born of a conviction that the truth must be told, even if it cannot always be told attractively.

The distinction Hardy draws between romance and reality does not appear only at the end of the book; it is worked into the scheme of the whole. In contrast to Gabriel Oak, the two other main male characters, Troy and Boldwood, one actively and the other passively, represent aspects of romantic unreality. Boldwood is the dreamer himself, and the unreality is in the way he approaches Bathsheba, seeing in her not a woman of flesh and blood, but a romantic dream. Troy, on the other hand, approaches Bathsheba realistically enough; but he is approached romantically *by her*: he seems to her a romantic figure and, initially, an escape from a dilemma into which the circumstances of her real everyday life have thrown her. Boldwood, for Bathsheba, has represented a certain social goal: propriety and respectability. For a short time, while he seems inaccessible, these things seem attractive to her; and it is these values that he tries to insist upon: the formal rightness of her keeping her 'promise', her duty to reciprocate the love she has aroused in him. There is cruelty in Boldwood's romanticism, in the way he insists that she shall adhere to his idea of her (as there is cruelty in Angel's romanticism, and Knight's and Clym's); but Boldwood suffers more than he makes Bathsheba suffer, and the wildness and unhappiness of his love is conditioned by his dream and his distance from reality:

The great aids to idealization in love were present here: occasional observation of her from a distance, and the absence of social intercourse with her . . . the pettinesses that enter so largely into all earthly living and doing were disguised by the accident of lover and loved-one not being on visiting terms; and there was hardly awakened a thought in Boldwood that sorry household realities appertained to her . . .   [ch. XIX]

But Boldwood remains just as blind to realities when he gets to know her. After the disappearance of Troy, he again nourishes his love, but 'almost shunned the contemplation of it in earnest, lest facts should reveal the wildness of the dream' [ch. XLIX]. It is a 'fond madness': and the anticlimax is the discovery (while Boldwood is in prison, awaiting trial) of all the jewellery and clothing labelled 'Bathsheba Boldwood', bought for a woman who had never promised to marry him [ch. LV].

Hardy is disparaging romance, the dream and the dreamer. He is suggesting, instead, that one should live – not in accordance with nature – but in accordance with reality. And this point is made clearly by the three choices open to Bathsheba: Oak, Boldwood and Troy. Boldwood, of course, ceases to attract her as soon as he forces his attentions on her: and there is a gentle irony in the fact that she sees in Troy, who has taken her away from Boldwood, something of what Boldwood has seen in her: a figure of romance, someone from another world. But it is not only Troy's glamour; it is also that 'arch-dissembler' Nature that prompts Bathsheba to love Troy. She goes to meet him, hesitates, and then surrenders her heart, in the chapter called 'The Hollow amid the Ferns'. The scene is one of great natural beauty, of lush growth:

... tall thickets of brake fern, plump and diaphanous from recent rapid
growth, and radiant in hues of clear and untainted green.

At eight o'clock this midsummer evening, whilst the bristling ball of
gold in the west still swept the tips of the ferns with its long, luxuriant
rays, a soft brushing-by of garments might have been heard among them,
and Bathsheba appeared in their midst, their soft, feathery arms caressing
her up to her shoulders. She paused, turned, went back ... [ch. xxviii].

But again she changes her mind, and goes on to the meeting place,
a hollow where the fern

grew nearly to the bottom of the slope and then abruptly ceased. The
middle within the belt of verdure was floored with a thick flossy carpet of
moss and grass intermingled, so yielding that the foot was half-buried
within it

Nature is softly inviting and reassuring her. She surrenders to
Nature as much as to her lover – to her own natural womanliness
which, Hardy tells us, she normally had too much sense to be quite
governed by [ch. xxix]. The treatment of this theme is more subtle,
perhaps, and certainly more extended, in *Tess*; but it is effective in
Far from the Madding Crowd, all the same.

Bathsheba's third possibility is Oak; whose name at least cannot
be made to suggest *compliance* with nature, but rather sturdy
resistance, hard use and endurance. The distinction Hardy draws
at the beginning of the novel [ch. ii] between the intermingling
sounds of one vast integrated body of Nature over Norcombe Hill,
and the 'clearness' and 'sequence' of the 'notes of Farmer Oak's
flute', runs right through the book. Gabriel Oak is not a part of
Nature. He may be a countryman, but he is always a human being,
fully conscious of his human responsibility, always ready to modify,
to deflect, to improve, Nature's workings; always, that is, after his
first setback. A 'natural' sequence of events destroys his sheep; but
he does not see himself as a victim of fate – as Troy would have
done, or Henchard ('I am to suffer, I perceive'). He realises he is
ruined, and that, not having insured his sheep, he himself is to
blame. And his second thought is that things would be even worse
if Bathsheba had married him: ' "Thank God I am not married:
what would she have done in the poverty now coming upon me?" '

Thereafter he intervenes in the natural sequence of events in as
timely a fashion as he can. He prevents the fire from spreading to
the ricks and buildings of Bathsheba's farm [ch. vi]; he cures the
poisoned sheep [xxi]; he saves Bathsheba's harvest from the storm
[xxxvi, xxxvii]; and he tries to intervene, but unsuccessfully,
before Boldwood's optimistic dreams lead to disaster (lii, iii & vi),

and before Bathsheba gives way to her infatuation for Troy: '. . . But since we don't exactly know what he is, why not behave as if he *might* be bad, simply for your own safety? Don't trust him, mistress . . .' [xxxix]. – Gabriel's version of Hardy's own advice to take 'a full look at the Worst'. But Oak's attitude towards Nature is best seen in the account of the storm, because here Nature appears in her two aspects: creator and destroyer. She is prepared, but for Gabriel, to destroy the harvest she has bounteously created; and it is Gabriel's appreciation of the bounty, his sense of its meaning in terms of human life and sustenance, that makes him put forth all his strength to save the bounty from the destruction and to pit himself against the whole scheme of things, the whole trend of circumstance at that time. He fights not only against elemental nature, but against 'nature's' hold on the humanity around him: Troy's insidiously easy-going ways ('"Mr Troy says it will not rain, and he cannot stop to talk to you about such fidgets"'), the only too natural sleepiness and inertia of the drunken workfolk in the barn, and his own natural fears when the threat of the lightning becomes too great. The critics who suppose that Hardy shared and advocated the philosophic resignation of some of his rustics should read again the thirty-sixth and thirty-seventh chapters of *Far from the Madding Crowd*: if ever a man had the excuse of surrendering, of saying 'It was to be', Oak has the excuse on the night of the storm. Instead, he fights.

Yet throughout his fight, there remains a sense in which Nature's opposition is 'neutral'; nothing is purposely aimed against Oak. The chances mount against him; but they are still chances. And he seeks to keep ahead of them; he gets a lightning conductor improvised. Had there been any malicious purpose, an earlier flash of lightning would have struck him down. It is a fight between a man intelligently directing his efforts and 'senseless circumstance'. Oak persists; and he wins. He is not quite alone; in the latter part of the night he is helped by Bathsheba. The scene is one of many in the novels that vividly suggest the need of the human pair for each other, the individual's comparative – sometimes complete – helplessness alone.

There is another side to Gabriel's feeling for Nature: he fights her successfully because he understands and can sympathetically interpret the doings not only of his sheep, but also of Nature's smaller creatures – slug, spiders and toad [ch. xxxvi]. He seeks to learn from Nature; for instance, from the sprig of ivy that has grown across the door of the church tower, proving that Troy has *not* been in the habit of entering here modestly and unobserved (as

Bathsheba too readily believes), and that Troy is, therefore, a liar
[ch. xxix]. Nature is one of Gabriel's resources; but he is never
controlled by her, nor, in any Wordsworthian sense, does he ever
trust her. The essential thing about Gabriel is not that he is in
contact with Nature, but that he is in contact with reality. He
neither evades it nor resigns himself to it; he makes something out
of it.

This point is effectively made by a metaphor embodied in an
incident early in the book, just at the turning point of Oak's
fortunes, when he has proved he can survive even the worst that
life has to offer and when his luck (if such a word can be used) is at
last on the mend. He is drinking cider in the Malthouse, and has
just endeared himself to the Weatherbury folk by refusing the
luxury of a clean cup:

'And there's a mouthful of bread and bacon that mis'ess have sent,
shepherd. The cider will go down better with a bit of victuals. Don't ye
chaw quite close, shepherd, for I let the bacon fall in the road outside as I
was bringing it along, and may be 'tis rather gritty. There, 'tis clane dirt;
and we all know what that is, as you say, and you bain't a particular man
we see, shepherd.'
'True, true – not at all', said the friendly Oak.
Don't let your teeth quite meet, and you won't feel the sandiness at all.
Ah! 'tis wonderful what can be done by contrivance!'
'My own mind exactly, neighbour.'   [ch. viii]

The incident is a precise metaphor of what Oak has been doing in
the wider sphere of his life: he has had his share of 'unpalatable
reality', but by contrivance he has managed to find life's grittiness
not so 'unpalatable' after all.

Hardy's attitudes and themes in this novel are, indeed, typical;
what is not typical is the method: he is presenting his main theme –
the value of pessimism as a practical policy ('. . . You cannot lose
at it, you may gain . . .') through a pessimist, a central character
who is successful. He is presenting it, that is, positively, instead of
through the failure of a hero who is too optimistic or unrealistic.
The total pattern, however, is not so different: there are unrealistic
people (as we have seen) who are foils to Oak, just as in the other
novels there are realists, like Farfrae [in *The Mayor of Casterbridge*],
who are foils to the unsuccessful heroes. An advantage of *Far from
the Madding Crowd* as an introduction to Hardy's novels is just that
it *is* positive, and provides a basis for understanding the irony of
most of the others.

Despite Meredith's advice that he should avoid the direct and
positive method, Hardy has given us, in Gabriel Oak, as positive a

model – after one or two initial overconfident slips – as Egbert Mayne. I see this as not without significance: Hardy wished, without doubt, to clarify the values for his readers. The fire in *Desperate Remedies* that seems to proceed haltingly, and to wait every now and then – but quite in vain – for some intelligent intervention, becomes the fire Oak sees at Weatherbury [ch. VI]: it has already reached the stage of accelerated climax; but, even so, a man like Oak who can act promptly and courageously, is able to intervene, and to organise the fire-fighting, and he is just in time to prevent the spread of the flames to the farm buildings and to other ricks.

But the Weatherbury fire can serve as an illustration of Hardy's development in a more important respect. The point of the incident is not only to show how the courage and intelligence of a superior man can help the ordinary community when by itself that community is helpless; but also to show how that man gets a job. Oak has failed to get work at the hiring fair, and he is in desperate straits; but through the fire, and his ability to swallow his pride even when he discovers that the owner of the farm is Bathsheba, the woman who once rejected him, he gets the employment he needs. Hardy here embodies in action and incident what in *Desperate Remedies* had to be expressed in an explicit statement. What Edward Springrove reminds Cytherea – '. . . that the fame of Sir Christopher Wren himself depended upon the accident of a fire in Pudding Lane' – is transposed from the key of the young architect to that of the countryman, and presented not in words, but in action. And there are other examples. We have already remarked [in an earlier chapter of Morrell's book – Ed.] that Hardy's note about the 'figure' that 'stands in our van with arm uplifted, to knock us back from any pleasant prospect we indulge in as probable' is paraphrased in *Desperate Remedies*, Hardy explaining that 'a position which it was impossible to reach by any direct attempt was come to by a seeker's swerving from the path'. Less than four years later, this does not have to be phrased at all. It becomes the sequence of events at the beginning of *Far from the Madding Crowd*: Gabriel, indulging in the 'pleasant prospect' of success as a sheep-farmer, and even at one point accepting as 'probable' his marriage with Bathsheba, is 'knocked back'. He is ruined. At Casterbridge hiring fair, subsequently, he fails to get a job as bailiff or even as shepherd. But then, 'swerving from his path', he gradually contrives to reach all his original objectives, one by one: he becomes a shepherd, a bailiff, the owner of Boldwood's farm, and eventually Bathsheba's husband.

Let us now consider such of Hardy's favourite narrative devices
as may be illustrated from *Far from the Madding Crowd*, beginning
with two of the most important: the highly-charged expressionistic
incidents that have been called 'grotesques', and his contrasts.
These ironical contrasts ... may be partly accounted for by
Hardy's modest wish – expressed indeed at this very period of life –
'to be considered a good hand at a serial'. But this is certainly not
the whole truth. Hardy's belief in the eternal possibility of change
was something fundamental; and some of the contrasts he suggests
are far more elaborate than anything required by the suspenses and
sequels of a magazine serial story. In *Far from the Madding Crowd* it
happens that one of the most extraordinary of Hardy's 'grotesques'
has an important place in one of his series of ironical contrasts; we
shall therefore be able to discuss them together. But first a word
about the 'grotesques', since they have proved to be critical
stumbling blocks: Hardy risked the sleepwalking scene in *Tess*, and
the trilobite and cliff rescue in *A Pair of Blue Eyes*, and other such
scenes, because he saw their function as transcending their
awkwardness and lack of realism. And they may fulfil their function
not despite their awkwardness, but because of it. Read in their full
contexts, they set chords vibrating through the whole novel. The
sleep-walking scene, with its central incident of Angel carrying
Tess precariously along the plank above the flooded waters of the
Froom, reminds us of Tess's complete helplessness in Angel's care;
and of Tess's responsibility too, since a false move on her part will
be fatal; above all, the precariousness is a reminder that the
happiness of both is in the balance; Angel's placing of Tess in the
coffin powerfully suggests that he is killing his love for her; and,
behind the mere fact of the sleepwalking, is the hint that Angel
does not know where he is going. It is Tess, indeed, who finally
takes control, leading Angel back to safety; this is an indication
that the salvation may be in Tess's own hands. Through the very
incident – if she tells Angel about it – she may help him to clarify
his feelings. The cliff scene in *A Pair of Blue Eyes* is less complex; but
this too might be taken primarily as an indication of the deep need
of Elfride and Knight for each other, while subsidiary details
suggest the completeness with which Elfride has renounced all
thought of marrying Stephen. These are but suggestions; with the
most interesting expressionistic scene in *Far from the Madding Crowd*
I will try to give the implications a little more fully: it is the scene
where the grotesque gurgoyle spouts water over Fanny's grave and
undoes all that Troy's remorseful labour has accomplished.

The first irony is Troy's astonishment. He feels he has turned

over a new leaf and made a virtuous show of remorse; but finds
that

... Providence, far from helping him into a new course, or showing any
wish that he might adopt one, actually jeered his first trembling and
critical attempt in that kind ...   [ch. XLVI]

But Hardy, in the preceding chapter, 'Troy's Romanticism', had
shown Troy's activities in a different light. After a long and tiring
day, in which he had walked to Casterbridge and back, arranged
for a headstone to be inscribed and dispatched, and finally toiled at
the grave late into the night, planting flowers by the light of a
lantern, Troy had taken shelter in the church porch, and fallen
asleep. 'Troy', Hardy remarks, 'had no perception that in the
futility of these romantic doings, dictated by remorseful reaction
from previous indifference, there was any element of absurdity.'
Here, then, is another and a greater irony: in the contrast between
the immense trouble that Troy takes, to prove his love for Fanny
now she is dead, and his neglect of her during her lifetime. Seen in
this light, the gurgoyle's mockery is but a picturesque projection,
an image, of Hardy's own feelings about Troy. But even if we share
Troy's view that Fate cruelly prevents him from adequately
displaying his remorse, we certainly cannot suppose it was Fate
that had stopped him from marrying Fanny: it was injured pride.
And is not this the explanation of his present defeat? His pride is
hurt; the approving pat on the back that he expects from Providence
has not come. If he had been thinking, not of the hurt to himself,
but simply of what could be done to repair the damage, he could
have done it; and with a quarter of the effort he had spent toiling
by lantern-light the night before. Hardy pushes this point home, as
there is no need to remind the reader, by showing Bathsheba doing
simply and easily what Troy thinks it is useless to attempt:
gathering up the flowers and replanting them, cleaning up the
headstone, and arranging for the pipe in the gurgoyle's mouth to be
deflected. For Troy such actions are impossible:

He slowly withdrew from the grave. He did not attempt to fill up the
hole, replace the flowers, or do anything at all. He simply threw up his
cards, and foreswore his game for that time and always ... Shortly
afterwards he had gone from the village.

He has no intention of returning to Bathsheba's farm; and surely
the greatest irony of all is that in his remorse for the past, he is
neglecting the present. He regrets having neglected Fanny when
she was alive; but, repeating the same pattern, he is neglecting the

woman – in every way Fanny's superior – whom he has actually
married.

Indeed, as one contemplates the situation, the ironies seem to
multiply. There is the fact that Troy, of all people, should not be
surprised at what the rain can do: only a few weeks before, the
storm he confidently predicted would not happen, did happen, and
would have ruined him and Bathsheba but for Oak's courage.
Then he had blamed the rain for all the money he had lost at the
Budmouth races. And this reminds us that the money he spent on
Fanny's grave, like that he lost on the horses, was not even his
own; it was Bathsheba's. And again the realisation is forced upon
us that from the rain and the gurgoyle Troy had suffered no
tangible harm; his ego was hurt, his gesture spoilt: nothing else.
But the world of *Far from the Madding Crowd* is, after all, one where
more is at stake, sometimes, than the success of a gesture; and
beyond the ironies of what Troy had left undone, and still leaves
undone, there is the further ironic contrast between the way Troy is
immediately and utterly defeated by the mere *appearance* of disaster
and difficulty, and the way Oak has fought against what might
have been a real disaster and at the real risk of his life. Many facets
of Troy's character are recalled as we ponder over the incident; and
in particular his weakness for display: a small point in the splendid
impossibility of the lie about his modestly entering the church in
such a way as to avoid being seen, and the blindness of Bathesheba
in believing him.

The occasional importance of images in Hardy's narrative
method is not likely to be overlooked. Discussion of these has
proved easy, and sometimes uninformative. When Bathsheba first
meets Troy, the gimp on her dress is caught in one of his spurs, and
as Troy seeks to disentangle it, the lantern throws their shadows
against the trees of the fir plantation so that 'each dusky shape'
becomes 'distorted and mangled till it wasted to nothing' [ch. xxiv].
It is easy to see this as a 'proleptic image', a hint of the trouble in
store for them when their lives become entangled. But why 'when'?
Why not '*if* their lives become entangled'? Why should Bathsheba
ignore a danger that almost everyone else in Weatherbury sees
clearly? There is no need to repeat what I have already stressed [in
earlier discussion – Ed.]: that far more striking images – such as
those which predict death and disaster for Gabriel before the
storm – indicate not a determined future, but undetermined
possible dangers that can be averted.

But there is one image in *Far from the Madding Crowd* on which it
is necessary to comment, since it has escaped the notice of other

critics. Gabriel is investigating an unfamiliar light [ch. II], and
finds that it comes from a shed set into the hillside. He peers
through a hole in the roof, and finds himself looking down upon a
young woman whom he at first does not recognise, seeing her 'in a
bird's eye view, *as Milton's Satan first saw Paradise*'. There are ways of
dealing with things as awkward as this: some critics may say that
Hardy does not know what he is doing; that he is writing here
without inner conviction; others may ridicule Hardy's attempt to
display his book knowledge. But there is only one way of reading
this in good faith: to assume that Hardy meant what he said. And
Hardy is not parading his own book knowledge: *Paradise Lost* was
one of Gabriel Oak's books, we discover later [ch. VIII]; and we are
following *Gabriel's* eyes, *his* impressions, *his* slight feeling of guilt, as
he peers into the hut. There is nothing satanic about Gabriel; and
indeed there is something very unsatanic about his name; all the
same, he would like to intrude, and does in fact later intrude, upon
this girl's life. The function of the image is, indeed, clear: it
strikingly raises the question whether the intruder is always evil, or
whether he can be – as Gabriel turns out to be, by and large – a
good angel.

It is through this image, in fact, that we approach the social
theme of the book – in so far as it has one: the strengthening of a
rather backward, pleasant, easy-going rural community by two
newcomers, two intruders. The Weatherbury folk are too close to
nature; ignorant, lazy, rather irresponsible, and superstitious: it is
significant that when Bathsheba, against her better judgement and
under Liddy's persuasion, consults the 'Sortes Sanctorum', a rusty
patch on the page indicates how often the Bible has been used
before for this purpose. In all kinds of small ways the country
people show that they are not adapting themselves for survival
under new conditions of life, and weaknesses are creeping in. They
need someone like Bathsheba, an unconventional woman, whose
parents were townsfolk, to come and take a personal interest in the
farm, to sack the dishonest bailiff and take full responsibility
herself. The workfolk are capable enough, but they are useless in
an emergency: they get flustered or they are tipsy; and they have
none of the new skills and scientific knowledge that enable Gabriel
Oak to operate upon the sheep that have poisoned themselves in
the young clover. But more than this, they need Oak's new
conscientiousness, his firmness, his readiness, his refusal to let
personal griefs affect his actions (he is contrasted strikingly in this
respect with Boldwood, whose preoccupation with grief – as we
learn when Gabriel meets him the morning after the storm – has

caused him to neglect his harvest). Neither Oak's new skills nor the qualities of his character were learnt from the Weatherbury community; he brings them – as Bathsheba brings her vitality and unconventionality – from outside. They are strangers in a sense that even Troy is not; Troy slips only too readily into the easy-going country morality. Gabriel and Bathsheba have all the strength of newcomers, outsiders, who rivitalise the old stock.

I have mentioned the fact that Bathsheba allows herself to be influenced by the irresponsible and romantic Liddy in the Sortes Sanctorum scene and the sending of the valentine. This does not contradict my argument: it is a lapse on Bathsheba's part, and she pays dearly for it. And every detail of the episode is interesting as revealing that Bathsheba is all the time aware of the more sensible course; for instance she reverses the conditions of the toss because she thinks the book is more likely to fall open: '". . . Open Boldwood – shut, Teddy. No; it's more likely to fall open: Open, Teddy – shut, Boldwood"' [ch. XIII]. It falls shut. And Bathsheba, who knows perfectly well what she wants to do, and what she ought to do, acts instead as she is directed by chance. It is an interesting illustration of the fact that human beings who are capable enough of acting independently of chance, and more intelligently, sometimes choose to put themselves in chance's hands. The relevance of this point to incidents in the other novels (for instance, Elfride's decision that her horse shall choose her direction for her) needs no emphasis; nor need we stress the irony with which Hardy links Bathsheba's foolish and, indeed, disastrous action with the Sortes Sanctorum and tossing of a hymn book, and so, by ironic implication, with the workings of Providence.

So often is Hardy's attitude to chance misunderstood, that it is perhaps worth adding that chances, in his books, are not always disastrous ones; and there is an instance in *Far from the Madding Crowd* of a singularly fortunate chance: Bathsheba happens to pass near Gabriel's hut and to notice that both ventilators are closed. Her chance discovery saves Gabriel's life:

'How did you find me?'
'I heard your dog howling and scratching at the door of the hut when I came to the milking (it was so lucky, Daisy's milking is almost over for the season, and I shall not come here after this week or the next). The dog saw me, and jumped over to me, and laid hold of my skirt. I came across and looked round the hut the very first thing to see if the slides were closed. My uncle has a hut like this one, and I have heard him tell his shepherd not to go to sleep without leaving a slide open . . .'   [ch. III]

But there is more to it than the lucky chance of Daisy's milking not being quite over: the event is nearly a disaster, and the disaster is prevented only because the person happening to come by was – by Wessex standards – remarkably responsible, and intelligently alert to the worst contingencies.

A final point: Hardy was much interested in what one may call the psychology of the 'object': the distress and sudden weakness felt by someone – often a woman – when she discovers she is being talked about, and has thus become an object in the eyes of others. Tess's 'feminine loss of courage' at Emminster is caused by overhearing Angel's brothers talking about her; Sue cannot ignore the gossip she overhears about herself and Jude; Elfride is horrified to find that Knight is writing an article about her; even Ethelberta is disconcerted at overhearing some gossip about her own future; and, as we might expect, Hardy explicitly theorises about this human weakness in *Desperate Remedies*. Bathsheba is vexed that Gabriel has seen her unconventional behaviour on horseback; and she is indignant at his tactlessness in letting her know. None the less, the fact she knows he has seen her, and is critical of her conduct, makes her a little dependent on him; she finds herself sounding him as to what others are saying about her, and seeking Gabriel's good opinion. Her self-justifications and confidences are not just a narrative device: Hardy is doing more than conveying to us a few facts we should otherwise not know – Bathsheba's doings in Bath, for instance – he is showing her becoming more and more dependent upon Gabriel and Gabriel's approval. At the same time Gabriel himself is becoming more and more the controlling centre of all the activity on the two farms; and from looking *to* him, Bathsheba gradually finds herself looking *up* to him.

Romantic Westerners are sometimes a bit surprised that Bathsheba marries Oak; but between the man we meet in the opening pages, pleasant and unassuming but tactless and just a shade too confident, and the Gabriel Oak of the last chapters, there are many subtle differences; and perhaps her choice is not so surprising. In the East, feelings are reversed: surprise is sometimes felt that *he* could have brought himself to marry *her*. She had slighted him, as Japanese and Chinese readers point out, and she was not an easily controllable woman. Not many English people react in this way because, I suppose, we share Gabriel's liking for a woman who is exceptional. And also, surely, because we have learnt to understand his great merits; first, he leaves pride and pique to fools like Troy, and second, we feel he can cope even with Bathsheba: there has been nothing so far that he has failed to cope

with. We have learnt to accept, as one of the greatest of qualities,
Oak's adaptability; and, at the end of the book, we take Hardy's
point that it is a special sort of goodness to arrange to go to
California, if that seems best, and then to be able, equally easily, to
cancel such plans when, at the last moment, the factors in the
situation change, and he can marry Bathsheba after all.

SOURCE: ch. v ('*Far from the Madding Crowd* as an Introduction to
Hardy's Novels') of *Thomas Hardy – The Will and the Way* (Kuala Lumpur,
1956), pp. 59–72.

John Lucas   'Bathsheba's Uncertainty of Self' (1977)

When we come to *Far from the Madding Crowd* we encounter a
heroine who is a good deal more difficult to place than is either
Fancy or Elfride. For one thing Bathsheba has no living parents,
and this is important because it means that she can have an
independence of behaviour and action which is new among Hardy's
women. For another, Hardy seems to me to be trying to do
something far more ambitious with her than anything he had
attempted with the earlier heroines. We can perhaps get some clue
to what he has in mind if we ask what kind of a woman Bathsheba
Everdene is (which includes asking what kind of a woman she
thinks she is). What are her origins, where are her roots, what is
her present social situation? Take the scene where she saves Gabriel
from suffocating in his hut. He tells her:

'I believe you saved my life, Miss – I don't know your name. I know
your aunt's, but not yours.'
'I would just as soon not tell it – rather not. There is no reason why I
should, as you probably will never have much to do with me.'
'Still, I should like to know.'
'You can enquire at my aunt's – she will tell you.'
'My name is Gabriel Oak.'
'And mine isn't. You seem fond of yours in speaking it so decisively,
Gabriel Oak.'
'You see it's the only one I shall ever have, and I must make the best of
it.'
'I always think mine sounds odd and disagreeable.'

'I should think you might soon get a new one.'

'Mercy! – how many opinions you keep about you concerning other people, Gabriel Oak.' [ch. III]

It may remind us of the great scene in *Our Mutual Friend*, where Eugene Wrayburn doesn't want to know Bradley Headstone's name, and reduces him to 'Schoolmaster'. Names suggest identity, so that to know the name is in some measure to know the person. Eugene doesn't want to know who Bradley is (his chosen ignorance produces, of course, disastrous consequences); and Bathsheba doesn't want to be known by Gabriel. 'You will probably never have much to do with me.' The voice of class speaks there as clearly as it does in Eugene's acceptance that Bradley's name doesn't 'concern' him. But the difference is that whereas Eugene chooses to have no doubts about his own identity, Bathsheba obviously has doubts about hers. It is hardly necessary to analyse in any detail that fragment of dialogue with Gabriel to recognise that she isn't entirely sure of herself or of her name. She thinks herself above him, wants to put him down, is warmed by his unshakeable self-reliance and composure to reveal something of herself and is then sufficiently discomposed by his familiarity to retreat into conventional flightiness and would-be acerbity. ('Mercy!' sounds to my ear slightly vulgar – as though Bathsheba isn't at all secure in the identity which she puts on when she tells Gabriel he will probably not have much to do with her.)

The point is that the impulsiveness and changes in manner of speaking that we can find in that dialogue point forward to such matters as the sending of the valentine to Boldwood and the elopement with Troy: they hint at Bathsheba's radical uncertainties about herself, which she tries to resolve by sudden action. To act is to discover herself. Or so she hopes. In short, Bathsheba offers Hardy a way of dramatising the nature of social movement, and of how it works through individuals. Jacob Smallbury says that her parents 'were townsfolk, and didn't live here. . . . I knowed the man and woman both well. Levi Everdene – that was the man's name, sure. "Man" said I in my hurry, but he were of a higher circle in life than that – 'a was a gentleman-tailor really, worth scores of pounds. And he became a very celebrated bankrupt two or three times' [ch. VIII]. And a little later, commenting on the coolness of her manner to Oak, Hardy remarks that 'perhaps her air was the inevitable result of that social rise that had advanced her from a cottage to a large house and fields'. But Bathsheba herself doesn't find it easy to cope with that advancement, and although she can adopt the air of Mrs Charmond (shall we say), it never becomes natural to her. When, much later, she learns of Troy's affair with Fanny Robin, we are told: 'Her simple country nature, fed on old-fashioned principles, was troubled by that which would have troubled a woman of the world very little ...' [ch. XLIII]. 'Simple country nature' is perhaps overdoing it, but one sees what Hardy means.

It is in Bathsheba's relationship with the three men, however, that Hardy's meaning emerges at its richest. Risking oversimplification for the moment we might say that Oak appeals to Bathsheba's 'simple country nature', Boldwood to that air that accompanies her social rise 'from a cottage to a large house and fields', and Troy to the improbable romanticism of town-bred bankrupt gentlemen-tailors. Oak and Boldwood both have visions of Bathsheba, and she nurtures a vision of Troy. All three visions have to be shattered before Bathsheba can achieve anything like a firm sense of self.

Gabriel's first sight of her is when, imagining herself alone on a wagon, she takes out a looking-glass and studies her reflection. It is a device which Hardy has already used with Elfride and Knight and here as there the question is how to 'read' the incident.

The picture was a delicate one. Woman's prescriptive infirmity had stalked into the sunlight, which had clothed it in the freshness of an originality. A cynical inference was irresistible by Gabriel Oak, as he regarded the scene, generous though he fain would have been. There was no necessity whatever for her looking in the glass. She did not adjust her hat, or pat her hair, or press a dimple into shape, or do one thing to signify that any such intention had been her motive in taking up the glass. She simply observed herself as a fair product of Nature in the feminine kind, her thoughts seeming to glide into far-off though likely dramas in which men would play a part – vistas of probable triumphs – the smiles being of a phase suggesting that hearts were imagined as lost or won. Still, this was but conjecture, and the whole series of actions was so idly put forth as to make it rash to assert that intention had any part in them at all.   [ch. i]

It is inevitable that Gabriel should interpret her actions as dictated by vanity, and right that Hardy should separate himself from that interpretation, and that we should therefore be left with an impression of Bathsheba that makes her something of a mystery: is she vain, shallow, coquettish; or is she trying to recognise, account for herself?

Gabriel creates her in his own image. His first vision of her is followed by another, at night, as she and her aunt tend a cow that has just given birth. He doesn't know it's her because of the 'hooding effect' of her cloak, and so, wanting

... to observe her features ... he felt himself drawing upon his fancy for their details. In making even horizontal and clear inspections we colour and mould according to the wants within us whatever our eyes bring in. Had Gabriel been able from the first to get a distinct view of her countenance, his estimate of it as very handsome or slightly so would have been as his soul required a divinity at the moment or was readily supplied with one. Having for some time known the want of a satisfactory form to fill an increasing void within him, his position moreover affording the widest scope for his fancy, he painted her a beauty.

The prose is pretty clumsy, but the reference to painting and the acceptance of the romantic credo about what we half-perceive and half-create make it clear that Hardy is drawing our attention to the inventiveness of Gabriel's vision. Immediately after this he recognises who she is, and then she and her aunt 'took up the lantern, and went out, the light sinking down the hill till it was no more than a nebula' [ch. II]. That the word should make its appearance here is, I think, a clear indication of Hardy's interest in Oak's mental processes, and the fact that he has now his fixed vision of the girl. As with Dick's vision of Fancy and Stephen's of Elfride, it has to be decreated. Gabriel has to become an ignorant man again, in the sense in which Wallace Stevens meant the phrase.

It is Bathsheba, of course, who does most to shatter his vision. There is a brilliant moment – it comes after a very clumsy description of her – when we are told of Gabriel's staring at her: 'Rays of male vision seem to have a tickling effect upon virgin faces in rural districts; she brushed hers with her hand, as if Gabriel had been irritating its pink surface by actual touch, and the free air of her previous movements was reduced at the same time to a chastened phase of itself' [ch. III]. An acutely imagined incident, and one that tells us much about the aggressive, possessive nature of Gabriel's vision of Bathsheba, and against which she fights back. Gabriel tells her he loves her and wants to marry her.

'Mr Oak', she said, with luminous distinctness and common sense, 'you are better off than I. I have hardly a penny in the world – I am staying with my aunt for a bare sustenance. I am better educated than you – and I don't love you a bit: that's my side of the case. Now yours: you are a farmer just beginning, and you ought in common prudence, if you marry at all (which you should certainly not think of doing at the moment), to marry a woman with money, who would stock a larger farm for you than you have now.'   [ch. IV]

The direct practicality of this speech, and the toughness of
Bathsheba's spoken thoughts, effectively destroy Gabriel's vision of
her. She has broken free of him. And as a result he can now deal
with her at a practical level. There is a telling scene where Gabriel
rebukes her for sending the valentine to Boldwood. 'Bathsheba
would have submitted to an indignant chastisement for her levity
had Gabriel protested that he was loving her at the same time. . . .
This was what she had been expecting, and what she had not got.
To be lectured because the lecturer saw her in the cold morning
light of open-shuttered disillusion was exasperating' [ch. xx]. The
camera has replaced the artist's eye. Vision cancelled by the
truthful clarity of the photograph: 'faithful as no art is'.
Understandable, therefore, that Bathsheba should feel pique at
being exposed to an eye 'that will not censor blemishes'. And of course
she knows she has behaved badly to Boldwood. Self-reproach has
much to do with her exasperation.

But why send the valentine? It's part of her restlessness, her
impulsiveness, and of her desire for a full – equal – relationship.
Education and station prevent such a relationship with Gabriel,
whereas she learns that Boldwood is a squire and a man of
learning. And, as she tells Gabriel when she rejects him, she also
wants to be tamed, is almost frightened of her independence. The
problem of finding herself, deciding who and what she is, tugs her
in different directions. And is the cause of the valentine.

Unfortunately for her, Boldwood is very like Henry Knight in his
romantic vision of women. Indeed, in many respects he is a
rewriting of Knight. He doesn't like to think of Bathsheba in the
market place: 'it was debasing loveliness to ask it to buy and sell,
and jarred upon his conceptions of her' [ch. xvii]. It is only when
she is away from work that she becomes a vision to him: 'Boldwood,
looking into the distant meadows, saw there three figures. They
were those of Miss Everdene, Shepherd Oak, and Cainy Hall.
When Bathsheba's figure shone upon the farmer's eyes it lighted
him up as the moon lights up a great tower' [ch. xviii]. It is an
extraordinary image, and a considered one. Radiance positively
flows from Bathsheba, bringing Boldwood into light. She has the
power to illumine him and yet at the same time he creates the light,
for in the market place she has no such effect on him.

When Boldwood proposes marriage, the decency and limitations
of his view of her become obvious.

I fear I am too old for you, but believe me I will take more care of you than
would many a man of your own age. I will protect and cherish you with all my

strength – I will indeed! You shall have no cares – be worried by no household affairs, and live quite at ease, Miss Everdene. The dairy superintendence shall be done by a man – I can afford it well –you shall never have so much as to look out of doors at haymaking time, or to think of weather in the harvest. . . . I cannot say how far above every other idea and object on earth you seem to me – nobody knows – God only knows – how much you are to me!

[ch. xix]

And there is the offer which will lead to her taming. Bathsheba is struck by it and entirely sympathetic to the 'deep-natured man who spoke so simply'. Left to herself, she muses that 'he is so disinterested and kind to offer me all that I can desire'. Yet she doesn't truly desire it. Though she may countenance this male vision of a woman's life she instinctively rebels against it, as Elfride had done. But where Hardy had occasionally cheapened Elfride in the interest of retaining our sympathy for Knight, he can now dramatise the tensions between Bathsheba and Boldwood without offending against the complexity of either. Both are treated with sympathy, and in the study of Bathsheba's agonised indecision over whether to accept or reject Boldwood's offer Hardy adroitly manages to reveal her struggle to keep free from a coercive vision of her that will separate her from herself. For the fact is that for her not to work amounts to self-separation. And indeed Boldwood's vision is of a woman parted from herself: 'you shall never have so much as to look out of doors at haymaking time, or to think of the weather in the harvest'.

Something of this comes out in the very beautiful chapter of the sheep-shearing supper, where the labourers are seated outside the house at a long table and 'an unusually excited' Bathsheba is inside the parlour window, facing down the table. The bottom place is left empty, until after the meal begins.

She then asked Gabriel to take the place and the duties appertaining to that end, which he did with great readiness.

At this moment Mr Boldwood came in at the gate, and crossed the green to Bathsheba at the window. He apologised for his lateness: his arrival was evidently by arrangement.

'Gabriel', said she, 'will you move again, please, and let Mr Boldwood come there?'

It is an image of contained harmony and order such as one associates with a whole tradition of English literature going at least as far back as 'To Penshurst'. On a lower scale, it is true, but identical in its feeling of achieved repose. Except, of course, for the moving of Gabriel. And that tiny moment neatly emblematises

Hardy's refusal to be taken in by the myth of agreed order. Gabriel
is shifted about at Bathsheba's whim; and is displaced by Boldwood,
though he has a fuller understanding of her than the gentleman-
farmer does. But she is the lady of the house, and her social
position is one that makes it possible for her to deny him the right
to be opposite her – to be her equal in love.

The twilight expands and, 'Liddy brought candles into the back
part of the room overlooking the shearers, and their lively new
flames shone down the table and over the men, and dispersed
among the green shadows behind. Bathsheba's form, still in its
original position, was now again distinct between their eyes and the
light, which revealed that Boldwood had gone inside the room, and
was sitting near her' [ch. XXIII]. The candle light shining out of the
house and over Bathsheba's employees is like that of the lares and
Penates: 'thy fires/Shine bright on every harth as the desires/Of the
Penates had been set on flame,/To entertayne. . . .' And the singing
of Coggan, Poorgrass and of Bathsheba herself remind us of that
notion of social harmony and order implicit in the music which flows
from the great house of Belmont: 'It is your music, Madam, of the
house.' Hardy pays his tribute to the idea of achieved harmony,
stability.

And at the same time he knows that it won't do. It is not merely
the moving of Gabriel that reminds us that order depends on
ordering; nor that Boldwood's going into the house can be seen as a
dangerous invasion. There is also the threat implicit in the song
Bathsheba sings. 'For his bride a soldier sought her,/And a winning
tongue had he. . . .' It hints at Bathsheba's dissatisfaction with
herself. As madam of the house she is separated from Gabriel; as
madam she equally doesn't want Boldwood's appropriation of her.

What does she want, then? Well, what she thinks she wants
turns up soon enough. The shearing-supper over, she walks round
her estate and in the darkness collides with a man.

The man to whom she was hooked was brilliant in brass and scarlet. He
was a soldier. His sudden appearance was to darkness what the sound of a
trumpet is to silence. Gloom, the *genius loci* at all times hitherto, was now
totally overthrown, less by the lantern-light than by what the lantern
lighted. The contrast of this revelation with her anticipations of some
sinister figure in sombre garb was so great that it had upon her the effect
of a fairy transformation.   [ch. XXIV]

This is her vision of Troy, a romantic one, of course, and one that
she has painfully to undo. For Troy is as utterly conventional in his
attitude to women as is Boldwood. This is revealed in the famous

sword-exercise display, in which Bathsheba is quite passive, 'enclosed in a firmament of light, and of sharp hisses'; and it is also revealed in Troy's relationship with Fanny Robin, sentimental and brutal as that is by turns.

What Bathsheba thinks to find in Troy is a certain excitement which has to do with sexual abandonment: he is her folly, 'lymph on the dart of Eros'. It may seem that Hardy intends a reproof to Bathsheba's sexuality: 'though she had too much understanding to be entirely governed by her womanliness, [she] had too much womanliness to use her understanding to the best advantage'. Yet I think that by womanliness Hardy means conventional 'romantic' femininity, which doesn't permit her to see that, like Isabel Archer, her choice of apparent unconventionality will lead her to be ground in the very mill of the conventional. We are told that after one meeting with Troy 'there burst upon [Bathsheba's] face when she met the light of the candles the flush and excitement which were little less than chronic with her now' [ch. xxx], and we need to recall that by the time Hardy came to use the word 'chronic' it meant not only constant, but bad, and was customarily applied to the condition of a disease (the word can be linked to the 'lymph on the dart of Eros' which Troy is for her). Troy's presence is an infection, a kind of sexual illness. It leads her to abandoning the affairs of her house, just as Boldwood's romantic love for her leads to the ruin of his harvests: between romantic love and the concerns of social life is another separation. What is apparently unconventional – the sexual excitement – is actually deeply conventional, and potentially disastrous to Bathsheba's full self-awareness.

Besides, it seems clear that she and Troy have no sexual life together. Later on we are told that Troy thought of how 'the proud girl . . . had always looked down upon him even whilst it was to love him . . .' and I detect there a hint that Troy feels himself incapable of sexual relationships unless he is the aggressor (as he certainly is with Fanny Robin).

Troy also threatens Bathsheba's social well-being, her being the madam of the house. And so we have the famous scene of the wedding-night drunkenness, and later we hear of Troy's gambling, which all but ruins her. Bathsheba's vision of him fades, and when that happens he disappears – for he is *only* vision, he himself recognises that he can't survive once he can no longer be a vision to her. He takes off, and when he belatedly returns to Boldwood's house and Boldwood tells Bathsheba she must go to her husband, 'she did not move. The truth was that Bathsheba was beyond the pale of activity – and yet not in a swoon. She was in a state of mental *gutta serena*; her mind was for the minute totally deprived of light at the same time that no obscuration was apparent from without' [ch. LIV].

I think that such a moment shows beyond all reasonable doubt how seriously Hardy took the psychological implications of vision and its loss. For I do not think that he is playing with words here. Bathsheba literally cannot see Troy because since he is no longer a vision to her he is nothing. He has ceased to have an identity which she can acknowledge.

By contrast, her relationship with Gabriel becomes anti-visionary because it is anti-romantic. Each comes to accept the other's social position, and their ripening friendship is dependent on the fact that Gabriel is once more a rising man, and has money. The relationship is solidly bourgeois.

He accompanied her up the hill, explaining to her the details of his forthcoming tenure of the other farm. They spoke very little of their mutual feelings; pretty phrases and warm expressions being probably unnecessary between such tried friends. Theirs was that substantial affection which arises (if any arises at all) when the two who are thrown together begin first by knowing the rougher side of each other's character and not the best till further on, the romance growing up in the interstices of hard prosaic reality. This good-fellowship – *camaraderie* – usually occurring through similarity of pursuits, is unfortunately seldom superadded to love between the sexes, because men and women associate, not in their labours, but in their pleasures merely. Where, however, happy circumstance permits its development, the compounded feeling proves itself to be the only love which is strong as death – that love which many waters cannot quench, nor the floods drown, beside which the passion usually called by the name is evanescent as steam.   [ch. LVII]

Substantial: 'having a real existence'. Not a vision, not steam. But such affection depends on 'happy circumstance' which, as Hardy's fiction shows, is very rare indeed. Class differences, expectation, change, the rise and fall of families and of individuals: all these matters typically forestall the circumstance which allows for the growth of substantial affection between Bathsheba and Oak. *Far from the Madding Crowd* is the last of the novels to deal with a centrally successful relationship, one in which both man and woman can allow for the substantiality of the other's identity – simply because 'the mass of hard prosaic reality' which largely forms their knowledge of one another has to do with an attained, and a rare, balance of social and economic quality as well as an unvisionary forbearance towards one another. (In the famous scene where they work side by side to save the harvest, Gabriel is still Bathsheba's 'hand', their togetherness no more than an interlude.)

In implying, through a narrative which elaborates on their separations, how unlikely is their coming together, Hardy seems to me finely to recognise and explore a subject that is crucial to nineteenth-century experience, and in no way to be thought of as exotic, pastoral or escapist.

SOURCE: section IV ch. 4 ('Hardy's Women') of *The Literature of Change: Studies in the Nineteenth-Century Provincial Novel* (Brighton, 1977), pp. 137–47.

Alan Shelston   'Narrative Security'   (1979)

... I want to emphasise the very basic point that Hardy's great qualities are those, purely and simply, of the story-teller. It is an anomaly of criticism of the novel that the novelist's role as story-teller has always been acknowledged, at best grudgingly. 'Yes – oh dear yes – the novel tells a story', wrote E. M. Forster apologetically in *Aspects of the Novel*. The function of the story-teller, with what Bayley has described in Hardy's case as his 'singular fancy feeding upon itself',[1] – seems to me not something for which the novelist should apologise: it is at the root of his art. And the art of story-telling is in itself, as Bayley suggests, self-generative and self-delighting: we tend to forget, I suspect, that the novelist writes as much to please himself as to please his reader, and that a measure of the reader's pleasure will always be a consequence of the author's pleasure in the act of creation. In *Far from the Madding Crowd* we are continually aware of Hardy's delight in his own achievement: it is a major source of the novel's attraction.

Arising from that sense of achievement on Hardy's part is an authorial confidence, or what I would want to call 'narrative security' which is at the heart of *Far from the Madding Crowd*, a novel in which we see Hardy completely in control of his medium and enjoying, as I say, the growth of his own creation. We find it immediately in the assuredness of the novel's opening sentence, introducing its first major character:

When Farmer Oak smiled, the corners of his mouth spread till they were within an unimportant distance of his ears, his eyes were reduced to chinks, and diverging wrinkles appeared round them, extending upon his countenance like the rays in a rudimentary sketch of the rising sun.

It might be observed, parenthetically, that a similar narrative security is a characteristic of Gray's *Elegy* from which Hardy took his title, and never more so than at the opening of the poem, and in a similar way the confidence with which Hardy unfolds the opening sequence of his novel over its first five chapters, establishing the basic characteristics of Oak and Bathsheba Everdene, instils in the reader a correspondent confidence in Hardy as narrator that allows him to place himself completely in Hardy's hands.

With narrative security go narrative poise and detachment, most notably in the creation of those scenes, often comic, which tell us exactly what we need to know with tactful economy of observation that again leaves us with a sense of the amused satisfaction of the author observing the workings of his own skill. Consider, for example, the brief dialogue between the keeper of the tollgate and Oak at the conclusion of that perfectly apposite opening chapter:

The gatekeeper surveyed the retreating vehicle. 'That's a handsome maid', he said to Oak.
　'But she has her faults', said Gabriel.
　'True, farmer.'
　'And the greatest of them is – well what it is always.'
　'Beating people down? ay, 'tis so.'
　'Oh no.'
　'What, then?'
Gabriel, perhaps a little piqued by the comely traveller's indifference, glanced back to where he had witnessed her performance over the hedge, and said, 'Vanity.'

The scene could be over-laden with portent, and indeed I suspect would have been had it appeared in one of Hardy's later novels. It obviously is significant, in terms of the future careers of Oak and Bathsheba, but here Hardy's sense of fictional tact, embodied in the economy and the comedy of his rendering of the scene, sustains the appropriate tone at this point in the novel. Tact, in the aesthetic sense, is not something we necessarily associate with Hardy's fiction, but it is a quality that we find throughout *Far from the Madding Crowd*.

Hardy's dexterity in the exercise of his craft is thus a major factor in the effect which *Far from the Madding Crowd* has upon the reader, and there is one further element to which I would refer, again choosing an example from the opening chapter, by which this sense of authorial enjoyment is conveyed. I have referred to the introduction of Oak in the novel's opening sentence: the conviction of the carefully measured prose in that instance is effectively a means of establishing that quality of reliability which Oak himself represents. When Bathsheba appears we find a different, but equally appropriate means of establishing her character.

Bathsheba is first seen on 'an ornamental spring waggon, painted yellow and gaily marked' and then, we are told,

It was a fine morning, and the sun lighted up to a scarlet glow the crimson jacket she wore, and painted a soft lustre upon her bright face and dark hair. The myrtles, geraniums and cactuses packed around her were fresh and green, and at such a leafless season they invested the whole concern of horses, waggon, furniture and girl with a peculiar vernal charm.

Bathsheba's 'vernal charm', of course, is to be exposed to a series of tragic experiences during the course of the novel, but at this point her fundamental nature, which may be modified but never changes in essence, is established by the suggestion of freshness and the references to the variety of colour which seems to surround her. And here we have an element in *Far from the Madding Crowd* which is not confined to Bathsheba alone: constantly throughout the novel we are made aware of the impact of colour.

We have, for example, the brilliance of the stars at night when Oak is guarding his flock – 'Capella was yellow, Aldebaran and Betelgueux shone with a fiery red'. There is Troy 'brilliant in brass and scarlet' as he meets Bathsheba. ('Dazzled by brass and scarlet', as Boldwood later protests of her surrender) and, pathetically, it is a 'blue spring wagon, picked out with red, and containing boughs and flowers' which collects the body of Fanny Robin from the Casterbridge Union-House for its last tragic – and sadly comic – journey. Colour is the embodiment of vitality, even in this last unhappy instance, and it is an important factor in Hardy's self-communicating narrative delight, as it is evidenced throughout this novel.

The opening chapters of *Far from the Madding Crowd* do much to set the tone of the novel, and it is fitting that Hardy should establish his narrative techniques so firmly at the outset. As the novel develops, however, the calm and stability of the opening develops into action that is highly dramatic, while the social and emotional perspectives of the novel widen. The first five chapters in a sense act as an overture, abruptly terminated by the tragedy of the loss of Oak's flock. (A structural analogy might be made with the first five chapters of *Great Expectations*, concluding with the capture of Magwitch.) Hardy may take his title from Gray's quatrain, which, we remember, concludes

Along the cool sequester'd vale of life
They kept the noiseless tenor of their way

but this can hardly be said of the characters of Hardy's novel. In musical terminology *Far from the Madding Crowd* may open 'moderato' but whereas Gray's *Elegy* is, in the precise sense of the word, 'monotonous', *Far from the Madding Crowd* employs the full musical range, and its great passages might be marked 'allegro assai'. Certainly Hardy's vale of life is far from cool and sequestered and the tenor of the way of his characters is scarcely noiseless. Whatever the development of the novel though, the basic qualities of narrative security, of fictional tact, and of life and excitement suggested in those opening chapters are never lost.

Hardy's control as narrator is in evidence not simply in isolated instances but in his overall handling of that recurrent movement from the static to the active narrative mode which is one of his novel's most distinguishing characteristics and which I would define, again using musical terminology, as its basic rhythm. Hardy achieves similar control in each aspect, whether describing the stillness and permanence of the natural world against which the melodrama takes place, or the startling incidents of the melodrama itself, and much of the overall effect of the novel comes from Hardy's success in sustaining the tension between these two fictional polarities. Again the point can best be made from specific examples.

What I have called the 'static mode' is clearly best represented by the sense of permanence in nature itself: in this novel, as elsewhere (most notably for example in the opening of *The Return of the Native*), Hardy tends to see individuals in isolation, set against a backcloth of universal permanence. Consider, for example, the description of Oak, watching his flock at midnight:

To persons standing alone on a hill during a clear midnight such as this, the roll of the world eastward is almost a palpable movement. The sensation may be caused by the panoramic glide of the stars past earthly objects, which is perceptible in a few minutes of stillness; or by the better outlook upon space that a hill affords, or by the wind, or by the solitude; but whatever be its origin the impression of riding along is vivid and abiding. The poetry of motion is a phrase much in use, and to enjoy the epic form of that gratification it is necessary to stand on a hill at a small hour of the night, and, having first expanded with a sense of difference from the mass of civilised mankind, who are dreamwrapt and disregardful of all such proceedings at this time, long and quietly watch your stately progress through the stars. After such a nocturnal reconnoitre it is hard to get back to earth, and to believe that the consciousness of such majestic speeding is derived from a tiny human frame.

Suddenly an unexpected series of sounds began to be heard in this place up against the sky. They had a clearness which was to be found nowhere in nature. They were the notes of Farmer Oak's flute.

Here the effect is initially one of relaxed philosophical reflection, arising from the description of a specific experience that has its own uniqueness. The philosophical element is never over-strained – again 'tact' is the word that comes to mind – and by the end of the first paragraph the reader comes naturally to accept the trance-like state suggested in its final sentence. This in its turn is broken by the sudden interjection of reality: 'the notes of Farmer Oak's flute'. The brevity, almost terseness of the second paragraph, is in direct contrast with the relaxed, reflective tone of the first, and its effect is two-fold. In terms of the progress of the story it brings the reader back to earth – literally, in fact, for we are now to move into the very realistic account of Oak's shepherding, which is to end in the first of those highly dramatised, but always authentic, agricultural disasters which punctuate *Far from the Madding Crowd*. At the same time the aesthetic effect of the juxtaposition of the two passages is to sustain exactly that quality of poise and detachment that contributes so much to the authority of Hardy's narrative.

The method used by Hardy here, that of suspending the process of the narrative by reflective description in order to introduce character and event, recurs throughout *Far from the Madding Crowd*. We have, for example, Fanny Robin's visit to the barracks in search of Troy at the beginning of ch. xi, where the descriptive introduction emphasises a dreariness of aspect which provides an atmospheric prelude to Fanny's tragedy. Here it is significant that Fanny herself is introduced simply as a 'form' moving 'by the brink of the river', and we read of her 'outline on the colourless background'. The presence of colour almost everywhere else in the novel gives added weight to that 'colourless'. Again we have Boldwood's meditative wanderings in the down after receiving Bathsheba's valentine [ch. xiv], with 'the sky, pure violet in the zenith . . . leaden to the northward, and murky to the east' and 'the only half of the sun yet visible . . . rayless, like a red and flameless fire shining over a white hearthstone'. And, involving the agricultural community as a whole, there is the introduction to the great sheep-shearing scene with its perfectly expressed conclusion: 'So the barn was natural to the shearers, and the shearers were in harmony with the barn.'

Here certainly it might be said that Hardy is whispering what
Lawrence might have shouted. In all these instances what we have
is a fictional mode perfectly adapted to the expression of what
Hardy sees as the especial quality of the world of *Far from the
Madding Crowd*: we are concerned here with tone, that most
undefinable of all literary qualities, and I cannot recall a single
instance in *Far from the Madding Crowd* where Hardy's sense of tone
is at fault.

The movement from the descriptive, or static, mode to the active
occurs in each of the cases mentioned: as I suggested the notes of
Oak's flute introduce action that quickly develops into tragedy. *Far
from the Madding Crowd* is a novel of highly-charged incident and
highly-charged relationship: if at one extreme we have descriptive
stasis, at the other we have dramatic action. This is why I have
referred to the controlling rhythm of the novel, rather than to its
structure. Under the permanence of Hardy's sky we have a series of
events such as the loss of Oak's sheep, the rick-fire which brings
Oak to Bathsheba's farm, the disease of her own flock and the
storm after the Harvest-supper, which serve to demonstrate not
only the characters of the protagonists, but in a more general sense
the impermanence of human experience against which Oak's
stoicism is the only defence. The assurance with which Hardy
moves from the static to the active mode can be demonstrated in
any of these instances and is at the heart of the novel's narrative
achievement, but it does yet more than this. It serves to remind us
repeatedly that while the novel embodies a morality that can be
assessed from an interpretative response, its overall effect on the
reader is far greater than that to be obtained from a reductive
moralistic interpretation.

The point can be clearly made with reference to perhaps the
most justly famous examples of Hardy's presentation of dramatic
incident, the early meetings, first in the fir-plantation, and then in
the hollow in the ferns, between Bathsheba and Troy. To obtain
the full effect of these passages one would need to quote them *in
extenso*, but in both passages we see the techniques which I have
already defined – the movement from suspended animation to
dramatic action. At the climax of each passage, relaxed description
is set against an economy of dialogue which achieves a kind of wit
in which, as elsewhere, we sense the author's delight in his
awareness that he is conducting his craft at the level of perfection.
(We remember, for instance, Bathsheba's response to Troy's
provocative offer to repeat his sword-exercise: 'I don't mind your
twos and fours; but your ones and threes are terrible!') Above all,

by the introduction of the action, Hardy is able to achieve, in both encounters, a sense of transformation, not simply in Bathsheba's experience, but in that of the reader, in terms of his total comprehension of the novel. In the darkness of her evening walk, Bathsheba's sight of Troy's brilliance is in fact described as a transformation: 'The contrast of this revelation with her anticipations of some similar figure in sombre garb was so great that it had upon her the effect of a fairy transformation' – and the reference is repeated when Troy comes to the climax of the sword-exercise:

> In an instant the atmosphere was transformed to Bathsheba's eyes. Beams of light caught from the sun's low rays, above, around, in front of her, well-nigh shut out earth and heaven – all emitted in the marvellous evolutions of Troy's reflecting blade, which seemed everywhere at once, and yet nowhere specially. These circling gleams were accompanied by a keen rush that was almost a whistling – also springing from all sides of her at once. In short, she was enclosed in a firmament of light, and of sharp hisses, resembling a sky-full of meteors close at hand.
> Never since the broadsword became the national weapon had there been more dexterity shown in its management than by the hands of Sergeant Troy, and never had he been in such splendid temper for the performance as now in the evening sunshine among the ferns with Bathsheba.

A scene such as this has obvious symbolic, moral and structural purposes. For those who delight in the mechanisms of Freudian symbolism, Troy's sword has obvious implications, and it is perhaps worth mentioning that in this novel we are to find that the flute is mightier than the sword – and for that matter the shot-gun as well. More seriously the moralist can point out that Troy's effect is magical, but ultimately illusory: we know already that he is a bad magician and it is part of Bathsheba's own moral development that she must find this out. But no interpretative account of these scenes, at whatever level, can do justice to their impact on the reader in imaginative terms. Furthermore the quality of that imaginative impact, and of our transformation as readers, forces us to reconsider the over-simplification of the morality that is produced by a reductive thematic or interpretative approach. In a recent study of the Victorian novel an American critic, John Halperin, points out that Troy's 'physical beauty is only another indication that (Bathsheba's) shallow vision still perceives surfaces but not depths. Troy interests Bathsheba initially by flattering her elaborately; she is both charmed and encouraging . . . Her self-absorption blinds her to his real nature, which is even more selfish than hers.'[2] This is true, of course, if somewhat hard on Bathsheba, and Hardy indicates clearly enough that Troy is ultimately the villain of the piece. No such account, however, can do justice to Hardy's dramatic presentation of the effect of Troy on Bathsheba, and by extension on the reader, in the passages I have referred to. Morality is rarely as simple a matter as literary criticism would have us believe, and one of the more useful reminders of this truism is the conflict between our imaginative and our literal responses in passages such as these.

I have concentrated on the qualities of Hardy's story-telling in *Far from the Madding Crowd* because it seems to me that it is in these qualities that the real attraction of the novel lies. In doing so, however, I would want to insist finally on the reality of the world in which the passionate relationships and the tempestuous events are set. I often suspect that the modern critic's dismissal of 'story' is only a sophisticated version of the old objection to fiction, namely that it involves fabrication and sets fantasy above reality. However that may be, what Hardy presents us with in *Far from the Madding Crowd* is a world in which a useless sheepdog must inevitably be shot and in which the irresponsibility of Troy, in his assumed role as gentleman-farmer, can result in the destruction not only of his crops, but also of the livelihood of his hands. Hardy's rural characters have often come under fire: Henry James cited them as evidence of the difference between 'original and imitative talent' [see review in Part Two, above – Ed.], while Chesterton referred scathingly to Hardy's self-projection as 'a sort of village atheist brooding and blaspheming over the village idiot'.[3] Chesterton, if given to prejudice, was an astute critic, and one can see what he means in certain instances in Hardy's fiction. But throughout *Far from the Madding Crowd*, Hardy holds in check his tendency to exact more from his setting and his characters than can decently be allowed, and he constantly reveals his awareness of the realities of life in a vale which, as I have said, is far from cool and sequestered. One thinks, for example, of the casual revelation during conversation with Oak, of the generational continuity of the Smallways family where, during the course of a few lines of dialogue, we move through five generations from Old Smallways himself to his grandson's grandson, recently christened. The potential for sentimentalisation is there, but not exploited: what we are offered is a matter-of-fact example of a reality of agricultural life in the Dorset of the early and mid-nineteenth century. The absence of sentimentality is never more clear than when Smallways, in recounting the details of his Methusalian career, includes the fact that he had been 'fourteen times eleven months at Millpond St

Judes . . . old Twills wouldn't hire me for more than eleven months at a time, to keep me from being chargeable to the parish.'

This is a particularly accurate sociological detail, for under the terms of the Old Poor Law, which would have been operating at the time of which the old man speaks, parish relief was not available to someone employed on this basis. Again we are reminded of the pressures brought to bear on the agricultural worker, a reminder made all the more potent by the very tangible presence in the novel of the Union-house to which Fanny Robin struggles on her last journey.

Details such as these establish realism by accuracy of observation and comment. Bathsheba, Boldwood, Troy and Oak may stand out as the major protagonists of *Far from the Madding Crowd*, but it must not be forgotten that their lives, like those of the people who work for them, are inextricably bound up with the normal activities of farming life, its accidents, hazards, disasters and celebrations. One thinks, for example, of the rick-burning, which introduces Oak to the work-men, and reveals the extent of Bathsheba's dependence upon him, a dependence that is confirmed on at least two more such occasions. Furthermore, if Bathsheba's emotional life is high-lighted in the novel, at least as much stress is placed on her self-chosen career as a farmer, surprising the men by her independence at Casterbridge market and demonstrating a courage equal to that of Oak as they struggle to save the ricks in the storm. As a parallel instance of the way in which the emotional drama of the novel is embodied in the realities of farming life we have the tragedy of Fanny Robin, a girl known amongst the working-community, who becomes the instrument of Bathsheba's tragedy, and who is conveyed to her last resting-place on a farm-waggon driven – until he renders himself incapable – by the farm labourer Coggan. Once again a major strand in the novel is presented as part of the rural norm and here also, at an appropriately subdued level, we are aware of Hardy's perfect authorial control over his narrative, his tact in this instance being deployed to achieve precisely the right emotional effect.

I began my discussion of *Far from the Madding Crowd* by referring to Hardy's narrative security and to his artistic tact. I am conscious of the vagueness of such terminology but what I am concerned with ultimately is the skill with which Hardy achieves the appropriate relationship between the substance of his narrative and the fictional techniques he deploys in the course of his narration. Such a relationship implies both restraint and vitality; the result is a story delivered with a confidence that comes from Hardy's acceptance of the story-telling role of the novelist, seeing it not as a limitation, but as an opportunity. We all know Lawrence's tag, 'Trust the tale and not the teller' – it is a corner-stone of our critical approach to fiction. It is a measure of the supremacy of Hardy's narrative skill in *Far from the Madding Crowd*, and of the positive pleasure that the novel gives, that in this instance we give all our trust to the teller, and leave him to get on with his tale.

SOURCE: extract from lecture at Mather College of Education (28 October 1974), published in *Thomas Hardy Year Book*, no. 7 (Guernsey, 1979), pp. 33–9.

NOTES

[Reorganised and renumbered from the original – Ed.]

1. John Bayley, Introduction to *Far from the Madding Crowd*, New Wessex Edition (London and Basingstoke, 1974), p. 15.
2. John Halperin, *Egoism and Self-Discovery in the Victorian Novel* (New York, 1974), pp. 221–2.
3. G. K. Chesterton, *The Victorian Age in Literature* (1913); reissued in paperback (Oxford, 1966), p. 62.

Andrew Enstice   The Farming Community   (1979)

The setting of *Far from the Madding Crowd* is the valley of the River Piddle, just upstream of Puddletown. (The latter spelling is a Victorian emendation.) The area was well-known to Hardy as a child, and features in his work throughout his life. His mother's younger sister, Martha, was married to a Puddletown man, John Brereton Sharpe (supposed to be the model for Troy), and the Hand family (related through Hardy's maternal grandmother, Elizabeth Hand) counted numerous Puddletown members: James Sparkes, a cabinet-maker, and the three uncles, all bricklayers, Henery, William and Christopher, as well as John Antell, the cobbler. Hardy paid frequent visits to his Puddletown relatives, at first in company with his mother, and later by himself, walking across the heath road between the village and his own home. He had no direct connection with the farms on which the main action of *Far from the Madding Crowd* is based, but must often have wandered along the line of the Ridgeway overlooking the Piddle valley, and watched the everyday life of the mixed farms below. He would have met the workers in the village itself, tired after a day's hard field work, cold from winter fencing and maintenance, or relaxing in times of ease. Animals seem to have become as familiar as people to him, but crops are treated sketchily in the novels, indicating that he never came to know man's plants as well as his creatures. Perhaps this comes from his early familiarity with a different kind of farming, that of the heath's-edge and the Frome valley. Apple and vegetable crops he knew, as also the dairy cattle of Lower Bockhampton (they are featured largely in *Tess of the d'Urbervilles*). He knew the trees and wild creatures of the heath, and encountered sheep in the sparse fields between Puddletown and Higher Bockhampton, but crops such as wheat and barley were confined to the richer soils north and south of his home, coming no nearer than Druce Farm, or the outlying fields of Higher Kingston, beyond the main London road. They seem to have impressed him more in the mass, as qualities of tone or movement ('the ground was melodious with ripples, and the sky with larks') – it was this characteristic that enabled Gustav Holst, many years later, to create such an evocative musical portrait of Egdon Heath – and as functions of economic necessity (as when Oak calculates the value of the threatened ricks) than as individual plants. They serve as a reminder that all Hardy's descriptions of nature and man are subservient to the landscape of general effect in his Wessex novels; nothing is included which is superfluous to that effect.

The detailed reality of the Puddletown Hardy knew is tempered in *Far from the Madding Crowd* by this artistic function. The basis of existence for the community is shifted, from the ancient square of Casterbridge's enclosed trading world, to the wider sphere of agriculture. The need for a concrete image of the community is changed, too, from buildings to fields, and the men and their actions alike take colour and life from the new landscape.

Although buildings are of minor importance in the novel, they do have a function, in agricultural terms. They are described in detail only when necessary, the necessity being dictated by the need to circumscribe certain functions of the agricultural community. In Norcombe, before the action shifts to Weatherbury, the only building given attention is the cow-byre on the slope of the down (the hut is more an extension of simple hurdle shelters than a building). It is the agricultural side of Bathsheba's life that is

emphasised, even Oak's courtship visit centring on the lamb, not
the interior of the cottage. At Weatherbury itself, where the world
to be encompassed is that of the mixed farm (the artisans,
dairymen, journeymen, woodsmen and other rural figures being
variously dealt with in other novels), a very limited range of
buildings is described, each serving a particular function of life on
the farm. Bathsheba's farmhouse is a type for the decayed properties
bequeathed to tenant farmers by landlords whose estates are grown
too large to manage personally:

> By daylight [it] presented itself as a hoary building, of the early stage of
> Classical Renaissance as regards its architecture, and of a proportion
> which told at a glance that, as is so frequently the case, it had once been
> the manorial hall upon a small estate around it, now altogether effaced as
> a distinct property, and merged in the vast tract of a non-resident landlord,
> which comprised several such modest demesnes.
>
> Fluted pilasters, worked from the solid stone, decorated its front, and
> above the roof the chimneys were panelled or columnar, some coped
> gables with finials and like features still retaining traces of their Gothic
> extraction. Soft brown mosses, like faded velveteen, formed cushions upon
> the stone tiling, and tufts of the houseleek or sengreen sprouted from the
> eaves of the low surrounding buildings. A gravel walk leading from the
> door to the road in front was encrusted at the sides with more moss – here
> it was a silver-green variety, the nut-brown of the gravel being visible to
> the width of only a foot or two in the centre. This circumstance, and the
> generally sleepy air of the whole prospect here, together with the animated
> and contrasting style of the reverse facade, suggested to the imagination
> that on the adaptation of the building for farming purposes the vital
> principle of the house had turned round inside its body to face the other
> way.

The description is subtly different from those employed in *The
Mayor of Casterbridge*, where buildings in the aggregate suggest age
and continuity. Here there is continuity, but of a kind that reminds
us of the vagaries of the rural world, based not on trade but on
nature and the sweat of man's brow. The simple affirmation of the
house's changed status might have been enough to place the thing
in an economic and social context, but Hardy's essential union, of
man and nature, dictates that mere social vagaries are not enough.
The weight and bulk of description are given to features which
bespeak the harmony of the building with its role – a harmony
born, not of design, but of necessary adaptation. As centre of a
small agricultural estate, the building had purpose; as the farmhouse
of a tenant farmer, it still has purpose, although altered. Nature
and time adjust what man has made, as long as the creation has a
function in harmony with nature. The mosses and sengreen become

symbols of the acceptance by nature of something that has a place in the rural world.

Bathsheba's farmhouse having been described, Boldwood's, which is of a similar status, is given the most cursory treatment. We are told it 'stood recessed from the road'. In a similar fashion, only one representative of the building most associated with farmwork is detailed – Bathsheba's barn:

> The vast porches at the sides, lofty enough to admit a waggon laden to its highest with corn in the sheaf, were spanned by heavy-pointed arches of stone, broadly and boldly cut, whose very simplicity was the origin of a grandeur not apparent in erections where more ornament has been attempted. The dusky, filmed, chestnut roof, braced and tied in by huge collars, curves and diagonals, was far nobler in design, because more wealthy in material, than nine-tenths of those in our modern churches. Along each side wall was a range of striding buttresses, throwing deep shadows on the spaces between them, which were perforated by lancet openings, combining in their proportions the precise requirements both of beauty and ventilation. . . .
>
> The lanceolate windows, the time-eaten arch-stones and chamfers, the orientation of the axis, the misty chestnut work of the rafters, referred to no exploded fortifying art or worn-out religious creed. The defence and salvation of the body by daily bread is still a study, a religion, and a desire.

Here, there is even more emphasis given to function and continuity, in a world of changing economic, social and spiritual values. This is the very heart of the farm world, and is made as concrete as possible, while fortifying the knowledge that it is as a symbol of function that it exists, not by its own right. Once again, the interior is given full treatment (something accorded only to the three main buildings of the novel – the farmhouse, the barn and the malthouse).

The porches are designed to admit fully-laden wagons, the roof is noble in its perfect interpretation of the simple necessity of protecting the food of man and beast for the winter, and buttresses and windows stand mute testimony to the balance between beauty and function – between art and simple survival – that, in *Far from the Madding Crowd*, is the study and joy of author and characters alike. In this novel, more than in any other, Hardy expresses his sheer (and short-lived) pleasure at the harmonies of man's agricultural partnership with nature.

The third member of the inanimate trio is Warren's Malthouse. Where the farmhouse bore in itself the harmony of natural adaptation and change, and the barn the rich beauty of continuing function, the malthouse radiates warmth and comfort, the symbol of man's continuing need to relax from his work, and commune with his fellow men:

There was no window in front; but a square hole in the door was glazed with a single pane, through which red, comfortable rays now stretched out upon the ivied wall in front. Voices were to be heard inside. . . .

The room inside was lighted only by the ruddy glow from the kiln mouth, which shone over the floor with the streaming horizontality of the setting sun, and threw upwards the shadows of all facial irregularities in those assembled around. The stone-flag floor was worn into a path from the doorway to the kiln, and into undulations everywhere.

Each building, as description progresses, is associated with men; they emerge from it as they emerge from the fields, a part of the landscape. But in the malthouse, the involvement of men with its atmosphere of hospitable warmth is so essential that their features are as naturally a part of its functional character as the undulations of a floor, worn by generations of malters stoking the kiln. The other two buildings retain their function and feeling even without immediate reference to men; the malthouse is virtually an extension of the men themselves, a shell of warmth emanating from their own companionship.

The farm life has been centred around farmhouse and barn, the companionship of the workers around the malthouse; the main social action takes place almost entirely in the open air. There remain, in terms of function, only the community's links with the trading community at Casterbridge to be rendered in physical form (cottages are virtually ignored, as having no more direct function to the community than shelters; the Buck's Head at Roytown and other buildings mentioned in Casterbridge and elsewhere are given cursory treatment, being introduced only for reasons of plot). This final building is the Corn Exchange at Casterbridge, where the scattered farming communities meet in economic need, and it is notable because it is given such concrete treatment while yet being hardly delineated. It receives the force of the same function and nature which brought men into the description of the malthouse; the actual appearance of the building matters less than the atmosphere it conveys, where is here associated with the coming-together of men in business, rather than companionship. The words devoted to the material of the building are few, but when its occupants are extensions of its function, the final effect is considerable:

The low though extensive hall, supported by beams and pillars, and latterly dignified by the name of Corn Exchange, was thronged with hot men who talked among each other in twos and threes, the speaker of the minute looking sideways into his auditor's face and concentrating his argument by a contraction of one eyelid during delivery. The greater number carried in their hands ground-ash saplings, using them partly as walking-sticks and partly for poking up pigs, sheep, neighbours with their backs turned, and restful things in general, which seemed to require such treatment in the course of their peregrinations. During conversations each subjected his sapling to great varieties of usage – bending it round his back, forming an arch of it between his hands . . . or perhaps it was hastily tucked under the arm whilst the sample-bag was pulled forth and a handful of corn poured into the palm, which, after criticism, was flung upon the floor.

The treatment of material here is reminiscent of the market-scenes in *The Mayor of Casterbridge*, but the detached objectivity of those street scenes has been altered, the men becoming living embodiments of the town's trading relationship with its rural neighbours. The mechanics of exchange are more important than the surroundings.

These are the only buildings which have a major function in the novel, and in keeping with this limited use of them, their physical position is of little relevance to the development of the novel. Where, in *The Mayor of Casterbridge*, physical reality is altered to create the landscape of the market-town, here the main work of this landscape-creation lies with natural features. In keeping with the idea that the farm community has a peripheral contact with Weatherbury, through the maltster's, the two farms are shifted about a mile from their true position, bringing into a single area of focus the river, the farms, the valley-edges with the bracken-fringed heath beyond, and the highway between Casterbridge and Weatherbury. However, no emphasis is given to this area as a unit, other than the slight emphasis on the single nature of the agriculture. The heath and woodland touch the edges of the community, but have little place in its life. . . .

. . . The first part of the novel, dealing with the development of the relationship between Oak and Bathsheba, is bound closely to their roles as young farmer and country girl who might have been a governess 'only she was too wild'. Events revolve around their respective farming roles, the two human figures as apparently unchangeable as the other elements of the natural scene. One juxtaposition, curious at first to ears unused to rural priorities, is reminiscent of John Clare's attempts to display man's indissoluble connection with the natural world by substituting simple reality for elegant logic: 'By making enquiries he found that the girl's name was Bathsheba Everdene, and that the cow would go dry in about seven days. He dreaded the eighth day.'

Semantically, the two facts are inelegant together in the one sentence. Realistically, there is nothing more reasonable than that the two should be taken in conjunction, in such a situation. By interrupting the flow of prose with this juxtaposition, Hardy forces our whole attention onto the necessarily close relationship between the courtship of this couple and their everyday agricultural lives.

Similarly, the description of Oak the suitor is constructed on the same lines as descriptions of other natural objects:

He . . . put on the light waistcoat patterned all over with sprigs of an elegant flower uniting the beauties of both rose and lily without the defects of either, and used all the hair-oil he possessed upon his usually dry, sandy, and inextricably curly hair, till he had deepened it to a splendidly novel colour, between that of guano and Roman cement, making it stick to his head like mace round a nutmeg, or wet seaweed round a boulder after the ebb.

It is hardly the mannered human vision of much Victorian literature, and the contrast is made the greater by the use of very similar terms to portray one of Oak's sheepdogs:

George, the elder, exhibited an ebony-tipped nose, surrounded by a narrow margin of pink flesh, and a coat marked in random splotches approximating in colour to white and slaty grey; but the grey, after years of sun and rain, had been scorched and washed out of the more prominent locks, leaving them of a reddish brown, as if the blue component of the grey had faded, like the indigo from the same kind of colour in Turner's pictures. In substance it had originally been hair, but long contact with sheep seemed to be turning it by degrees into wool of a poor quality and staple.

All the elements of involvement in the hard life of agriculture are evident in this nondescript dog (apparently largely of Old English strain, but as far removed from the modern collie as is the present Italian sheepdog, which may be of any convenient mixture of breeds). The weight given to picturing such a minor 'character' in the novel reminds us once more of man's relative stature in the farming world, reliant as he is at this period upon Nature's day-to-day organisation to make his own work prosper. Another image – a favourite of Hardy's – emphasises the harmony of man with his natural surroundings, and also his individual unimportance, as transient as the leaves on a tree; 'We thought we heard a hand pawing about the door for the bobbin, but weren't sure 'twere not a dead leave blowed across.'

This gentle reminder of man's transience, unobtrusive in the early part of the novel, marks Oak's changed character, saddened and wiser from the force of circumstance. He is aware now of his own frailty, and also of the strength he draws from his close association with nature. When we see him with Boldwood's eyes, the sunrise after St Valentine's Day, he seems, as a representative of Man, both to draw from and give to Nature: ' . . . on the ridge, up against the blazing sky, a figure was visible, like snuff in the midst of a candle-flame.' It is an idea developed more fully in *The Return of the Native*, but even here the sense of a perfect union between Man and Nature is very strong. Man casts the light of his understanding on the world, but to do so he must draw from Nature the fuel of that understanding.

The same glow goes on to touch Warren's malthouse, suggesting the same rooted harmony with nature as is given explicitly to the man; and the other major buildings in the novel share in this involvement as they are variously involved with men in their natural roles.

These roles come to life vividly in the most powerfully described event in the whole novel – the thunderstorm after harvest supper. Oak's weather-reading skills, like his ability in deciphering the stars, are evidence of the harmonious existence of such a community in nature. The landscape of fields and farm comes alive in detail, and acts in close harmony with the man whose life is a part of the same landscape. Even at the height of the storm, Oak emerges perfectly into the scene illuminated by each flash of lightning: ' . . . the rick suddenly brightened with the brazen glare of shining majolica – every knot in every straw was visible. On the slope in front of him appeared two human shapes, black as jet. The rick lost its sheen – the shapes vanished.'

When the rain at last comes on in earnest he becomes as one with the sky and the earth. 'The rain stretched obliquely through the dull atmosphere in liquid spines, unbroken in continuity between their beginnings in the clouds and their points in him.' It is not a struggle to oppose the elements, but to harmonise with them, taking their strength and using it, and turning aside their destruction when it comes. Oak is a focus for all that is best and most skilled in Man's efforts to achieve a perfect harmony in life. He has been through the personal tragedies that bring the realisation of weakness, and can temper the pride of ability with awareness. In him, Hardy displays all the qualities which combine to make the farming community function. Other characters are, by comparison, sketchy in treatment, since in them Hardy can concentrate on other aspects – of character, circumstance and function – which combine with Oak's skills to portray as fully as possible the whole community.

Bathsheba herself is in every way a farm girl, born into a family
of yeoman stock, and too taken up with the rather wild existence
she has led in the country to be concerned with advancing herself.
'She's so good-looking, and an excellent scholar besides – she was
going to be a governess once, you know, only she was too wild.'

When she takes over her uncle's farm, it is only her sex that
raises doubts as to her ability to run it herself, and those doubts she
soon dispels by an obviously competent management of affairs (her
dismissal of Oak, and subsequent re-hiring, are the result of
emotional involvement rather than evidence of lack of foresight in
farm matters). Throughout the novel, no matter how violent or
complicated her private affairs, she is able to recognise the
paramount needs of her farm. In the event, it is she, helping Oak to
save the ricks, who proves more reliably agricultural in mood than
the unfortunate Boldwood, who loses most of his crop in the
thunderstorm. Others rise and fall about her, but she, the perfect
successor to her uncle, maintains the steady middle course. Images
of her, though fewer and less prominent than those involving Oak,
are nevertheless entirely to do with Nature. Like Oak, she is a dead
leaf upon the wind: 'He heard what seemed to be the flitting of a
dead leaf upon the breeze, and looked. She had gone away.' In her
passage through the woods on horseback, 'The rapidity of her glide
into this position was that of a kingfisher – its noiselessness that of
a hawk.' And when courted by the brilliant Troy, 'No christmas
robin detained by a window-pane ever pulsed as did Bathsheba
now.'

In many ways, she is the perfect counterpart to Oak. Her
emotional uncertainty, her forwardness, her apparent recklessness,
are all tempered by an inborn respect for the way of life she leads,
and an instinctive knowledge of how far she can bend the day-to-
day rules of the farm. Mistakes, when she makes them, are
personal; in business matters she takes no decision that is
irreversible. (The one mistake that might have harmed the farm,
her marriage to Troy, is prevented from large-scale damage by
circumstance. It can be argued that it would have led to disaster
eventually, but in the context of the novel the question does not
arise.)

Boldwood receives even less attention from imagery than
Bathsheba, his place in the community being implied rather than
stated. His farm, scarcely mentioned, is apparently successful
(though he is only a tenant), since he is described by Liddy as 'a
gentleman-farmer at Little Weatherbury', and the occasion of his
neglect of the ricks occasions much comment locally, being

produced as evidence of his temporary insanity in the appeal to the Home Secretary after the killing of Troy. Occasional images seem to reflect the comfortable union of the farming and genteel ways of life; 'Boldwood went meditating down the slopes with his eyes on his boots, which the yellow pollen from the buttercups had bronzed in artistic gradations.' In the passage describing his impression of the frozen morning, images of the drawing room combine easily and naturally with images of the farm. His standing is rather like that of the successful Henchard in *The Mayor of Casterbridge*, at the highest social level which still admits of personal involvement in a working community.

Other, less important, characters also centre on Oak as the symbol of farm life, drawing a personal involvement with nature from occasional strong images, '. . . his frosty white hair and beard overgrowing his gnarled figure like the grey moss and lichen upon a leafless apple-tree' describes the maltster at our first meeting with him. As with the images of Bathsheba (of wild birds) and Boldwood (the juxtaposition of farm and drawing room) the images are suited to the character, being of old apple trees, the staple of his involvement with the community. Fanny, fleeing to meet Troy, is compared to the lambs of the farm on which she worked: 'He had frequently felt the same quick, hard beat in the femoral artery of his lambs when overdriven.' Like them, she is a victim of circumstance, whose brief span of years is soon terminated by the harsher realities of life in the rural world.

More happily, the minor characters appear together at the shearing supper, and twilight touches the revellers with a soft light that emphasises the utter harmony of their celebrations with a natural world that provides the bounty they celebrate:

> The sun had crept round the tree as a last effort before death, and then began to sink, the shearers' lower parts becoming steeped in embrowning twilight, whilst their heads and shoulders were still enjoying day, touched with a yellow of self-sustained brilliancy that seemed inherent rather than acquired.

Troy is locally supposed to be the illegitimate son of the Earl of Severn, but born into the family of a poor doctor. As with all the major characters except Boldwood (whose long standing in the community seems to serve as sufficient local connection), great care is taken to emphasise his family links with the area. Bathsheba's deceased uncle is discussed at length at the malthouse (her parents are mentioned, but are of considerably less importance, having died early), as also are the close connections of Oak's family with the maltster's, a circumstance which confers on him familiarity by association.

Hardy is working here to establish something of that 'class of stationary cottagers' on whom this farming world is stated to depend, in the Preface. So too, when he describes the ancient barn, he is at pains to point out the static nature of rural society:

The citizen's *Then* is the rustic's *Now*. In London, twenty or thirty years ago are old times; in Paris ten years, or five; in Weatherbury three or four score years were included in the mere present, and nothing less than a century set a mark on its face or tone. Five decades hardly modified the cut of a gaiter, the embroidery of a smock-frock, by the breadth of a hair. Ten generations failed to alter the turn of a single phrase.

However, having demonstrated the element of continuing change which kept Casterbridge pulsing with life, it seems unlikely that Hardy would have been so insensitive to the more familiar farm world, even allowing for his relative literary immaturity. The Preface seems, by its bland contradiction of the reality of the novel, to be more of a sop for the Victorian reading public, who could comprehend a rustic idyll, but not a working rural community. . . .

SOURCE: extracts from ch. 3 of *Thomas Hardy: Landscapes of the Mind* (London and Basingstoke, 1979), pp. 48–53, 57–62.

3. THE WOODLANDERS

Douglas Brown   'Transience Intimated in
Dramatic Forms'   (1954)

. . . *The Woodlanders* is the novel that most comprehensively expresses Hardy's feelings towards agricultural life, and his sense of its resistance to despair. It is his most fluid book; the talk and the activities of the lesser country folk are joined into the rhythm of the whole, and not contrived as an episodic chorus or commentary. The writing finds and states its objects with more confidence; the writer, one feels, is clearer in his own mind about his personal predicament. 'It was one of those sequestered spots outside the gates of the world', he begins. And when that spring is released again, later in the story, you feel something like exultancy in the nostalgia.

Day after day waxed and waned; the one or two woodmen who sawed, shaped, or spokeshaved on her father's premises at this inactive season of the year, regularly came and unlocked the doors in the morning, locked them in the evening, supped, leant over their garden-gates for a whiff of evening air, and to catch any last and furthest throb of news from the outer world, which entered and expired at Little Hintock like the exhausted swell of a wave in some innermost cavern of some innermost creek of an embayed sea. . .

Like *Far from the Madding Crowd*, the tale tells of the choice between agricultural life and the lure of the town, the lure of 'rising in the world', confronting a country girl; and the outcome of the story embodies imaginatively the implications of the choice made. Grace Melbury is a second Bathsheba, a quieter, subtler study, less vividly drawn, but drawn with a rather deeper respect for human complexity. Giles Winterborne re-enacts the function of Gabriel Oak, while Marty South resumes Venn's function. In her the resilient local community takes personal form and skill. She is 'rooted in one dear perpetual place' and she disengages herself at the end from the individual lives and destinies of the surviving protagonists, and – so to say – simply continues to be. Egdon was a darker image of the rural environment than the hillsides and farms

of Weatherbury; now in the woods of the *The Woodlanders*
Weatherbury and Egdon seem to fuse together, the open loveliness
and the bounty of the first, and the overshadowing presence so
intimately declared, and the inner fecundity, of the second. In *The
Return of the Native* every insect and creature is alive, stirs, troubles
the eye. In *The Woodlanders* every footfall crushes leaves, every touch
and smell is of twigs and trees. Moreoever the woods combine
suggestions of long generations, of near-agelessness, with particular
moments in the community's past (when this plantation was made,
when the great gale blew). And they continually remind us of
human cultivation, human participation in the slow work of time.

But in one important particular this tale of choice stands apart
from the earlier ones. Bathsheba finally chose the agricultural order
and married Oak. When Winterborne, in *The Woodlanders*, the
representative woodman, dies, Grace fulfils her father's social
ambition and accepts the rôle she has been trained for. A diminished
person, she returns to Fitzpiers; and Hardy lays firm but varied
stress upon that choice as an issue of life-commitment. He also
made it clear, in private comment, that he envisaged no happiness
for her. *Far from the Madding Crowd* reflects through its fable
turbulence and insecurity, but *The Woodlanders* reflects defeat. The
last voice in the novel is Marty's, and a lonely devotion and loyalty
speak in one who incarnates the finest part of country attitudes.
Grace has turned to Fitzpiers, a Fitzpiers who has made the
accommodating gesture (and how revealing a gesture!) of renouncing
his studies. Marty takes Venn's place. What was projected before
in the active, resilient practitioner of a dying trade, is projected now
in the strong-willed, but lonely, impotent mourner, who polishes a
dead man's tools and tends his grave. A richer, more personal and
truthful apprehension underlies the second figure.

Fitzpier's renunciation takes it origin from a more obvious kind
of honesty in Hardy. He knew well where studies of that kind led. At
this very time of his life he himself was renewing his efforts to
master German metaphysics. Studies were the heart of his
experience of the 'outer' world. But such a renunciation is, of
course, no way of dealing with the situation; it is a gesture of
despair, of abandonment. And this is not like the despair of the
countryman, which does not stunt the pursuit of activity, even vain
activity. Grace makes the paralysing choice, and (as in *The Mayor of
Casterbridge*) the future seems to offer no happiness or resolution. In
Clym's last vocation and Venn's trade, in the life and death of the
Mayor, you have the feeling that theirs is a dying way of life. Now,
in the union of Grace and Fitzpiers after the death of Giles, the

feeling gets clearer definition. This story deals more subtly than its predecessors with personal and social relations, at some sacrifice of the sharp, hard edges of the character-drawing in the other books. Social status is integral to the pattern of the story; its protagonists each love 'above' himself or herself. That, too, indicates one facet of the impending collapse of the closed, compact agricultural communities. There are passages in *The Woodlanders*, however, where Hardy stands aside from his invention in a new way, and provides a troubled, intrusive commentary, one that speaks for the despair from outside, not the despair of the country which is able to endure patiently and hope on. It seeps into the movement of the novel. In the phrase of Mr Eliot, the man who suffers is less well separated from the mind that creates. Canalised nostalgia gives place, occasionally, to a coarser indulgence of bitterness.

But we find here some of Hardy's finest things. Marty South is perhaps the most moving of his characters, and two special reasons for the success suggest themselves. First, she is constantly present in scenes of activity and skill, sharpening spars, or planting young trees. Second, her speaking is often contrived with lovely imaginative truth, and a very personal movement. 'Her face', Hardy says,

had the usual fulness of expression which is developed by a life of solitude. Where the eyes of a multitude continuously beat like waves upon a countenance they seem to wear away its mobile power; but in the still water of privacy, every feeling and sentiment unfolds in visible luxuriance. . . .

'Mobile', it would be. Serenity and happiness seem to exist, for Hardy, in consonant and harmonious activities. Notice, too, how the solitude of seclusion from the urban world conditions the natural expressiveness. This 'still water of privacy' must remind us of 'sequestered spots' and the 'embayed sea': that note is insistent.

But the figure of Marty is no simple invention. A daydream character, you think. The wonderful hair, though it may help to express the physical fineness of the country girl, completes the daydream quality. Then she is robbed of her claim to comeliness, and robbed in order to add a biting touch of falsity to Mrs Charmond, the invader, the bewitching visitor in the agricultural group. And in fact, wherever Marty moves and speaks and works, as the novel develops, you become aware of a valuable mode of living. Hardy makes his most moving effects with just an air of adding corroboratory detail. He is absorbed in his object.

'It will be fine to-morrow', said Marty, observing them with the vermilion light of the sun in the pupils of her eyes, 'for they are a-croupied down nearly at the end of the bough.'

Marty South was an adept at peeling the upper parts; and there she stood encaged amid the mass of twigs and buds like a great bird, running her ripping tool into the smallest branches, beyond the furthest points to which the skill and patience of the men enabled them to proceed. . . .

'You seem to have a better instrument than they, Marty', said Fitzpiers.

'No, sir', she said, holding up the tool, a horse's leg-bone fitted into a handle and filed to an edge; "tis only that they've less patience with the twigs, because their time is worth more than mine.'

Hardy's appraisal of the worth of agricultural life is never far removed from his appreciation of agricultural economics.

Marty South embodies, then, a wholly fresh expression of Hardy's intelligent appraisal of the human possibilities of this way of life, with all its limitations. An ideal figure, we may say; but Hardy does present her, with conscious art, precisely as that. She brings to dramatic life, out of her close involvement in each facet of the novel, one possibility of meaning and worth. Her plain dignity, quite without pretension, defines one element of potential good inherent in the Little Hintock world, a good that matters even more than a single life, or two lives, spent and lost in affirming and celebrating it. There is tenderness in the way Hardy presents her, and there is more than a hint of nostalgia. But the language that brings her to life is careful and never false. She cuts spars with blistered hands. She is hired out for her living.

Is it possible to be more explicit about this 'good'? In part, certainly, it consists in intimacy with the plenitude of the natural order. We perceive it in the descriptions of Oak before and after the storm, of Clym at night upon Egdon and by day among the furze. Here is an illuminating passage.

The casual glimpses which the ordinary population bestowed upon that wondrous world of sap and leaves called the Hintock woods, had been with these two, Giles and Marty, a clear gaze. They had been possessed of its finer mysteries as of commonplace knowledge; had been able to read its hieroglyphs as ordinary writing; to them the sights and sounds of night, winter, wind, storm, amid those dense boughs, which had to Grace a touch of the uncanny, and even of the supernatural, were simple occurrences, whose origin, continuance, and laws they foreknew. They had planted together, and together they had felled; together they had with the run of the years, mentally collected those remoter signs and symbols which seen in few were of runic obscurity, but all together made an alphabet. From the light lashing of the twigs upon their faces when brushing through them in the dark, they could pronounce upon the species of tree whence they stretched; from the quality of the wind's murmur through a bough, they could in like manner name its sort afar off. They knew by a glance at a trunk if its heart were sound, or tainted with incipient decay; and by the state of its upper twigs the stratum that had been reached by its roots. The artifices of the seasons were seen by them from the conjuror's own point of view, and not from that of the spectator.

The unevenness of this passage makes it less than fairly representative of *The Woodlanders*; but it is uneven in illuminating ways. As you read the opening sentences, the prose seems like a laboured translation out of another language, and the trite handling of words is quite disconcerting. Periphrasis masquerades as impressiveness, the repetition is trying. Yet the very laboriousness has to do with an integrity the mannerisms would deny. With *To them, the sights and sounds* . . . the fluency of the movement and the solemnity of the cadence give you pause; Hardy is not always most trustworthy when most fluent. Then the odd phrase *mentally collected* jars the attention. Here is Hardy's sort of vigour, the elusive thing tightly gripped, at whatever cost in suavity. The earnest emphatic manner reappears, and then suddenly, with *From the light lashing of the twigs* . . . the intended movement is under way. Statement is left behind, and the perceptions act out the insight; and with this language of perceptions Hardy can speak like a master. Even then, he falters again, turns to his reader and explains – with a false analogy. Then see how beautifully he recovers his poise, with Marty's voice.

'He ought to have married you, Marty, and nobody else in the world!'
. . . .
Marty shook her head. 'In all our outdoor days and years together, ma'am', she replied, 'the one thing he never spoke of to me was love; nor I to him.'
'Yet you and he could speak in a tongue that nobody else knew – not even my father, though he came nearest knowing – the tongue of the trees and fruits and flowers themselves.'

Grace's reply is serious and sincere, yet laboured. But Marty's effort to sound a responsive note of adequate dignity gives a human implication to the experience of sensitive harmony with woodland life. Consider the delicacy of these words 'outdoor days', how they at once separate Marty from Giles, and bring them together not as lovers but as labourers. Then the gently deferential 'ma'am' reminds us of what now divides the two women also: the tragic marriage, and the way things have gone. Continually, in ways like this, Hardy has the delicate adjustment of individuals to local life and work issue in an equivalent delicacy of human feeling and relationship. You feel this quality in some measure whenever the woods come to life in the narrative, their sights and sounds, their growth and abundance, and whenever the novelist records intimations of the life and uniqueness of the trees.

A lingering wind brought to her ear the creaking sound of two overcrowded branches ... which were rubbing each other into wounds, and other vocalized sorrows of the trees, together with the screech of owls, and the fluttering tumble of some awkward wood-pigeon ill-balanced on its roosting-bough.

True, the sense of intimacy sometimes proves a temptation to that intrusive commentary I have mentioned.

Here, as everywhere, the Unfulfilled Intention, which makes life what it is, was as obvious as it could be among the depraved crowds of a city slum. The leaf was deformed, the curve was crippled, the taper was interrupted; the lichen ate the vigour of the stalk, and the ivy slowly strangled to death the promising sapling.

But such passages suggest also the honesty with which Hardy wanted to assess the country consolation. The insights he brings from outside probe at the sheltered world and give to the prose a shabby violence. Something of the kind happens whenever Hardy seeks to come to terms artistically with complexities his art as a novelist is insufficient to focus. For the most part of the book, he expresses something quite different.

The holes were already dug, and they set to work. Winterborne's fingers were endowed with a gentle conjuror's touch in spreading the roots of each little tree, resulting in a sort of caress under which the delicate fibres all laid themselves out in their proper directions for growth. He put most of these roots towards the south-west; for, he said, in forty years' time, when some great gale is blowing from that quarter, the trees will require the strongest holdfast on that side to stand against it and not fall.

'How they sigh directly we put 'em upright, though while they're lying down they don't sigh at all', said Marty.

'Do they?' said Giles. 'I've never noticed it.'

She erected one of the young pines into its hole, and held up her finger; the soft musical breathing instantly set in, which was not to cease night or day till the grown tree should be felled.

The feeling is for growth, for life. And its intimate quality is inseparable from the activities and skills of woodland living. The novel is not a collection of private descriptive set pieces; they have dramatic validity. The feeling towards the woods wells up from within the frame of the narrative.

The scene of the gathering around the woodfire after the bark-ripping, in chapter XIX, is a fine illustration. It forms an image at a point of rest, where the themes of the novel gather.

Melbury mounted on the other side, and they drove on out of the grove, their wheels silently crushing delicate-patterned mosses, hyacinths, primroses, lords-and-ladies, and other strange and common plants, and cracking up little sticks that lay across the track. Their way homeward ran along the western flank of Dogbury Hill. . . .

It was the cider country, which met the woodland district on the sides of this hill. . . . Under the blue, the orchards were in a blaze of pink bloom. . . . At a gate, which opened down the incline, a man leant on his arms, regarding this fair promise so intently that he did not observe their passing.

'That was Giles', said Melbury, when they had gone by.

'Was it? Poor Giles', said she.

'All that apple-blooth means heavy autumn work for him and his hands. If no blight happens before the setting, the cider yield will be such as we have not had for years.'

Grace has hitherto been poised uncertainly between Winterborne and Fitzpiers. Now she leaves the firelit circle where the human and social implications of her impending choice became so clear. Her father is carrying her away; the wheels of the gig crush the miniature world of green growth. They glimpse a distant Winterborne gazing out, absorbed, upon the tokens of abundant apple harvest. They are separated by their separate commitments, he to cultivation and the returning seasons of Hintock, she to her father's social ambition and the fruition of her civic and 'foreign' education. Dully she sets the yeoman aside. 'Was it? Poor Giles.' Her choice numbs her sensitiveness. Her loss of interest in and intimacy with the world of undergrowth and apple harvest becomes a withdrawal of personal warmth. But her father's deepest commitment is still to Hintock: this is part of the suggestive force of that promise to the dead father which still binds him to the son. He sees the yeoman, and feels the bond which unites them. Alongside the waste and pathos implied by the girl's curt dismissal, he brings into play feelings of a contrary order. The seasonal plenitude of earth and tree, and the labour which is the human response to it, these will persist.

The relation with the natural agricultural order which Hardy brings to life, reflects itself in many ways, but especially in the conduct of personal relations. Sensitiveness to people is an echo of a person's sensitiveness in the rural order. At one extreme is Mrs Charmond. 'As a rule she takes no interest in the village folk at all . . . she's been used to such a wonderful life, and finds it dull here.' Of her it is curtly noted – 'hardly knowing a beech from a woak'. Marty is at the other extreme, alert as even Giles is not, hearing the sound the young trees set up. Consider how the connection of that intimacy with degrees of human sensitiveness declares itself as that very passage continues.

'It seems to me', the girl continued, 'as if they sigh because they are very sorry to begin life in earnest – just as we be.'

'Just as we be?' He looked critically at her. 'You ought not to feel like that, Marty.'

Her only reply was turning to take up the next tree; and they planted on through a great part of the day, almost without another word. Winterborne's mind ran on his contemplated evening party, his abstraction being such that he hardly was conscious of Marty's presence beside him.

From the nature of their employment, in which he handled the spade and she merely held the tree, it followed that he got good exercise and she got none. But she was a heroic girl, and though her outstretched hand was chill as a stone, and her cheeks blue, and her cold worse than ever, she would not complain whilst he was disposed to continue work. But when he paused she said, 'Mr Winterborne, can I run down the lane and back to warm my feet?'

'Why, yes, of course', he said, awakening to her existence. 'Though I was just thinking what a mild day it is for the season. Now I warrant that cold of yours is twice as bad as it was. You had no business to chop that hair off, Marty; it serves you almost right.'

This quiet-voiced ironical commentary upon their differing sensitiveness is well-judged. One flinches at the callousness of the concluding remarks, and though that callousness is unconscious, Giles is found wanting.

There is a richer passage earlier, where Giles awaits Grace's homecoming, in Sherton Abbas – her return to the country. He has been sent by Melbury, and stands watching for her. For the very beginning of the episode Hardy has worked in a metaphorical way, as Melbury saw Giles out of sight. When the actual encounter comes, the metaphorical quality is plain and vivid.

Standing, as he always did, at this season of the year, with his specimen apple tree in the midst, the boughs rose above the heads of the farmers, and brought a delightful suggestion of orchards into the heart of the town.

When her eye fell upon him for the last time he was standing somewhat apart, holding the tree like an ensign. . . .

While she regarded him, he lifted his eyes in a direction away from Marty and his face kindled with recognition and surprise. She followed his gaze, and saw . . . Miss Grace Melbury, but now looking glorified and refined to much above her former level. Winterborne, *being fixed to the spot by his apple tree, could not advance to meet her:* he held out his spare hand with his hat in it, and with some embarrassment beheld her coming on tiptoe through the mud to the middle of the square where he stood . . . the little look of shamefacedness she showed at having to perform the meeting with him under an apple-tree ten feet high in the middle of the market-place.

The verve of the imagery displaying the encounter is naïve and delightful: Giles with his ensign, the tree; Giles turning away from Marty; Giles unable to move towards the glorified and refined Grace because of the tree – although there is no subtlety, phrase after phrase proves touchingly suggestive. Then the quality of the personal relations comes out more evidently, and what those relations imply.

'Don't Brownley's farm-buildings look strange to you, now they have been moved bodily from the hollow where the old ones stood to the top of the hill?' . . . .
'They had a good crop of bittersweets, they couldn't grind them all' – nodding towards an orchard where some heaps of apples had been left lying ever since the ingathering.
She said 'Yes', but looking at another orchard.
'Why, you are looking at John-apple trees! You know bittersweets – you used to well enough?'
'I am afraid I have forgotten, and it is getting too dark to distinguish.'

Hardy spares Grace nothing of the consequences of that darkness. The nerve of her insensitiveness to Giles and to Giles's world has been touched. It was getting too dark to distinguish. We recall an earlier colloquy. Mr Melbury had prepared Giles.

'We, living here alone, don't notice how the whitey brown creeps out of the earth over us; but she, fresh from a city – why, she'll notice everything!'
'That she will', said Giles.

Giles may be said to stand in somewhat the same relation to Grace – the real Grace – as Marty towards himself. But Giles is a woodlander, a protagonist in the story, and before us more often; so while Marty represents an ideal possibility beyond him, Giles in practice represents the worth of the agricultural life and skills and the worthiness of the traditional virtues – chivalry, loyalty, devotion. His symbolic function shows clearly at certain points in the novel; once or twice the feeling towards him is almost anthropological. There is first the passage where he stands with his apple tree in the market place. Then this:

An apple-mill and press had been erected on the spot, to which some men were bringing fruit from divers points in mawn-baskets, while others were grinding them, and others wringing down the pomace, whose sweet juice gushed forth into tubs and pails. The superintendent . . . was a young yeoman. . . . He had hung his coat to a nail of the outhouse wall, and wore his shirt-sleeves rolled up beyond his elbows to keep them unstained while he rammed the pomace into the bags of horsehair. Fragments of apple-rind had alighted upon the brim of his hat – probably from the bursting of a bag – while brown pips of the same fruit were sticking among the down upon his fine round arms, and in his beard.

It is much more than picturesque. Giles is not a daydream figure. The whole context is rich with sensuous and mobile suggestion. A virile pleasure in the activities directs the nostalgic emotion: the verbs and participles make the effect – *grinding, wringing, gushed, rammed, sticking*. Then, much later in the tale, comes a third construction:

Winterborne walked by her side in the rear of the apple-mill. He looked and smelt like Autumn's very brother, his face being sunburnt to a wheat-colour, his eyes blue as cornflowers, his sleeves and leggings dyed with fruit-stains, his hands clammy with the sweet juice of apples, his hat sprinkled with pips, and everywhere about him that atmosphere of cider which at its first return each season has such an indescribable fascination for those who have been born and bred among the orchards.

This remarkable passage forms part of the prolonged study of Grace's restoration, one of the finest sequences in the book. (This restoration, by a new immersion in agricultural life, cleansing, refreshing and renewing resource for living, is woven into the texture of each of Hardy's major novels. Bathsheba, Clym, and Grace all experience it; so, once, and then again, in a harsher way, does Tess.) The sensuousness here is more vital than before, and the range of suggestion – *wheat colour, blue as cornflowers, dyed with fruit-stains, return each season, orchards* – is wider.

When Giles dies, the loss is communal. Marty's elegy for him is well known; Creedle's speech is important too.

'Forgive me, but I can't rule my mourning nohow as a man should, Mr Melbury', he said. 'I ha'n't seen him since Thursday se'night, and ha' wondered for days and days where he's been keeping. There was I expecting him to come and tell me to wash out the cider barrels against the making, and here was he. . . . Well, I've knowed him from table-high; I knowed his father – used to bide about up on two sticks in the sun afore he died! – and now I've seen the end of the family which we can ill afford to lose, wi' such a scanty lot o' good folk in Hintock as we've got. And now Robert Creedle will be nailed up in parish boards a' b'lieve; and nobody will glutch down a sigh for he!'

Hardy uses the local idiomatic word with restraint: when he brings it in, it carries special force. Creedle gives us a sense of the interdependence of the labouring lives in Hintock, and of solicitude for old age. Hardy works close to the economic grain of this labouring life. The haunting figure of old South, for instance, identifies the close connection between the labourer's livelihood and provision for the future, and the tenure of land and home. The chapters that present him, XII to XIV, belong to Hardy's own realm of narrative art: he is a ballad figure accommodated in fiction, whose bizarre impotence gives a nightmare shape to Hardy's darker apprehensions. His obsessions turn upon tenure and the tree's life is his life.

Indeed the whole tale turns upon these issues, and upon the power so to dissolve old local ties and commitments now vested in the mildly, stupidly predatory figure of Mrs Charmond, the interloper. Marty is deprived. Giles is made dependent upon the representative of the new and alien squirearchy, and loses his home. These are the mainsprings of the fable. When Giles becomes a wanderer, Hardy drives home the gravity of the predicament. (Both the use of Mrs Charmond in this context, and the theme of deprivation look forward to the alien squire of *Tess of the D'Urbervilles*, and the homeless plight of the family at the end of that novel.)

Winterborne walked up and down his garden next day thinking of the contingency. The sense that the paths he was pacing, the cabbage plots, the apple-trees, his dwelling, cider-cellar, wring-house, stables, weathercock, were all slipping away over his head and beneath his feet as if they were painted on a magic-lantern slide, was curious. . . .

When he returns to his home later, a visitor in the twilight, the shapes of things past discernible in the gloom, and the unharvested apples, speak eloquently. And when Mrs Charmond's carriage crashes into the ruins of Giles's cottage and overturns, the narrative assumes vivid poetic force. Quite evidently the whole episode engaged Hardy's most powerful feelings.

Finally, Giles stands for traditional agricultural codes of conduct, and these codes too have their part in the 'good' which *The Woodlanders* seeks to embody. Ponderously, at one point, Hardy stresses his intention.

The wrong, the social sin, of now taking advantage of the offer of her lips, had a magnitude in the eyes of one whose life had been so primitive, so ruled by household laws, as Giles's, which can hardly be explained.

The conviction is real; and the tenderness with which Hardy treats of Giles in the final chapters flowers from this conviction. 'Her timid morality had indeed underrated his chivalry.' Thus Grace is criticised; and the chivalry by which she is judged has its origin not in 'Victorian morality' but in customs of behaviour sanctioned by immemorial household laws of village communities.

I have tried to express something of the body behind such a
phrase as 'He looked and smelt like Autumn's very brother'. Let us
now consider Grace Melbury a little further. Bathsheba was most
impressive in repentance and restoration. For Grace, no such
complete restoration is possible, but Hardy feels very tenderly
towards her when gradually she comprehends her predicament. The
moving passage that describes her silent watching of Giles, the prince
of Autumn, is illuminating here. The apprehensions are exact, but the
driving force is nostalgic, the backward look across time and space
from the point of exile, when 'Home over there' can no more be
brought into adequate relation with 'Out here'.

> Her heart rose from its late sadness, like a released bough; her senses
> revelled in the sudden lapse back to Nature unadorned. The consciousness
> of having to be genteel because of her husband's profession, the veneer of
> artificiality which she had acquired at the fashionable schools, were thrown
> off, and she became the crude country girl of her latent early instincts.
> Nature was bountiful, she thought. No sooner had she been cast aside
> by Edred Fitzpiers than another being, impersonating chivalrous and
> undiluted manliness, had arisen out of the earth ready to her hand.

You cannot feel that the writer here stands sufficiently at a distance
from the experience his art deals with; but that does not diminish
its importance for the novel as a whole. Grace, we are told,
'combined modern nerves with primitive feelings'. In some ways
she stands near to her creator, and she is used, constantly, to
sharpen our response to the novel's meaning. At several points in
the story, she recalls earlier memories, and the passages serve to
recapitulate the main themes and developments of the composition.
Here, for instance, she remembers Giles.

> He rose upon her memory as the fruit-god and the wood-god in
> alternation: sometimes leafy and smeared with green lichen, as she had
> seen him amongst the sappy boughs of the plantations: sometimes cider-
> stained and starred with apple-pips, as she had met him on his return from
> cider-making in Blackmore Vale, with his vats and presses beside him. . . .
> From being but a frail phantom of her former self, she returned in
> bounds to a condition of passable hopefulness. She bloomed again in the
> face. . . . She thought of that time when he had been standing under his
> apple-tree on her return from school, and of the tender opportunity then
> missed through her fastidiousness. Her heart rose in her throat. She
> abjured all fastidiousness now. Nor did she forget the last occasion on
> which she had beheld him in that town, making cider in the courtyard of
> the Earl of Wessex Hotel, while she was figuring as a fine lady on the
> balcony above.

Mr Melbury appears a more subtly observed character than his forerunner, Mrs Yeobright. Hardy grasps so well the strong country passion for 'betterment', and its bitter outcome. The blindness of Melbury's ambition finds expression in his personal tragedy: the obligation towards Giles's father, the betrayal of trust, and the recognition of irreparable error. Indeed, the more closely one inspects *The Woodlanders*, the more admirable appears its structure both in the subtle blending of the tale with its woodland soil, and in the metaphorical detail of the tale itself. A vivid instance of that blindness is Melbury's trust in the new divorce law, in rescue, so to speak, from outside the village walls; and the sorry frustration of that trust. The outer world is constantly like that: fair in promise, but bitterly deceptive. Coming upon such a passage as this one, we remember Mrs Hardy's note: 'If he could have had his life over again, he would prefer to be a small architect in a country town, like Mr Hicks at Dorchester, to whom he was articled.'

'I wish you had never, never thought of educating me. I wish I worked in the woods like Marty South! I hate genteel life, and I want to be no better than she!'

'Why?' said her amazed father.

'Because cultivation has only brought me inconveniences and troubles. I say again, I wish you had never sent me to those fashionable schools you set your mind on. It all arose out of that, father. If I had stayed at home I should have married –'

She closed up her mouth suddenly and was silent; and he saw that she was not far from crying.

Melbury was much grieved. 'What, and would you like to have grown up as we be here in Hintock – knowing no more, and with no more chance of seeing good life than we have here?'

It isn't a subtle irony. Yet these effects of Hardy's achieve a simple but considerable poignancy, like his strong, dramatic conceptions. He saw the blindness of the Melburys as instrumental in the collapse of the agricultural societies; he found the 'more perfect insight into the conditions of existence' which education brought to bear, to be stunting to life; and the transience of those societies, with their valid, if limited 'good life', a transience intimated in dramatic forms throughout his best fiction, is his essential theme.

The counterpart to Melbury, fumbling in the great world without, is Mrs Charmond fumbling in the village world, or lost in Hintock Woods, helpless and terrified. Her meeting there with Grace is one of Hardy's most imaginative contrivances. Grace is heavily committed in Mrs Charmond's world, and she too loses herself in those woods. But though she is tired and frightened too, she knows these woods, they are her home. It is she who leads the stranger out, and her resource and poise offset Mrs Charmond's bewilderment.

SOURCE: extract from chapter ('Novels of Character and Environment') of *Thomas Hardy* (London, 1954; reissued 1961), pp. 70–89.

Merryn Williams 'A Post-Darwinian Viewpoint of Nature' (1972)

It is easy to use a novel like *The Woodlanders* to support stereotyped ideas of the relationship between country and town. The woods can be seen as a place of innocence, safety and natural fertility; the 'good' characters as simple country people, and Fitzpiers and Mrs Charmond as urban interlopers (in Brown's view their sinister qualities are heightened by Fitzpiers's being an intellectual). Grace is then the pivotal figure, who has to choose between town civilisation and country life in choosing between Fitzpiers and Giles.

Yet this interpretation of the novel is much too simple. The woods are productive and fruitful in certain seasons and under certain aspects, but this is only part of the truth:

Here, as everywhere, the Unfulfilled Intention, which makes life what it is, was as obvious as it could be among the depraved crowds of a city slum. The leaf was deformed, the curve was crippled, the taper was interrupted; the lichen ate the vigour of the stalk, and the ivy slowly strangled to death the promising sapling.

The flowering or fruit-bearing orchards are contrasted with dead and dying trees; during the storm which kills Giles the woods assume a quality of terror:

Dead boughs were scattered about like ichthyosauri in a museum ... Next were more trees close together, wrestling for existence, their branches disfigured with wounds resulting from their mutual rubbings and blows ... Beneath them were the rotting stumps of those of the group that had been vanquished long ago, rising from their mossy setting like black teeth from green gums.

Nature is seen here from a post-Darwinian viewpoint; the trees have to struggle with their 'neighbours' in order to stay alive. And in some respects nature is not life-sustaining or even neutral but actively hostile to human beings, like the tree that kills John South: 'He says that it is exactly his own age, that it has got human sense, and sprouted up when he was born on purpose to rule him, and keep him as its slave.'

To South this tree has become 'an evil spirit', and when it falls 'my poor life, that's worth houses upon houses, will be squashed out o' me'. Yet the relationship is more complex than that of destroyer and victim; South has perversely *identified* with the tree, which he claims was born at the same time as him, and when it is chopped down he dies. And his consciousness that his life is worth 'houses upon houses' reminds us that the tree is the landowner's property, which cannot legally be cut down without her permission, and that human lives and destinies (Giles's loss of the houses and Grace with them) are tied up inextricably with money and land. The woods belong to Mrs Charmond who can fell both trees and houses according to her caprice. When Giles is turned out of his cottage after South's death it is pulled down, and the apples in his garden rot. The wastage spreads in a reciprocal process from human to natural life; human beings, trees and houses are all connected with each other through the 'closely-knit interdependence of the lives' in the tiny village. The woods, like Egdon, are not a background but a complex and changing entity through which individual characters define themselves. Marty says that the young trees 'are very sorry to begin life in earnest – just as we be.' Grace is described to Fitzpiers as 'the tree your rainbow falls on' by Giles. The trees, whether viewed as subjects or as objects, are the medium through which the community lives and expresses itself.

The culture of this community is not merely simple, but primitive. Grace, at the rituals on Midsummer Eve, feels 'as if she had receded a couple of centuries in the world's history'. In fact a belief in the supernatural is deeply rooted among the less educated; hence the popular legends of 'white witches and black witches', 'equestrian witches and demons', John South's obsession about the tree, and the people's rationalisation of their instinctive distrust of Fitzpiers by claiming that he has 'sold his soul to the wicked one'.

Fitzpiers is also the centre of another kind of superstition, owing to his aristocratic descent. People value this quality, irrationally:

That touching faith in members of long-established families as such, irrespective of their personal condition or character, which is still found among old-fashioned people in the rural districts, reached its full perfection in Melbury.

Melbury's admiration for the upper classes and what he considers their superior refinement and culture leads him to sacrifice his daughter. Grace, too, is partly fascinated by the romantic aura from the past which surrounds Fitzpiers. Fitzpiers, despite his claims to be an emancipated intellectual, accepts this homage complacently: 'I feel as if I belonged to a different species from the people who are working in that yard.' His instinctive recoil from the normal patterns of life in the village makes him feel 'a profound distaste for the situation' and react boorishly when the neighbours come to congratulate him and Grace on their return from honeymoon. 'There must be no mixing in', he insists, 'with your people below'. His feeling of superiority to ordinary people is based much more on snobbishness than on intellectual pride.

The aristocratic background reminds us of Troy, whose behaviour to women is very like that of Fitzpiers. But in general he is even more like Wildeve, more subtly and fully portrayed. Like him, he is a 'man of sentiment', who is only stung into being interested in his wife when he thinks she has been unfaithful – 'he cultivated as under glasses strange and mournful pleasures that he would not willingly let die.' Hardy is echoing Wildeve's description of himself when he explains how Fitzpiers can feel attracted to Grace and other women simultaneously:

Yet here Grace made a mistake, for the love of men like Fitzpiers is unquestionably of such quality as to bear division and transference. He had indeed once declared, though not to her, that on one occasion he had noticed himself to be possessed by five distinct infatuations at the same time.

His attitude to women is that of the typical aristocrat; the episode with the 'hoydenish maiden of the hamlet' Suke Damson is strongly similar to Alec d'Urberville's behaviour with the Trantridge girls. Suke is a new type in Hardy's work, though one that was to become prominent in his next two novels – the amoral, noisy, casually promiscuous girl, totally realistically drawn with all 'the scratches and blemishes incidental to her outdoor occupation' who is as much a recognisable type of village girl as Marty. The harmful social effects of this liaison are emphasised; Suke's husband is forced to emigrate to conceal the disgrace and Fitzpiers, by way of retribution, narrowly escapes being caught in the hideous man-trap which was set to mutilate poachers only a generation before the novel begins. Indeed it is noteworthy that this, one of the most 'idyllic' of all Hardy's pictures of country life, contains the figure of

Suke, the man-trap and the operations of a primitive code of revenge.

Fitzpiers's affair with Mrs Charmond is quite different – not a casual sexual encounter but a decadent and sentimental romance. It subsists on 'infinite fancies, idle dreams, luxurious melancholies, and pretty, alluring assertions which could neither be proved nor disproved'. It is broadly similar to the relationship of Eustacia and Wildeve, and Mrs Charmond is recognisably a development from Lucetta – the rich, sophisticated, irresponsible woman who is destroyed through her sexual sins. She is 'a body who has smiled where she has not loved, and loved where she has not married', who has been an actress (this is associated here, as in Troy and Eustacia, with an inauthentic personality) but having married money can find nothing to interest her. Her sole idea of occupying herself when she is not flirting is to travel about the continent and write a diary of her impressions – 'but she cannot find energy enough to do it herself'. Her interests are as futile as her emotions, and these are both artificial and shortlived. 'Now for a winter of regrets and agonies and useless wishes, till I forget him in the spring.'

The essential falsity of the relationship is stressed from the beginning when she summons Fitzpiers to treat her for a non-existent ailment, as an excuse to flirt. We feel that in doing this she is making a mockery of his skill as a doctor, the one really valuable thing he possesses. Douglas Brown regards Fitzpiers as a typical useless intellectual, who eventually, to be reconciled with Grace, has to make the 'gesture (and how revealing a gesture!) of renouncing his studies' [see preceding excerpt – Ed.]. But the trouble with Fitzpiers is that he is only playing at being an intellectual, allowing his desultory reading to divert him from his real work:

Dr Fitzpiers was a man of too many hobbies . . . In the course of a year his mind was accustomed to pass in a grand solar sweep through the zodiac of the intellectual heaven . . . One month he would be immersed in alchemy, another in poesy; one month in the Twins of astrology and astronomy; then in the Crab of German literature and metaphysics. In justice to him it must be stated that he took such studies as were immediately related to his own profession in turn with the rest.

His metaphysical speculations, as reported by Grammer Oliver, sound rather empty: 'Let me tell you that Everything is Nothing. There's only Me and Not Me in the whole world.'

However, his real intellectual achievements command admiration:

One speciality of Fitzpiers was respected by Grace as much as ever: his professional skill. In this she was right. Had his persistence equalled his insight instead of being the spasmodic and fitful thing it was, fame and fortune need never have remained a wish with him.

After he has saved Grace's life she reflects: 'why could he not have had more principle, so as to turn his great talents to good account!' In fact there are indications towards the end that he means to lead 'a new, useful, effectual life' as a doctor. Fitzpiers can, with a little effort, find a positive role in the community; Mrs Charmond cannot. 'It seemed to accord well with the fitful fever of that impassioned woman's life that she should not have found an English grave.'

Mrs Charmond has another role in the novel, that of the non-productive landowner whose relationship with the land and her tenants is entirely predatory. This is not an exaggeration; her treatment of Giles over the houses is typical of the worst landlords. She owns the woods but dislikes and does not know her way round them. It is taken for granted that people in the Hintocks should work for her but – 'she takes no interest in the village folk at all'. When she is forced into a direct relationship with any of them it is because she wants to deprive them of something – Marty's hair, Giles's home, Grace's husband. In each case she is acting not out of need but in order to gratify some trivial emotion – vanity, resentment, or sentimentality. Nothing is so important for her as to satisfy her caprice.

Contrasted are Giles and Marty, each of whom submits stoically to circumstances. Both of them endure a hopeless love without complaining and both can lose sight of their own suffering, physical and mental, in concentrating on the work which always has to be done. This work is not mechanical but as much of a skill as is Fitzpiers's; it is 'intelligent intercourse with Nature'. They understand the life of the trees, which to other people are only scenery, as no one else can:

The casual glimpses which the ordinary population bestowed upon that wondrous world of sap and leaves called the Hintock woods had been with these two, Giles and Marty, a clear gaze. They had been possessed of its finer mysteries as of commonplace knowledge; had been able to read its hieroglyphs as ordinary writing; to them the sights and sounds of night, winter, wind, storm, amid those dense boughs, which had to Grace a touch of the uncanny, and even of the supernatural, were simple occurrences whose origin, continuance and laws they foreknew.

The second sentence indicates that their work, despised by the sophisticated, is actually very difficult and complex. The description of how they are not afraid of the woods under any aspect reminds us of Thomasin's fearlessness on Egdon Heath. Nature is frequently destructive but it has to be come to terms with because it is the basis of life (the false reaction is Mrs Charmond's drawing the curtains because she is depressed by a rainy day). Giles's wonderful skill, and his instinctive understanding of nature, are shown through his ordinary work in the woods with Marty:

He had a marvellous power of making trees grow . . . There was a sort of sympathy between himself and the fir, oak or beech that he was operating on; so that the roots took hold of the soil in a few days . . . He put most of these roots towards the south-west; for, he said, in forty years' time, when some great gale is blowing from that quarter, the trees will require the strongest holdfast on that side to stand against it and not fall.

Giles's work is thus set in its perspective in history (for history is no less real in the woods than in Casterbridge). He feels that he is working for something beyond himself and that the trees have a relation to other human beings, some of them not yet born, besides him. His work extends through the generations; this is what gives it its value. Although he is a much more tragic figure, Giles is very similar to the other skilled countrymen in Hardy's earlier novels, Oak and Diggory Venn. He has the same patience, the same skill, the same incapacity to love more than one person. This single-heartedness, while it makes him ready to die for Grace, is fatal to Marty's hopes, since she is no more capable than he is of transferring her love.

Marty is as skilled at copse work as Giles – she can make excellent spars with no practice – but this does not mean she is incapable of the kinds of work which society values more highly:

Nothing but a cast of the die of destiny had decided that the girl should handle the tool; and the fingers which clasped the heavy ash shaft might have skilfully guided the pencil or swept the string, had they only been set to do it in good time.

It is continually stressed that she is a person of vivid intelligence and great human potential. But her possibilities are never fulfilled, because of her subordinate social position and her unreturned love, and she remains 'always a lonely maid' up to the end. Other people usually forget or ignore her claims as a person – 'everybody thought of Giles; nobody thought of Marty'. Unlike Grace, and unlike Mrs Charmond – who, at the other extreme of the social scale, needs to think about nothing but her femininity – she is shut out from love and marriage. She desexualises herself (like Tess when she is abandoned by Angel) by sacrificing her hair to deck another woman. By the end of the novel this process has been completed:

The contours of womanhood so undeveloped as to be scarcely perceptible ... she touched sublimity at points, and looked almost like a being who had rejected with indifference the attribute of sex for the loftier quality of abstract humanism.

Marty exists only through her work and is allowed no self-realisation apart from it. She carries 'the marks of poverty and toil', her arm is covered with 'old scratches from briars ... purple in the cold wind'. Although Giles never loves her, she is 'his true complement in the other sex' through the language and values they share. Her final speech over his grave brings out the reality of their relationship, one built out of the homely details of common work and experience:

Whenever I plant the young larches I'll think that none can plant as you planted, and whenever I split a gad, and whenever I turn the cider wring, I'll say none could do it like you.

It is symbolic, too, that she should finally take over his tools and his work. Giles's character is ultimately made clear through his actions – 'you was a good man, and did good things'.

Grace, an almost neutral figure 'who combined modern nerves with primitive feelings', is balanced between these two groups. Her 'primitive feelings' are her love for the woods and for Giles; her 'modern nerves' are the false codes of conduct which have been instilled into her at school and also partly at home. Her father, believing that the idle 'refined' world of Fitzpiers and Mrs Charmond is intrinsically superior to that of the woodlanders, gives her an expensive education and, when this process is completed, cannot bear her to be reabsorbed into his own way of life. For Grace, who knows nothing about manual work, marriage is the only conceivable destiny, and marriage is more closely bound up with social status in this than in any other of Hardy's works. Melbury thinks that Grace is too fine for Giles, while Fitzpiers is not sure if she is fine enough for himself (the idea of 'a vulgar intimacy with a timber-merchant's pretty daughter' is the first one that crosses his mind). But Grace has been trained up to a point where she is indistinguishable on the surface from a member of Fitzpiers's own class: 'Won't money do anything', Giles says, 'if you've promising material to work upon?' Grace is in the position of a second-generation *nouveau riche* who is expected to ratify her position by marriage; as such she cannot help feeling that she is being treated as a commodity: ' "I, too, cost a good deal, like the horses and waggons and corn!" she said, looking up sorrily.' Her father replies with no ironic intention: ' "Never mind. You'll yield a better return." ' He sees a marriage with the aristocratic though impecunious Fitzpiers as the crown of his hopes for his daughter, and indeed the transaction is mutually beneficial: 'Fitzpiers . . . while despising Melbury and his station, did not at all disdain to spend Melbury's money.' What Melbury has no idea of ('in the simple life he had led it had scarcely occurred to him that after marriage a man might be faithless') is that the ethos of the class which he so admires includes an exceedingly lax sexual code.

Grace, of course, is not just a tool of her father's, but the comparative weakness of her emotions makes her submit almost passively while her destiny is arranged for her. She has not the deep feelings of Giles or Marty; while she is still free to marry Giles she hesitates and lets the opportunity go. On the other hand she does have several positive feelings of affinity with the upper class; she is strongly attracted not only by Fitzpiers but also in the beginning by Mrs Charmond. It should incidentally be stressed that her education on which so much emphasis is laid, seems to have been a paltry affair. She has read the right books and can juggle with the names of foreign authors (hence her enthusiasm for Mrs Charmond's silly scheme to publish a diary) but she has no genuine love or desire for knowledge as such. Her education is essentially a badge of social superiority; she has been to school with girls 'whose parents Giles would have addressed with a deferential Sir or Madam', and as Giles himself says, 'She's been accustomed to servants and everything superfine'. This accounts for her recoil from the jolly uninhibited manners at Giles's Christmas party (so similar to Fitzpiers's distaste for the neighbours' celebration) and from the tavern where Giles takes her, even after she thinks she has broken with her husband for good. Her sympathy with the world of Mrs Charmond and Fitzpiers does not of course mean that she can tolerate its sexual mores. On the contrary she has imbibed a prim boarding-school morality which makes her consider everything in the light of whether or not it is 'proper'. This helps to bring the tragic climax about.

Hardy had dealt with unhappy marriages several times in his earlier fiction – Bathsheba, Thomasin, Clym and Farfrae all make them – but in each case the unsuitable partner dies and the other is

set free, usually to marry again. In *The Woodlanders* for the first time
Hardy rejects this easy novelistic solution; Fitzpiers stays alive and
Grace has to make the best of a bad job. Instead it is Giles who
dies, and Grace is forced to realise that she has probably killed
him. Naturally frigid, she has rejected him before her marriage,
kept him at a distance afterwards ('I wish to keep the proprieties as
well as I can') and finally driven him into the storm. There is a
blinding moment of illumination when she understands what she
has done:

'How selfishly correct I am always – too, too correct. Can it be that cruel
propriety is killing the dearest heart that ever woman clasped to her own?
. . . O, my Giles', she cried, 'what have I done to you!'

Her 'selfish correctness' is, in its own way, as negative and cruel as
Fitzpiers's promiscuity. They are, in fact related, as both of them
spring from a fear of deep commitments. Having been used with
undeserved contempt by Fitzpiers, Grace is treated by Giles with
an equally undeserved reverence. In sacrificing himself for the sake
of her modesty he is treating her less like a human being than a
plaster saint.

Grace's moment of insight cannot last, her feelings are too
shallow. Almost immediately after Giles dies her false consciousness
reasserts itself; she consoles herself by reciting prayers from the
book 'which poor Giles had kept at hand mainly for the convenience
of whetting his penkife'. The same book, later on, convinces her
that she ought to go back to her lawful wedded husband. Her
religiosity reaches its final point of fatuousness when she declares,
after the man-trap incident: 'O, Edred, there has been an Eye
watching over us tonight, and we should be thankful indeed!'

When she goes back to Fitzpiers, Grace is, as Douglas Brown
says, 'a diminished person'. After the first agonising remorse she
ceases to worry about the extent of her responsibility for Giles's
death. Indeed, once she is again on semi-flirtatious terms with her
husband Giles has become a mere object to bait him with. 'I don't
see why you should mind my having had one lover besides yourself
in my life, when you have had so many.' The same is true of her
pretence that she had been having an affair with Giles; this is
prompted solely by spitefulness and in fact she realises that in
making it she had 'wronged Winterborne's memory'. Her final
reconciliation with Fitzpiers is not convincing; we have no reason
apart from his own protestations to think he has changed:

'Well – he's her husband', Melbury said to himself, 'and let her take him
back to her bed if she will! . . . But let her bear in mind that the woman

walks and laughs somewhere at this very moment whose neck he'll be coling next year as he does hers tonight; and as he did Felice Charmond's last year, and Suke Damson's the year before! . . . It's a forlorn hope for her, and God knows how it will end!'

Grace will be unhappy, we can scarcely doubt, and yet not much more unhappy than she deserves. The workmen's tart comments make it clear enough that what we are seeing is no triumphant vindication of the marriage-vow but a compromise; something shoddy and mean. And Marty's comment at Giles's grave finally puts Grace into the right perspective. 'She has forgot 'ee at last, although for her you died'.

So the novel appears to end on a note of defeat. Indeed one of the saddest things about *The Woodlanders* is that the community, unlike those in the earlier novels, seems to have almost no capacity for resistance. Its attitude towards those who exploit it is one of passive criticism or, worse still, of passive acceptance; the people cannot even imagine an active defiant revolt like the Casterbridge skimmity-ride. The only exception is Tim's man-trap, which is almost a joke. Natural laws fail to assert themselves. Fitzpiers gets off scot-free while the pure in heart suffer or die. And yet, at the very end, we feel that there is still an unspoken resilience which goes beyond individual lives, or the destruction of individual hopes. It is personified in Marty's lonely figure with her fresh flowers and her determination to continue Giles's work; it is felt on the morning of death through the trees which will live after Giles:

The whole wood seemed to be a house of death, pervaded by loss to its uttermost length and breadth. Winterborne was gone, and the copses seemed to show the want of him: those young trees, so many of which he had planted, and of which he had spoken so truly when he said that he should fall before they fell, were at that very moment sending out their roots in the direction that he had given them with his subtle hand.

The defeat seems total, but it is not total. Individuals are destroyed and yet the work which creates life continues; in the midst of death, there is life.

SOURCE: ch. 7 ('*The Woodlanders*') of *Thomas Hardy and Rural England* (London and Basingstoke, 1972), pp. 157–68.

Michael Squires   Arcadian Innocents   (1974)

... The novel's pastoral motifs derive from both classical and Renaissance pastoral. The theme of eviction or dispossession of property, realistic and threatening as it is, occurs twice in Vergil's *Eclogues* [1 and 9], and provides a model for realistic pastoral. (One of the first books Hardy owned was Dryden's *Virgil*) ... With equal force, this situation recurs in *The Woodlanders*: by chance, Giles Winterborne is dispossessed of his ancestral home by a foreigner. A chance failure to renew the lifehold leases that John South held, leases passed from Winterborne's mother (a South) to his father and then to him, ends his tenancy in Little Hintock and much of his income, whereupon he must depart from Mrs Charmond's estate. Robert Creedle explains: 'the law ordains that the houses fall without the least chance of saving 'em into Her hands at the House'. In this highly Vergilian novel, Hardy intensifies the realism he finds in Vergil's *Eclogues*: if Marty is dispossessed of her hair by Mrs Charmond, Giles is dispossessed not only of his property but of his emotional ties to Grace as well; we shall return to Giles's emotional dispossession later.

The dispossession theme, though central, is not the only pattern of classical pastoral that attracted Hardy's imagination. Hardy fuses patterns from both Vergil and Theocritus. From Theocritus's *Idyll* 7 he takes the pattern of sophisticated urbanites who journey into the country and eventually return to the city, as the substance of his 'intruder' plot. But Hardy's attitude toward the intruder plot is not positive like the Greek poet's; in every scene the narrator of the novel mistrusts the intentions of the sophisticated intruders, who practise deception and enjoy idle leisure. At the heart of his 'rural' plot, on the other hand, one finds the pattern of Vergil's *Eclogues* 1 and 9 – in which exile, dispossession, time, unrest and hints of labor move into the foreground; one finds also the elegiac pattern of *Eclogue* 5, a lament for the dead shepherd Daphnis. Hardy then welds together these pastoral patterns, or plots. Once they are recognised, the novel emerges as more *purely* pastoral than has heretofore been imagined. If he reorders and adapts the special conditions of the bower, his vision retains its strong pastoral bias.

More central to the action of the novel is the pastoral motif of extreme plot complication, a convention of Renaissance pastoral romance. Unlike the brief compass of pastoral poetry, the length of the pastoral novel requires the variety and tension supplied by a plot: a division of emotional loyalties of course quickly injects conflict and interest into a long fictional form. Robert Drake, following the lead of Hallett Smith, recognises that the romantic ties of *The Woodlanders* fall into the Renaissance pattern of 'cross-eyed Cupid' in which A loves B, B loves C, C loves D, and D loves A: Marty loves Giles, Giles loves Grace, Grace loves Fitzpiers, Fitzpiers loves Mrs Charmond. The arrangement of emotional relationships progresses like links of a chain, from rural Marty to urban Mrs Charmond, spanning nicely the distance between simplicity and sophistication, poverty and wealth, toil and idleness – a distance continually exploited in the novel. If the motif of plot complication reflects the novel's pastoralism, so does the motif of the rejected swain or constant lover, which Hardy uses with total seriousness to trace the parabola of Giles's short life. The motif, though it is especially clear in the *Aminta*, occurs in Guarini's *Pastor Fido*, Daniel's *The Queen's Arcadia* and *Hymen's Triumph*, Fletcher's *The Faithful Shepherdess*, Randolph's *Amyntas*, and Jonson's *Sad Shepherd*. In Tasso's pastoral romance the *Aminta* (publ. 1580), the woodlander Aminta, spurned by his beloved but too-modest Silvia, seeks his own death. His pure constancy, heightened by rejection, leads him to a cliff in the woodland from which he leaps, yearning for death. Instead, his fall is broken and he is gradually restored to health by the repentant Silvia, who at last conquers her cruel modesty. Giles Winterborne, a constant but unaggressive lover, updates Aminta. Reserved and upright, honest and pure, he has loved Grace Melbury since childhood (he is 'one who had always been true'), and until she leaves Little Hintock to acquire her education, she loves him in return. But her training and her travels modernise her outlook, they deracinate her loyalties. When she returns home at last, 'she had fallen from the good old Hintock ways'. Persuaded by her ambitious father that her training has rendered her 'too good' for Giles, Grace discourages his attentions: ' "I am assured [marriage] would be unwise" '. Giles, forced to 'make the best of his loss', endures with feigned indifference her ensuing marriage to Dr Fitzpiers and its collapse. Soon after hopes for a divorce collide with social law, Giles, living in exile in a hut near Little Hintock, takes sick. His fever 'seemed to acquire virulence with the prostration of his hopes'. When Grace, fleeing from her husband, seeks temporary refuge at Giles's hut, Giles's modesty allows him to expose himself, in a 'strange self-sacrifice', much like Aminta's, to the cold damp. By the time Grace, herself a version of Silvia, overcomes her modesty, 'cruel propriety' has, if only in part, felled her Giles. The rejected-swain motif, employed traditionally to show the cruelty of a beloved, permits Hardy to use Giles as his protagonist and to link the cruelty of love to larger social evils – divorce laws, urban invasion and declining rural strength. We therefore see the pastoral bower from the innocent view within and from the sophisticated view without.

But parallel patterns reflect clusters of vertical weight rather than the horizontal complexity of verbal texture. Many pastoral elements appear in modern costume, and others, such as *otium*, undergo total metamorphosis.

Like many novels, *The Woodlanders* has both a male and a female protagonist. But unlike *Tom Jones* or *Pride and Prejudice* or *Adam Bede*, the two protagonists do not marry at the close of the novel. The relationship shared by Giles Winterborne and Marty South, like that between Catherine and Heathcliff or Jude and Sue, is more spiritual than sensual. Though Giles and Marty differ in some important respects from shepherds of classical or Renaissance pastoral, they are *pastoral* heroes. Giles bears the marks of pastoral in his innocence, altruism, honesty, relative poverty, intimate relationship with nature, chastity, humility, simplicity, meditativeness. To these we must certainly add his delight in his work. These qualities preserve *otium* or tranquillity, perhaps the most essential characteristic of the traditional pastoral lyric.

Living in 'one of those sequestered spots outside the gates of the world', says Hardy, the inhabitants of Little Hintock exhibit 'more meditation than action, and more listlessness than meditation': physical location and human response thus conjoin. Circumscribed by shady boughs – shade is the sine qua non of classical pastoral – and seldom in contact with the outer world of money and power, Giles and Marty live pure, initially uncomplicated and tranquil lives. 'Hardly anything could be more isolated or more self-contained than the lives of these two', remarks Hardy early in the novel. A 'reticent woodlander', Giles is 'pure and perfect in his heart'. Until his death, even Grace had not understood the 'purity of his nature, his freedom from the grosser passions, his scrupulous delicacy'. Marty South, solitary and sublime in character, possesses little of the narrative yet objectifies, with Giles, the novel's moral vision, its ethic of man and nature fusing harmoniously, each dependent on the other and linked together by an unwritten language. Hardy demonstrates this ethic in an important passage analysing imaginatively the ideal relationship among Giles, Marty and nature:

Marty South alone, of all the women in Hintock and the world, had approximated to Winterborne's level of intelligent intercourse with Nature.

In that respect she had formed his true complement in the other sex, had lived as his counterpart, had subjoined her thoughts to his as a corollary.

The casual glimpses which the ordinary population bestowed upon that wondrous world of sap and leaves called the Hintock woods had been with these two, Giles and Marty, a clear gaze. They had been possessed of its finer mysteries as of commonplace knowledge; had been able to read its hieroglyphs as ordinary writing; to them the sights and sounds of night, winter, wind, storm, amid those dense boughs, which had to Grace a touch of the uncanny, and even of the supernatural, were simple occurrences whose origin, continuance, and laws they foreknew. They had planted together, and together they had felled; together they had, with the run of the years, mentally collected those remoter signs and symbols which seen in few were of runic obscurity, but all together made an alphabet. From the light lashing of the twigs upon their faces when brushing through them in the dark either could pronounce upon the species of the tree whence they stretched; from the quality of the wind's murmur through a bough either could in like manner name its sort afar off. They knew by a glance at a trunk if its heart were sound, or tainted with incipient decay; and by the state of its upper twigs the stratum that had been reached by its roots. The artifices of the seasons were seen by them from the conjuror's own point of view, and not from that of the spectator.

Hardy's generous use of anaphora ('They had been . . . had been . . . . They had . . . together they had . . . together they had. . . . From the . . . from the . . .') implies, rhetorically, his deep emotional commitment to the kind of interaction or 'intercourse' between man and nature that functions for Hardy as an imaginative ideal. With hints of Platonism perhaps derived from Shelley, Hardy stresses the role of intelligent perception in penetrating the 'finer mysteries' which may be hidden to the insensitive or the unsympathetic. Like Gabriel Oak, these two figures understand natural processes and readily decipher nature's alphabet. As Grace says to Marty, 'you and he could speak in a tongue that nobody else knew . . . the tongue of the trees and fruits and flowers themselves'. Dispossessed of nature's language, Mrs Charmond can hardly distinguish a beech from an oak. The knowledge, understanding and sympathy with which Giles and Marty are able to approach nature allows them to form a unique, asexual alliance with nature: a marriage. Both renounce human sexuality: Giles is free from gross passion and at the hut observes a severe propriety; at the moonlit close, Marty 'looked almost like a being who had rejected with indifference the attribute of sex'. By embracing an 'intelligent intercourse with nature' and by establishing a spiritual empathy between themselves, both characters illustrate the separation (frequent in pastoral) of sexual from spiritual love.

The intimacy of Giles and Marty with nature expresses itself not only in a conscious mental awareness of the interaction, but also in physical interaction with nature in the form of work. Normally the mention of work in pastoral is enough to shatter *otium* [ease, leisure – Ed.]. In this respect Hardy breaks with traditional pastoral to make an important change: in his treatment of rural life, he moves toward the georgic, ranking useful labor above *otium*. Traditionally, leisure and tranquillity merge in the bower. But in *The Woodlanders* Hardy splits them. To Giles and Marty he gives considerable tranquillity *and* work. To Mrs Charmond and Grace, he gives idle leisure; to Fitzpiers, the pursuit of whim. Unlike traditional pastoral, leisure arouses, paradoxically, not *otium* but *negotium* – an emotional turbulence mild in Grace, pronounced in Fitzpiers, feverish in Mrs Charmond.

For Giles and Marty, work is satisfying because it orders their world. Like Adam Bede, Giles 'found delight' in his work. Later, when Marty travels in the autumn with Giles's cider-press, she too will find satisfaction and purpose in her work. Early in the novel we find Giles and Marty preparing to plant trees:

What he had forgotten was that there were a thousand young fir trees to be planted in a neighbouring spot which had been cleared by the woodcutters, and that he had arranged to plant them with his own hands. He had a marvellous power of making trees grow. Although he would seem to shovel in the earth quite carelessly there was a sort of sympathy between himself and the fir, oak, or beech that he was operating on; so that the roots took hold of the soil in a few days. When, on the other hand, any of the journeymen planted, although they seemed to go through an identically similar process, one quarter of the trees would die away during the ensuing August.

Hence Winterborne found delight in the work even when, as at present, he contracted to do it on portions of the woodland in which he had no personal interest. Marty, who turned her hand to anything, was usually the one who performed the part of keeping the trees in perpendicular position whilst he threw in the mould.

. . . . .

The holes were already dug, and they set to work. Winterborne's fingers were endowed with a gentle conjurer's touch in spreading the roots of each little tree, resulting in a sort of caress under which the delicate fibres all laid themselves out in their proper directions for growth.

That Giles and Marty work, as in the georgic, does not in any way negate the pastoral vision of man in harmony with nature. The 'sympathy between himself and the fir, oak, or beech' differs little from the shepherd-piper teaching the woods to sing [Vergil's

Eclogue 6, e.g.] or the trees lamenting the death of the shepherd-hero Daphnis. Like the pastoral piper, he is a 'gentle conjurer'. In the same way that nature in classical pastoral reciprocates by echoing the musician's melody, the roots, touched by Giles, 'took hold of the soil in a few days'. True to the pastoral vision, moreover, delight in nature is divorced from money or personal gain: Giles, a minister of nature, had no 'personal interest' to serve. Out of his delight springs a good measure of pastoral tranquillity. Later, Hardy expresses this idea of interaction between man and nature in mythological terms, using both anaphora and Grace's point of view: 'He rose upon her memory as the fruit-god and the wood-god in alternation: sometimes leafy and smeared with green lichen, as she had seen him amongst the sappy boughs of the plantations: sometimes cider-stained and starred with apple-pips, as she had met him on his return from cider-making in Blackmoor Vale, with his vats and presses beside him'. A Pan figure put to work, Giles, whether fruit-god or wood-god, is still the 'conjurer' of the preceding passage – still the figure who has entered the heart of natural processes and who provides the *locus amoenus* [loved place – Ed.] with its divinity.

In another passage Giles's kinship (quite literally) to nature expresses itself in flashes of poetry, bathed with gentle feeling, that characterises Hardy's pastoral fiction: 'He looked and smelt like Autumn's very brother, his face being sunburnt to wheat-colour, his eyes blue as corn-flowers, his sleeves and leggings dyed with fruit-stains, his hands clammy with the sweet juice of apples, his hat sprinkled with pips, and everywhere about him that atmosphere of cider which at its first return each season has such an indescribable fascination for those who have been born and bred among the orchards.' The quickest index to the depth of nostalgic 'fascination' in this portrait is again the use of anaphora, a rhetorical scheme that Hardy regularly employs in passages to which he, or the implied author, commits himself emotionally. The identification of Giles with an organic process imagined as bountiful and benevolent achieves no simpler or purer form than it does here. The opening figure is instructive: a brother represents one's likeness or similarity; in this case the human figure manifests endless visual and gustatory parallels to nature. At one point Giles even assumes 'the colour of his environment'. If he is called a conjurer and a god, Giles is also, here, demythologized and brilliantly painted, the portrait seizing the whole man: seizing his internal beauty and innocence, and the external equivalents of his internal state. Hardy immerses him in the harvest, perfuming Giles's visual exterior with the redolent atmosphere of crops, much as Lawrence immerses George Saxton [in *The White Peacock*] in the heavy perfume of the harvest field.

But if Giles delights in his work, Marty does not. His work is never tedious; hers is. Despite her absorption in natural occupations, she emerges as a realistic figure. This fact, in the way it distances the novel from pastoral, should not go unobserved. Skilled at her work and uncomplaining and heroic, yet poor and sombre and sometimes listless, Marty South finds life 'a hard struggle'; and as the novel opens, we find her working all night, making spar-gads for Melbury. As faithful to Giles as he is to Grace, Marty is 'always doomed to sacrifice desire to obligation'. Stoic rather than epicurean, Marty approximates figures of the georgic, a genre in which the farmer, treated seriously, is glorified as he performs the hard tasks of planting or trimming trees or pressing apples into cider. The pastoral novel in the nineteenth century moves clearly in the direction of the georgic.

In *The Woodlanders* what Hardy does to pastoral is most interesting. We can discover a clue to his conception of modern pastoral in a phrase he uses to describe Marty's journey to Sherton Abbas. Her steadfast concentration, he says, 'means purpose and not pleasure'. For the pleasure or leisure he finds traditionally in pastoral, Hardy substitutes *purpose* – a purposive relationship with the natural world from which a livelihood, enjoyment and emotional tranquillity are derived. The observation that purpose is moral and pleasure or leisure immoral can be readily illustrated in the novel. The failure to find meaning through one's work is equated by Hardy, as by George Eliot, with moral and ethical failure. While Giles lived, Marty and Grace enjoyed 'no anticipation of gratified affection' in their relationship with Giles. On the other hand, Hardy observes with dismay the tattooed marks of cloying leisure on Mrs Charmond and, to a slightly lesser extent, Fitzpiers. The ironic name 'Felice' hints at her pleasurable, leisure-loving *modus vivendi* [way of living – Ed.], one that dreads contact 'with anything painful'. Mrs Charmond, 'always with a mien of listlessness', murmurs to Grace: ' "I am the most inactive woman when I am here", she said. "I think sometimes I was born to live and do nothing".' Fitzpiers, who too 'did not study economy when pleasure was in question', always finds Mrs Charmond 'reclining on a sofa', indulging 'in idle sentiments', and arousing for him an 'indefinite idle impossible passion'. In a marvellously inverted sentence, loaded with artifice, Hardy remarks that, while holding her cigarette, Mrs Charmond 'idly breathed from her delicately curled lips a thin stream of smoke towards the ceiling'. Even Fitzpiers contemplates a distant scene in an 'idle way'. Stripped of purposive direction, Fitzpiers enjoys 'too many hobbies' to reach professional eminence, reading books of 'emotion and passion as often as ... science'. Pastoral leisure, condemned as it is by the implied author, unlocks the characters' idle indulgence, which then breaks loose to destroy the simplicity and tranquillity of the innocent pastoral characters. Idleness in turn fertilises those emotions that eventually blossom into consuming passions. Fearing 'his own rashness', Fitzpiers 'allowed himself to be carried forward on a wave of his desire'. When he initiates the 'impassioned enterprise' of paying Grace Melbury a social call, he senses 'that he was casting a die by impulse which he might not have thrown by judgment'. Mrs Charmond, Byronic rather than pastoral, is 'capriciously passionate', like Trollope's Madeline Neroni in *Barchester Towers*. Acting always 'on impulse', she possesses a heart 'passionately and imprudently warm'. Hintock bottles up her emotions, and neither she nor Fitzpiers can outgrow 'the foolish impulsive passions' of their youth. Having no means of ordering their emotions, they enter upon agitated misalliances that plunge them, to use the surgeon's phrase, into 'sorrow and sickness of heart at last'. Their withdrawal into a lovely place, directed by their idle and passionate natures, propels them downward into a churning vortex in which order – both personal and social – is lost. Fitzpiers, like [George Eliot's] Arthur Donnithorne, ignores social barriers and allows his professional practice to decline; Mrs Charmond, in practising adultery, breaks legal barriers and in the scene of Fitzpiers's rumored death witnesses the crumbling of her self-respect. Throughout the novel these fluctuating passions and shifting alliances find their scenic equivalent in the frequent changes of light intensity – flaring matches, swinging lanterns, fleeting shadows, moving candles, dying fires, dawn turning to day and day to dusk – thus explaining in part Hardy's unusual concern with light.

Despite the moral hiatus between purpose and work on the one hand, and idle leisure and romance on the other, Hardy does connect both admired and unadmired characters by using romantic love and physical setting as connective agents. In the seventeenth century, Fontenelle theorised that pastoral results from a marriage between love and idleness; love, that is, prevents leisure from turning to sloth, and enlivens *otium*. Hardy will tolerate love in the pastoral world (provided it is chaste) but not idleness. The result is that the idle, whimsical characters intrude unnaturally into the *locus amoenus* and violate its purity. The motif of intrusion, producing imaginatively a reaction of fear and anxiety, dominates the novel and requires us to look briefly at the U-shaped curve of the action it originates.

As intruders, both Fitzpiers and Mrs Charmond (and to a much lesser extent Grace) hail from urban climes. Edred Fitzpiers, 'of late years a town man', comes to the secluded village as a surgeon reportedly in league with the devil. Having chosen the shady woodland hamlet arbitrarily, he had quit the urban world on a mere impulse, 'in a passion for isolation, induced by a fit of Achillean moodiness after an imagined slight'. Not long afterward, Grace Melbury, daughter of a prosperous Hintock timber merchant, returns home, her education complete. Fashionable and refined, though 'not ambitious', Grace has acquired a 'veneer of artificiality' that quite appeals to Fitzpiers and that provides a welcome contrast to the 'crude rusticity' of Hintock, although unlike Arthur Donnithorne, Fitzpiers hesitates but a moment to seduce Suke Damson, a lusty village plum. Quickly wooing Grace from Giles, to whom her father had promised her many years before, Fitzpiers manipulates Grace into his wife only a few months before he encounters the sophisticated widow, Mrs Felice Charmond, a woman with a mysterious past, 'a charmer in her time', a one-time actress, 'who has smiled where she has not loved, and loved where she has not married'. To the surgeon's joy, she returns his passion with fervor. In their 'erratic abandonment to doubtful joys', they make easy conquests of each other and, without sanctions, elope to the continent, where they had met earlier. Fitzpiers, stationed at the center of romantic complications, thus conquers a woman from each level of society: rural, rural/urban, urban. As Hardy portrays them, the two intruders invade Little Hintock like an army, leave with the spoils, and cause others to leave – Giles, Suke and Tim, Grace. We never see a conflict among the villagers that has not its roots in urban culture or (much more frequently) the aliens. Thus, in modifying pastoral, Hardy has not only shifted sympathy from the disguised rustics of tradition to actual rustics of his observation, but he has illustrated that the novel's moral hierarchy is inversely related to class structure: the characters who command the narrator's admiration are those without property or rank. Hardy makes no attempt, as pastoralists often have and as Lawrence does in *Lady Chatterley's Lover*, to remove barriers between classes. Instead, his deep sympathy for country people encourages what Lawrence in his study of Hardy calls 'moral antagonism' toward the aristocrat. . . .

... Alien not to the woodlanders alone, Fitzpiers and Mrs Charmond – like the gentleman from South Carolina – are alien to their setting as well, which in typically pastoral fashion refuses to harmonise with their unnatural natures. For them, lacking as they do Wordsworthian memories of their present environment, Little Hintock and its woods are lonely and monotonous. Hintock House, for example, reveals its unfitness 'for modern lives' like Mrs Charmond's. Fitzpiers 'hated the solitary midnight woodland', and his mate in passion, because she hates solitude, also 'disliked the woods'. If the tricks of the weather 'prevented any sense of wearisomeness' in the natives of Hintock, Fitzpiers requires some romantic diversion 'to relieve the monotony of his days'. Because they fail to harmonise with their setting, nature does not excite their interest, but tricks them instead. Fitzpiers, 'ever unwitting in horseflesh', mistakes his horse because of the gloom; and shortly thereafter, Blossom unseats this 'second-rate' equestrian. Both Mrs Charmond and Grace lose their sense of direction (physical *and* moral) in the 'umbrageous surroundings' of the wood. In like surroundings, Fitzpiers experiences 'a sudden uneasiness' at the contrast of nature's 'great undertakings' and his own idleness. Nature exerts a moral force, as it does when Troy plants flowers on Fanny's grave. This kind of oppression arises from lack of sympathy with one's environment: Mrs Charmond must, for example, counteract 'the fine old English gloom' of Hintock House. Fitzpiers, already 'oppressed' by Hintock, suffers an 'indescribable oppressiveness' near the end of his wedding journey and later feels 'doomed' to Hintock. This place 'oppresses me', Mrs Charmond cries to Grace. Although Grace 'never got any happiness outside Hintock', Fitzpiers wants to 'get away from this place for ever'. The failure of the invaders to appreciate the woods and the woodlanders confirms their anti-pastoral function, which is heightened in *The Woodlanders* nearly to obsession. The invaders' inability to sympathise genuinely with whatever, natural or human, lies outside the confines of the self corrodes their humanity, and the negative landscape descriptions beautifully reflect the corrosive texture of their minds.

These quotations document the anti-pastoral pattern of disharmony and intrusion that persistently counterpoints the pastoral pattern of happiness, tranquillity, harmony with nature, and spiritual love. The intruders permit Hardy to make explicit the conservative moral vision that controls the novel: the man who allows license (or, departure from Christian codes) to guide his actions lives *immorally*; the man who comprehends nature, rejects ambition, embraces altruism, and favors reticence lives *morally*. In using his villains to represent a vision of immorality, Hardy encounters the problem that Lawrence faced with Clifford Chatterley: how to prevent the novel from becoming morally schematic and therefore weakening its reality. I do not think that Hardy, like Lawrence, entirely surmounts this difficulty. Because he allots much space to Mrs Charmond and Fitzpiers, so that their villainy becomes exaggerated, his indictment of their idle passion and their devotion to pleasure loses, finally, some of its force. There are two reasons for this critical imbalance: whereas the reticence of Marty, Giles and Grace tends to deny life, the passion of Mrs Charmond and Fitzpiers asserts life; it becomes, finally, more attractive to the reader than perhaps it should if we are to remain persuaded by the novel's moral vision. More troublesome, I think, is the treatment accorded the characters who exemplify moral and immoral visions. Unlike Sergeant Troy, Felice Charmond and Fitzpiers indulge their passions with no worse effects than the characters who refuse indulgence. Chastity and honor, while praised by the narrator, merit punishment; virtue enjoys no clear sustained value. The unchaste and dishonorable, while censured, are punished with no more severity; although Fitzpiers promises to pass through 'a long state of probation', his dishonorable character, the narrator implies, will endure. Now, it will be objected that in this Hardy simply gives us a picture of an unschematised reality, or that he admits no inherent moral system to order human life – that the Unfulfilled Intention manifests itself indifferently. But values that a reader is persuaded to accept at the start of a novel lose their power and their sense of moral precision when they are compromised, to the extent that Hardy allows, by an opposing scale of values. Hardy's art, fascinating but also disturbing in its lack of moral coherence between plot strands, does not provide the intellectual subtleties we relish in George Eliot or Conrad. To say so is not to criticise but to try to seize upon the novel's distinctive features.

Earlier I said that Hardy's moral vision was conservative and traditional rather than innovative; and, with the exception noted, his vision is consistent with the pastoral vision. But like Sidney or Spenser or Marvell, Hardy had little fear of innovation in pastoral and, without reluctance, mixed genres – readily fusing pastoral themes with realistic techniques. His conception of the pastoral novel permitted substantial innovation in his focus on Grace as a bridge character between rural and urban, and in his use of the principle of *division* as the template for the narrative.

Although Grace functions as the valence of the novel, tautly joining city to country, Hardy provides her until the end of the novel with clear moral direction. When she returns 'from the world to Little Hintock', she had 'fallen from the good old Hintock ways' to become 'well-nigh an alien'. Like Cyril in *The White Peacock*, Grace, longing for simplicity and even physical labor, upbraids her father: '"I wish you had never, never thought of educating me. I wish I worked in the woods like Marty South! I hate genteel life, and I want to be no better than she!".' Despite Grace's cultured refinement, she emerges like Bathsheba Everdene as young and naive, a girl deceived by alcoholic sophistication. Fitzpiers acts upon her 'like a dram, exciting her' and produces 'intoxication' in her brain, metamorphosing her into a wasp 'which had drunk itself ... tipsy'. Juxtaposed to Mrs Charmond, Grace becomes a 'simple school-girl'. Her schooling and her susceptible nature, however, divide her loyalties and deflect the 'natural course' of her love for Giles. Directed toward simplicity by her varied experience of both rural and urban and then (when she returns) of her experience of rural-from-urban perspective, Grace at last finds virtue only in the hearts of 'unvarnished men'. Her discovery of virtue, 'her widening perceptions of what was great and little in life', hastens her progress from refined accomplishment and acquired tastes to simplicity. This progression reaches its climax when she recognises Giles as Autumn's brother: 'Her heart rose from its late sadness like a released bough; her senses revelled in the sudden lapse back to Nature unadorned. The consciousness of having to be genteel because of her husband's profession, the veneer of artificiality which she had acquired at the fashionable schools, were thrown off, and she became the crude country girl of her latent early instincts.' Hardy traces the trajectory of pastoral innocence on the path toward knowledge and culture; he then reverses directions in order to observe the truncation of the movement. The cultural process or trajectory brings not insight, as it does in Austen or Dickens or Henry James, but regret. Virtually every journey away from Hintock ends in failure: Grace's repeated journeys to a fashionable school, Melbury's to London, Fitzpiers's and Mrs Charmond's to Germany. An adequate guide to conduct must, the novel suggests, emerge from innocence, instinct, 'nature'; it is 'nature' that 'had striven to join together' Grace and Giles. In *The Woodlanders* knowledge warps consciousness, deflects or weakens moral impulses. The implied tragedy of the novel is not, I believe, Giles's death but

Grace's inability to return to her native Hintock. Like Cyril Beardsall or Clym Yeobright, Grace possesses firm rural roots; but her return to pastoral contentment is diseased by what Lawrence calls in *The White Peacock* 'the torture of strange, complex modern life', a torture Grace must ultimately face. By dissecting the 'pastoral' collision between two differing sets of values, Hardy can, by castigating one set, heighten the significance of the other, even though we sense clearly the power of sophistication over innocence. More important, he can use a single main character, of 'modern nerves' and 'primitive feelings', as the vehicle to express his pastoral theme of art versus nature. Grace's characterisation, then, defines Hardy's theme; and the varied *directions* of her characterisation do much artistically to define value in the novel.

One other innovation that illustrates Hardy's altered conception of the pastoral form is his insistence on division – physical, social, emotional – as the principle basic to the novel's texture and theme. It is well known that the book is divided between early conception (1874) and late execution (1885–87), and divided again between pastoral and realism. But, that the principle of division controls theme, characterisation, quality of diction, and representation of physical objects has not been recognised. The sharp central division between *rus* and *urbem*, which Hardy insists on, easily subsumes other kinds of division. Both the book's moral vision and its theme of art versus nature or sensual versus spiritual love depend on the city-country contrast of their sustained effectiveness. From a social standpoint, Grace and her father are both divided between rural and urban affinities. From a romantic or emotional standpoint, characters are nicely split between one lover and another, as we have seen: Grace between Giles and Fitzpiers; Fitzpiers between Suke and Grace and Mrs Charmond; and Suke between Tim and Fitzpiers. Melbury is socially divided between Fitzpiers and Giles, Marty is separated from Giles by Grace and by death, Giles is exiled from his ancestral homeplace, John South is tortured by a tree he loves. Nature herself divides her work between displays of beauty and revelations of cruelty or unfulfilled intentions. These assorted divisions, while they sustain the plot and give significance to the theme, produce tension rather than pastoral stasis. Similarly, what the bark-rippers do to the branches of the trees or what the surgeon does to John South's brain or what nature does to itself when the ivy strangles a sapling, the characters do to each other. . . .

. . . The novel closes, after a lengthy denouement, with a muted pastoral elegy, spoken by Marty, that has inspired the admiration of the novel's commentators. If nature's lamentation does not form part of Marty's elegy, something certainly akin to lamentation occurs a little earlier and reinforces the pastoral harmony between character and setting. As Grace and her father walk away from the hut after Giles has died, 'the chilling tone of the sky was reflected in her cold, wet face. The whole wood seemed to be a house of death, pervaded by loss to its uttermost length and breadth. Winterborne was gone, and the copses seemed to show the want of him.' If the sky finds its image in Grace's chilled features, Giles's death finds its reflection in the grieving wood. But Hardy heightens still more the pastoral intimacy between dead hero and nature. During their walk home, Grace and her father had seen 'but one living thing on their way, a squirrel, which did not run up its tree, but, dropping the sweet chestnut which it carried, cried chut-chut-chut and stamped with its hind-legs on the ground'. Hardy shows a frequent fondness for using animals to comment on human folly (earlier a bird complains sarcastically as Fitzpiers and Suke make love on the moonlit hay). His use of the squirrel implies the criticism of Grace that as narrator he refrains from expressing. As in traditional pastoral – in Theocritus's *Idyll* 1 or briefly in *Idyll* 7, for example – Hardy allows nature to alter her course because of the death of the pastoral hero: the squirrel, which would normally head for the safety of the tree, stops to complain of Giles's death. The participation of a sympathetic nature, though separated from Marty's elegy, is properly a part of it.

The elegy is preceded by the periodic visits of Marty and Grace to Winterborne's grave. The visits form the processions of mourners, one of the conventions of the pastoral elegy. Like those who lament the death of the gamekeeper in *The White Peacock*, the mourners lay flowers on the grave. Marty and Grace follow their weekly ritual 'for the purpose of putting snowdrops, primroses, and other vernal flowers thereon as they came' until Grace, at last, rediscovers, 'the arms of another man than Giles' and is accused by the narrator of neglect, the accusation being still another convention of the pastoral elegy. Marty alone remains loyal: ' "whenever I get up I'll think of 'ee, and whenever I lie down I'll think of 'ee again. Whenever I plant the young larches I'll think that none can plant as you planted; and whenever I split a gad, and whenever I turn the cider wring, I'll say none could do it like you. If ever I forget your name let me forget home and heaven! . . . But no, no, my love, I never can forget 'ee; for you was a good man, and did good things!" ' Remarkable here is Hardy's use of two more conventions of the pastoral elegy – the praise of the dead hero and the consolation of the aggrieved friend. Like the rites of praise that Menalcas in Vergil's *Eclogue* 5 promises to the dead hero Daphnis, Marty also promises a ritual of remembrance and praise.   . . .

. . . Marty's vow expresses her commitment in a more personal way: '"If ever I forget your name let me forget home and heaven!"' In a view more pagan than Christian – a view true to the pastoral vision – death is absorbed into the continuing cycle of planting and harvesting, the seasonal duties themselves serving as reminders of Giles's goodness and deeds; Giles is finally integrated into the larger sphere of animal and vegetable life.

If Hardy lingers awhile inside the hut, it is to renew the conflict between Grace and Fitzpiers, not to sentimentalise the death of Giles. In fact, although Hardy's sacrifice of his hero on the altar of propriety has in it the sting of social criticism, Giles's death is muted, the narrator is detached, the tragic implications are unnoted. T. G. Rosenmeyer [*The Green Cabinet* (1969), p. 112] has commented that in the pastoral lyric the peace and gentleness and simplicity of the bower have the effect of muting the pathos of death. Hardy's elegiac close unfolds from similar assumptions: the quiet seclusion of the graveyard, the intimation (both earlier and at the close) of cycles larger than a single life, compress grief into its proper perspective. If immortality is passed over, yet the simple and homely elegy murmured by Marty succeeds in assuaging sorrow and revealing to man his place in the universe.   . . .

SOURCE: extracts from ch. 7 ('*The Woodlanders*: Arcadian Innocents') of *The Pastoral Novel* (Charlottesville, Va., 1974), pp. 151, 151–61, 162–6, 170–1, 171–2.

Shelagh Hunter   'The Implications of *Impressionism*'   (1984)

. . .

After looking at the landscape ascribed to Bonington in our drawing-room I feel that Nature is played out as a Beauty, but not as a Mystery. I don't want to see landscapes, i.e., scenic paintings of them, because I don't want to see the original realities – as optical effects, that is. I want to see the deeper reality underlying the scenic, the expression of what are sometimes called abstract imaginings.

The 'simply natural' is interesting no longer. The much decried, mad, late-Turner rendering is now necessary to create my interest. The exact truth as to material fact ceases to be important in art – it is a student's style – the style of a period when the mind is serene and unwakened to the tragical mysteries of life; when it does not bring anything to the object that coalesces with and translates the qualities that are already there, – half-hidden, it may be – and the two united are depicted as the All.

[*The Life of Thomas Hardy*]

The comparison of Realism and Impressionism in painting, in the terms which Hardy uses here, may furnish a means of comparing *The Woodlanders* and *Under the Greenwood Tree*. The 'rural painting of the Dutch school' is a Realist picture; *The Woodlanders* was written at a time when Hardy was not only exploring the implications of Impressionism, but extending them to literature as well. Alastair Smart comments that any doubt of the completeness of Hardy's understanding of Impressionist technique can be dispelled by an examination of his handling of detail in *The Woodlanders*. He cites the passage in which Mr Percomb watches Marty, where 'such telling use is made of one of the principal canons of Impressionist theory – that all forms lying outside the immediate focus of the gaze are inevitably blurred and indistinct and that it is therefore legitimate for the particular painter having selected his focal point, to treat them as such'. And as an instance of the use of reflected light he quotes the picture of Grace as 'a sylph-like and greenish white creature, as toned by sunlight and leafage'. Hardy's grasp of the technique is, I believe, observable on a wider scale than this – the detail in such instances supports a conception of the whole structure as Impressionist in outlook, as *Under the Greenwood Tree* is Realist. To stop in Hardy's diary entries is to be reminded how privately functional they were intended to be; there are no concessions here to a reader presuming to read concurrent thoughts as a surrogate preface. But what Hardy seems to imply of the different relation between inner and outer reality in Realism and Impressionism illustrates the difference in technique and simultaneous closeness of conception of the two novels. Presumably Hardy would not have characterised the Dutch school as a 'student style', but in his own chosen medium *Under the Greenwood Tree* is a young man's book in the terms of Hardy's definitions in this passage from *The Life*. The external world as the subject of artistic representation is, he implies, separate from the interpretive mind, but in Realism object and significance are, nevertheless, *presented* as one. The picture of the world in *Under the Greenwood Tree* is, as it were, a static picture of movement. The picturesque Dewy cottage is picturesque precisely because it bears the marks of time; it can only, however, stay as it is for the briefest of moments. The gnarled and pocked tree in the Days' garden shelters the wedding party, observed with humour and humanity; here, not the manner of description but the pressure of the antecedent story suggests that Fancy is one of the last brides who will make the choice to marry in the old way. The interlocking of picture and process, stasis and movement, is characteristic of *Under the Greenwood Tree*. It can show in the delicate suggestion of movement by which first the candle and then Fancy herself appears at the window on Christmas Eve, or it can show under the total pressure of the story, as an old way of life pictured at the very moment of its passing. In Impressionistic art, the more mature art as Hardy presents it, the artist has grown so aware of his consciousness of inherent mystery that it takes precedence for him over the surface of things and his art becomes, though not necessarily in T. S. Eliot's pejorative sense, self-expressive. The story of *The Woodlanders* shows the woodland life invaded to a more dramatic or startling effect. The old ways of life are under severe strain, but there must, in spite of the descriptions of forest work, be as little sociological emphasis in this as in any of Hardy's novels. The preface suggests that the divorce laws are of central importance, but they do not seem so in the reading. *The Woodlanders* records an awareness of a 'tragical mystery' underlying appearances, whether fictional, historical or natural. The human and the natural world are shown as alike subject to decay even while life itself goes on. The undramatic continuity of life removes the possibility of a formally tragic ending and it remains for the narrator to present his morbid perception without resolution.

The technique by which the prevailing gloom of the abstracted point of view is transformed into the mellowness of the total effect of *The Woodlanders* ought to be capable of formal description. David Lodge, in his preface to the New Wessex Edition considers it as a 'novelistic adaptation of the pastoral elegy'. His argument is sharp and interesting. Cyclic nature, the close association of Giles with the vegetation, the 'religious and ritual overtones' attached to Marty's and Grace's mourning, the verbal play on the idea of resurrection in the course of the reconciliation of Grace and Fitzpiers – all these elements in the novel, together with the external evidence of the appearance in *Macmillan's Magazine* during the serialisation of *The Woodlanders* of a new translation of Moschus's 'Lament for Bion', are related in Professor Lodge's preface to the pastoral elegy. But they remain, to my mind and, ultimately, in the preface's final view of the novel, elements rather than generic signals which can inform our response to the whole book. In the splitting of the conventionally upbeat ending to a classical pastoral elegy into two, so that 'Grace and Fitzpiers go off to "fresh woods and pastures new" . . . with their love at least temporarily revived and renewed, while Marty is left behind in Hintock woods to nourish the memory of Giles', it seems to me that the conventions of realism have 'displaced' (Lodge uses Northrop Frye's word) the elegiac mode so successfully that the two halves do not unite to make a common effect. They are so separate as almost to seem to comment on one another, but the comment does not bridge the gap. The two endings are divergent and each separately is unresolved. Grace's future happiness is problematic and it is not as Nature God or vegetation spirit that Giles is remembered (that is an image that belongs to Grace's convalescence), but as a skilled rural workman. It was always their unthinking skill that Marty and Giles shared. When they plant the trees [ch. VIII] the narrator describes the 'sympathy between [Giles] and the fir, oak or beech that he was operating on', but Giles 'seems' careless of what he is doing and at this time is thinking of Grace and Mrs Charmond and his evening party. Marty heroically holds one tree upright after another, but is absorbed in her miseries, a bad cold, a dying father and unrequited love. Giles's epitaph is spoken with a moving but none the less restricted understanding entirely in character. Of the five main characters, two are now dead and the three remaining ones hardly closer together than any of the combinations of the five have been in the rest of the book. No element of the ending corresponds to the formal demands of the elegy. The consolation at the end of Moschus's 'Lament for Bion' is in terms of the myth of the descent of heroes into Tartarus – Orpheus, Odysseus and Hercules. The continuation of Bion's 'music' is assured by the power of the stories to draw the imagination of the reader to a sense of continuation beyond death. As a Christian adaptation of the form, 'Lycidas' is a complex blending of separate elements. Lycidas has 'mounted high / Through the dear might of him that walked the waves', a literally everlasting life had been vouchsafed the poet's friend. The poet himself is left not only to sing the passing of the shepherd, but to continue his pastoral care of the sheep in a way both like and unlike that of the dead shepherd. Neither the imaginative transfiguration of grief accorded by myth nor the combined resignation and self-involvement possible to the Christian poet with his acute sense of what is God's and what is Caesar's is available to Hardy. The realistic parts of the ending remain resolutely separate. Michael Millgate says the novel ends in 'narrative irresolution'; David Lodge describes the power of the book as residing in the 'delicate, precarious balance which Hardy manages to hold between those conflicting and logically incompatible value systems and knowledge systems that makes *The Woodlanders* the powerful, absorbing and haunting work of fiction it is'. The living Giles is the centre of a part of the action, which is a part of the 'web' of the whole, but he is not the centre of the book. Pastoral elegy as much as tragedy requires for formal resolution a concentration of interest at the centre.

The diffusion of interest over five characters in *The Woodlanders*, Ian Gregor says, 'makes way for the author', who sets his characters in a 'setting' of 'pervasive melancholy' suggested by the woods. The line between this argument and mine is a fine one, but I see the interest as diffused not simply over five characters but equally over their story and its setting, which makes the woods, although a setting for the story, an equal component in the view presented by the narrator. The 'purely descriptive' mode of the idyllium allows for diffusion of interest, 'irresolution' or ambiguity in the ending and the precarious balance of the whole. The balance, of 'incompatible value-systems and knowledge systems', is a balance of inner or interpreted realities. The narrator, with the resigned, mature melancholy of a man 'awakened to the tragical mysteries of life', presents an Impressionist picture of the world to which his sensibilities are open. Behind the natural world of the setting and the human world of the story lies the same pattern of decay, adaptation and endurance. The techniques of *Under the Greenwood Tree* maintain a constant tension between the still surface of the Realist painting of the Dutch school and the movement of historical as well as fictional time. In the Impressionist technique of *The Woodlanders* the separate parts of the total vision – the natural and the human – are brought together in a multiplicity of facets which produces an amazing uniformity of tone and mood. A truly 'mad, late-Turner effect' is hardly possible within the confines of realistic fiction; the human situations emerge with a form and definition which inevitably tones down the hectic vision. The shimmer is maintained in *The Woodlanders* by the constant but surprising interplay of story and setting over the time, which, of its nature, the fiction requires to unfold itself.

The pattern of the narrator's mediation of this vision is set very early in chapter I; in the opening paragraphs, in fact, the narrator has revealed himself. The chapter begins with a generalised evocation of a past time and as little temporal precision as there is sign of a single person with whom the reader may identify. There is, in fact or fiction, no rambler, 'who, for old association's sake, should trace the forsaken coach-road', no dreaming and responsive loiterer. The narrator invents him to say some things he wishes to say himself without engaging himself in generalities of that kind. The scene itself is described partly in scientific/geographic language – the road 'running almost in a meridonial line', 'the trees, timber or fruit-bearing as the case may be'. This cool approach throws into sharper relief the poetic description which works through all the senses. 'The trees ... make the wayside hedges ragged by their drip and shade' is both visual and tactile. The next sentence works by sight and sound:

At one place, on the skirts of Blackmoor Vale, where the bold brow of High-Stoy Hill is seen two or three miles ahead, the leaves lie so thick in autumn as to completely bury the track.

The sound of the words, 'bold brow', alerts the reader to a sense of muffled footsteps on the thick leaves which are not described, but are picked up implicitly in 'the loiterer's' sense of all the perished wayfarers. There is a suggestion here of the pattern of clear distance and enclosed autumnal foreground which is, of course, an important element in the whole book. Here too, as in well-developed ways later, the personified external world has an active, independent life. The distant hill has a 'bold brow', the trees *make* the wayside hedges ragged, *stretch* their lower limbs across the way' as though '*reclining* on the insubstantial air'. The deserted highway has a 'physiognomy' which addresses the observer, bespeaking 'a tomblike stillness more emphatic than glades and pools'. This stance is typical of the narrator of *The Woodlanders*. The passive recipient of active impression he, most characteristically, takes on a reflective role. Without seeming to shape the actual impression he allows his thoughts to run on in response to it. About the 'tomblike' stillness of the highway he says, in the tone of a man required to explain facts, 'The contrast of what is with what might be, probably accounts for this.' And he continues, putting himself in the place of someone who might, in stepping out of the woods on to the road, if he paused 'amid its emptiness for a moment ... exchange by the act of a single stride the simple absence of human companionship for an incubus of the forlorn'. The move into story at this point is effected by the introduction of a man in just this situation. But if he was affected in any way as the narrator was by the scene, it lasts only a moment. His 'finical' dress labels him out of place and he is 'mainly puzzled about the way'. It seems that this is not an introduction to anyone who is going to be important in the story. He is picked up in a lumbering van with an old horse and quaintly dressed carrier, all described so minutely that it seems completely natural in its time and place and grotesque at the same time. As the van lurches towards 'the little Hintock of the master-barber's search' it becomes increasingly clear that the object of his search rather than the barber himself is going to interest us as readers, that and the place where he expects to find it.

It is the narrator's description of that place which has led many to the assumption that Hardy conceived *The Woodlanders* as a tragedy:

> Thus they rode on, and High-Stoy Hill grew larger ahead. At length could be discerned in the dusk, about half a mile to one side, gardens and orchards sunk in a concave, and, as it were, snipped out of the woodland. From this self-contained place rose in stealthy silence tall stems of smoke, which the eye of imagination could trace downward to their root on quiet hearthstones, festooned overhead with hams and flitches. It was one of those sequestered spots outside the gates of the world where may usually be found more meditation than action, and more listlessness than meditation; where reasoning proceeds on narrow premisses, and results in inferences wildly imaginative; yet where, from time to time, dramas of a grandeur and unity truly Sophoclean are enacted in the real, by virtue of the concentrated passions and closely-knit interdependence of the lives therein.

With another writer the inference that this is a hint, even a statement, that the ensuing story will be such a Sophoclean drama, might well be justified. Here such an inference misreads this narrator and Hardy's habitual opening methods. Detached and meditative, the narrator first describes the signs of Little Hintock as they appear to the traveller, 'gardens and orchards sunk in a concave' and 'tall stems of smoke'. 'The eye of imagination' follows the smoke down to the hearths, but the live eye retains the impression of enclosure. The cultivated spaces seem only 'clipped out of the woodland'. Just as the lonely highway struck him as like the tomb of countless buried travellers over time so the almost hidden village suggests by the scant signs of its existence which penetrate the encompassing woodland the nature of the lives half-buried there. The possibility of Sophoclean intensity of passion is not more emphasised in this sentence than the suffocated mental life with which it coexists. Light does not penetrate to the mind in this dark place – the imagination may soar without any sense of its baselessness; the passions may well reach Sophoclean intensity 'by virtue of the closely knit interdependence of the lives'. The point is a Wordsworthian one, that remoteness and enclosure dull the mind and intensify the passions. The story we are to read will surely be about life in this place, probably a dark story of people with unenlightened minds and a potential intensity of feeling. The misleading 'Sophoclean' describes the feelings not the form of the story which is to follow.

The way in which this narrator will tell the story is more clearly indicated by the ending of the chapter from this point. The barber descends from the van and plunges into the 'umbrageous nook'. The things he is not interested in are described by the narrator as the barber passes them by. The end of the search is bathed in light, but it is hardly the eye of the purposeful barber that is caught by the picture, nor by the stray moth or two in the single shaft of light from the door:

> Half a dozen dwellings were passed without result. The next, which stood opposite a tall tree, was in an exceptional state of radiance, the flickering brightness from inside shining up the chimney and making a luminous mist of the emerging smoke. The interior, as seen through the window, caused him to draw up with a terminative air and watch. The house was rather large for a cottage, and the door, which opened immediately into the living-room, stood ajar, so that a riband of light fell through the opening into the dark atmosphere without. Every now and then a moth, decrepit from the late season, would flit for a moment across the outcoming rays and disappear again into the night.

The only personality to emerge from the first chapter is that of the narrator. He is a perceptive, brooding and humane man and one, we might think, 'who used to notice such things'. Only at the beginning of *The Woodlanders* and *Under the Greenwood Tree* does the narrative persona emerge as central in this way. In the dramatic presentation of a strong situation in a well-realised social setting in *The Mayor of Casterbridge*, in the 'sublimely' atmospheric and animating description of Egdon Heath, or in the sardonic little sketch of the drunken John Durbeyfield, the parson and the little boy, the narrator is subordinated to what he chooses to present. In chapter I of *Jude the Obsure* the narrator is a felt presence, but it is the strength of his sympathy with the sharply focused child at the well which sets the mournful tone of the opening. If maturity is, as Hardy described it, being awake to the 'tragical mysteries of life' then *Jude* is obviously from the opening going to be a very grown-up book indeed, but it presents the reality and the interpretation as one coherent whole and is thus a picture in a 'student' or realistic style. At the time of writing *The Woodlanders*, to judge from the diary entries, he would have regarded the style and content of *Jude* as incompatible, and the whole novel an attempt to present a mature sense of ineluctable tragedy fused in a stylistically youthful way with the 'real' surface of things. The coherent Impressionistic picture of a struggling world governed by the Unfulfilled Intention painted in *The Woodlanders* is built up, paradoxically, by a pervasive instability in the detail of the vision.

SOURCE: extract from ch. 5 of *Victorian Idyllic Fiction: Pastoral Strategies* (London and Basingstoke, 1984), pp. 186–94.

SELECT BIBLIOGRAPHY

For further reading, students are advised to consult: firstly, F. E. Hardy, *The Life of Thomas Hardy, 1840–1928* (1928, 1930); one-volume edition (Macmillan, London, 1962) – also edited and revised by Michael Millgate as *The Life and Work of Thomas Hardy* by Thomas Hardy (Macmillan, London, 1984) – and *Thomas Hardy's Personal Writings*, ed. Harold Orel (Macmillan, London, 1967). Secondly, the complete books from which extracts have been reprinted in this collection.

For consultation, the following editions of the 'pastoral novels' are recommended: *Under the Greenwood Tree*, New Wessex Edition, Introduction by Geoffrey Grigson (Macmillan, London, 1974); *Under the Greenwood Tree*, World's Classics Edition, edited with an Introduction by Simon Gatrell (Oxford University Press, 1985); *Far from the Madding Crowd*, New Wessex Edition, Introduction by John Bayley (Macmillan, London, 1974); *The Woodlanders*, New Wessex Edition, Introduction by David Lodge (Macmillan, London, 1974); *The Woodlanders*, edited by Dale Kramer (Oxford University Press, 1981).

The following books and articles are also recommended:

Alcorn, John, *The Nature Novel from Hardy to Lawrence* (Macmillan, London, 1977).

Babb, Howard, 'Setting and Theme in *Far from the Madding Crowd*', *English Literary History*, 30 (1963), pp. 147–61.

Brooks, Jean, *Thomas Hardy, The Poetic Structure* (Paul Elek, London, 1971).

Carpenter, Richard C., *Thomas Hardy*, Twayne's English Authors Series (Twayne, New York, 1964).

Cox, R. G., *Thomas Hardy: The Critical Heritage* (Routledge & Kegan Paul, London, 1970).

Draffan, Robert A., 'Hardy's *Under the Greenwood Tree*', *English*, 22, (Summer 1973), pp. 55–60.

Draper, R. P., *Far from the Madding Crowd*, recorded discussion (Norwich Tapes, Battle, Sussex, 1985).

——, *The Woodlanders*, recorded discussion (Norwich Tapes, Battle, Sussex, 1985).

——, 'Hardy and Respectability' (includes comment on *Under the Greenwood Tree* as pastoral), in Brian S. Lee (ed.), *An English Miscellany* (Oxford University Press, London and Cape Town, 1977), pp. 179–207.

Gatrell, Simon, 'Thomas Hardy and the Dance', *Thomas Hardy Year Book*, no. 5 (Toucan Press, Guernsey, 1976), pp 42–7.

Gittings, Robert, *Young Thomas Hardy* (Heinemann, London, 1975); paperback edn (Penguin, Harmondsworth, 1978).

——, *The Older Hardy* (Heinemann, London, 1978); paperback edn (Penguin, Harmondsworth, 1980).

Halperin, John, *Egoism and Self-Discovery in the Victorian Novel: Studies in the Ordeal of Knowledge in the Nineteenth Century* (Burt Franklin, New York, 1974).

Hannaford, Richard, 'A Forlorn Hope? Grace Melbury and *The Woodlanders*', *Thomas Hardy Year Book*, no. 10 (Toucan Press, Guernsey, 1981), pp. 22–6.

Hardy, Barbara, '*Under The Greenwood Tree*: A Novel about the Imagination', in Anne Smith (ed.), *The Novels of Thomas Hardy* (Vision Press, London, 1979), pp. 45–57.

Howe, Irving, *Thomas Hardy* (Weidenfeld & Nicolson, London, 1966).

Page, Norman, *Thomas Hardy* (Routledge & Kegan Paul, London, 1977).

Pinion, F. B., *A Hardy Companion* (Macmillan, London, 1968).

Stewart, J. I. M., *Thomas Hardy, A Critical Biography* (Longman, London, 1971).

Toliver, Harold E., 'The Dance under the Greenwood Tree: Hardy's Bucolics', *Nineteenth-Century Fiction*, 17 (1962–63), pp. 57–68.

Vigar, Penelope, *The Novels of Thomas Hardy: Illusion and Reality* (Athlone Press, London, 1974).

NOTES ON CONTRIBUTORS

SIR JAMES M. BARRIE (1860–1937): novelist, playwright and essayist; his many works include *Peter Pan* and *The Admirable Crichton* (play).

JOSEPH WARREN BEACH (1880–1957): Professor of English, University of Minnesota, 1924–48; in addition to his study of Hardy, he wrote on Meredith and Henry James when they also might have been regarded as contemporary novelists.

DOUGLAS BROWN: formerly Senior Lecturer in English, University of Reading, and, at his death in 1964, Professor-elect at the University of York; author of *Thomas Hardy* (1954) and of a study of *The Mayor of Casterbridge* (1962).

PETER J. CASAGRANDE: Professor of English, University of Kansas; his publications include *Unity in Hardy's Novels* (1982).

JOHN DANBY (died 1972): formerly Professor of English, University College of North Wales, Bangor; author of studies of Shakespeare and Wordsworth.

ANDREW ENSTICE: his publications include *Thomas Hardy: Landscapes of the Mind* (1979).

SHELAGH HUNTER: Lecturer in English, Yale University; her publications include *Victorian Idyllic Fiction* (1984).

HENRY JAMES (1843–1916): American novelist and critic, and a powerful influence on the development of modern fiction; he took British nationality in 1914.

JOHN LUCAS: Professor of English, University of Loughborough; author of books on Dickens and Arnold Bennett, and of *Literature and Politics in the Nineteenth Century* (1971), *The Literature of Change* (1977), *The 1980s: A Challenge to Orthodoxy* (1978) and *Romantic to Modern Literature* (1982).

MICHAEL MILLGATE: Professor of English, University of Toronto; his contributions to Hardy studies include *Thomas Hardy: His Career as a Novelist* (1971) and *Thomas Hardy: A Biography* (1984), and the editorship of *The Life and Works of Thomas Hardy* by Thomas Hardy

(1984) and (with Richard L. Purdy) *The Collected Letters of Thomas Hardy* (1978–present).

HORACE MOULE (died 1873): scholar, critic and journalist; an early friend of Hardy's who committed suicide.

ROY MORRELL: formerly Professor of English, University of Malaya; author of *Thomas Hardy: The Will and the Way* (1965).

NORMAN PAGE: Professor of English, University of Nottingham (and formerly teaching at the University of Alberta); his publications include books on Kipling, A. E. Housman and Hardy; he is also editor of *Thomas Hardy Year Book* and of the Casebooks on Dickens: *Hard Times, Great Expectations & Our Mutual Friend*, on Golding: *Novels, 1954–67* and on *The Language of Literature*.

ALAN SHELSTON: Senior Lecturer in English, University of Manchester; his publications include works on Biography and on Mrs Gaskell, and on Thomas Carlyle, and the Casebooks on Dickens: *Dombey and Son & Little Dorrit* and on Henry James: *Washington Square & The Portrait of a Lady*.

MICHAEL SQUIRES: member of the English Department of the University of Virginia; his publications include *The Pastoral Novel* (1974) and *The Creation of 'Lady Chatterley's Lover'* (1983).

MERRYN WILLIAMS: tutor for The Open University; author of *Revolutions, 1775–1830* (1971), *Thomas Hardy and Rural England* (1972), *A Preface to Hardy* (1976) and *Women in the English Novel, 1800–1900* (1984).

VIRGINIA WOOLF (1882–1941): novelist and critic.

ACKNOWLEDGEMENTS

The editor and publishers wish to thank the following who have given permission for the use of copyright material: James M. Barrie, for an article on 'Thomas Hardy: The Historian of Wessex' in *Contemporary Review* (1899), by permission of Samuel French Ltd on behalf of the Estate of the author; Douglas Brown, for an extract from *Thomas Hardy* (1954), by permission of Longman Group UK Ltd; Peter J. Casagrande, for an extract from *Unity in Hardy's Novels* (1982), by permission of Macmillan Publishers; John F. Danby, for an article on 'Under the Greenwood Tree' in *Critical Quarterly* (Spring, 1959), by permission of the author's widow; Andrew Enstice, for extracts from *Thomas Hardy: Landscapes of the Mind* (1979), by permission of Macmillan Publishers Ltd; Shelagh Hunter, for an extract from *Victorian Idyllic Fiction: Pastoral Strategies* (1984), by permission of Macmillan Publishers Ltd; John Lucas, for an extract from *The Literature of Change* (1977), by permission of The Harvester Press Ltd; Michael Squires, for extracts from *The Pastoral Novel* (1974), by permission of the University Press of Virginia; Michael Millgate, for an extract from *Thomas Hardy: His Career as a Novelist* (1971), by permission of A. D. Peters & Co Ltd on behalf of the author; Roy Morrell, for an extract from *Thomas Hardy: The Will and the Way* (1965), by permission of the author; Norman A. Page, for an extract from 'Hardy's Dutch Painting: *Under the Greenwood Tree*' in *The Thomas Hardy Yearbook*, No. 5 (1975), Toucan Press, by permission of the author; Alan Shelston, for an extract from 'The Particular Pleasure of *Far from the Madding Crowd*' in *The Thomas Hardy Yearbook*, No. 7 (1979), Toucan Press, by permission of the author; Merryn Williams, for an extract from *Thomas Hardy and Rural England* (1972), by permission of Macmillan Publishers Ltd; Virginia Woolf, for extracts from her essay, 'The Novels of Thomas Hardy', 1928, from *Collected Essays Vol. 1*, by permission of the Author's Literary Estate and The Hogarth Press Ltd.

Every effort has been made to trace all the copyright holders but if any have been inadvertently overlooked the publishers will be pleased to make the necessary arrangement at the first opportunity.

INDEX

Page numbers in **bold** type relate to essays or excerpts in this Casebook. Entries in SMALL CAPS denote characters in the three Pastoral Novels.

Addison, Joseph 78

Aldeclyffe, Cytherea (*Desperate Remedies*) 98

Allenville, Geraldine (*An Indiscretion in the Life of an Heiress*) 112, 114

Allenville, Squire (*An Indiscretion in the Life of an Heiress*) 114

Amiens (*As You Like It*) 9

Antell, John 146

Arden, The Forest of (*As You Like It*) 9, 11

Aristotle 47

Aurelius, Marcus 38

Austen, Jane 191; *Pride and Prejudice* 182

Avice III *see* Caro, Avice III

Barn, the Great 149

Barnes, William 37, 56, 99

Barrie, James M. **59–64**

Barthélémon, François-Hippolyte 32

BATHSHEBA *see* EVERDENE, BATHSHEBA

Bayley, John 137, 146

Bazin, René 67

Beach, Joseph Warren 13, 15, **64–82**

Bellini, Giovanni 38

Bible, the 13, 52, 65, 66–7, 68, 125

Bion 197

Blackmore, R. D., *Lorna Doone* 61

Blackmore, Vale of 56, 168, 185, 199

Bockhampton 32, 33, 34, 37, 147

BOLDWOOD, FARMER 12, 15, 47, 49, 52, 65, 67, 68, 69, 70, 116, 117, 118, 121, 125–6, 129, 130, 132–3, 134, 135, 139, 141, 145, 149, 153, 154–5

Bonington, Richard Parkes 19, 194

BOWMAN, JOSEPH 77, 91

Bridehead, Sue (*Jude the Obscure*) 68, 127, 182

Brontë, Emily, *Wuthering Heights* 90, 97, 182

Brown, Douglas 16–17, **157–70**, 173, 178

Browne, Sir Thomas 74

BROWNJOHN, MRS 92

Bubb-Down Hill 29, 30

Buck's Head Inn 53, 79, 82, 150

Budmouth 124

Bulbarrow 30

Byron 187

CALLCOMBE, NAT 102

Cantle, Christopher (*Return of the Native*) 62, 78

Caro, Avice III (*The Well-Beloved*) 109

Casagrande, Peter J. 12, **111–15**

Casterbridge 60, 61, 79, 102, 121, 123, 139, 145, 147, 150, 151, 156, 175, 179

CHARMOND, FELICE 17, 57, 59, 130, 159, 163, 167, 169–70, 173, 174, 175–6, 177, 179, 180, 181, 183, 184, 186–7, 188, 189, 190, 191, 192, 197

Chesterton, G. K. 144, 146
Chromis 65
Clare, Angel (*Tess*) 68, 117, 122, 127, 176
Clare, John 151
CLARK, MARK 79
COGGAN, JAN 46, 55, 79, 81, 85, 134, 145
COGGAN, TEDDY 126
Collins, Wilkie 106
Comte, Auguste 36
Coney, Christopher (*Mayor of Casterbridge*) 62
Conrad, Joseph 190
Contemporary Review 59–64
Corn Exchange (Casterbridge) 15, 150–1
Cornhill 8, 33, 34, 35, 36
CREEDLE, ROBERT 57, 59, 166, 180
Critical Quarterly 10, 89–97
Crivelli, Carlo 38

DAMSON, SUKE 172, 173, 179, 188, 192, 193
Danby, John F. 10–11, **89–97**
Daniel, Samuel 181
Darwin, Charles 17, 170
David, King 66, 67
DAY, BESSIE 110
DAY, FANCY 11–12, 13, 43, 44, 45, 60, 62, 90, 92, 93, 95, 96, 97, 98, 99, 100, 101, 102, 103, 104, 105, 109, 110, 111, 112, 113, 114, 115, 128, 131, 196
DAY, GEOFFREY (Keeper) 43, 44, 45, 62, 102, 104, 105, 108, 112, 114, 115, 196
DAY, MRS 62, 102, 104
Desperate Remedies 43, 61, 98, 106, 107, 111, 114, 121, 127
DEWY, ANN, MRS 77, 92, 93, 94, 95, 96, 101
DEWY, DICK 10, 11–12, 13, 43, 44, 45, 60, 62, 90, 91, 92, 93, 95, 96, 97, 98, 99, 100, 101, 102, 105, 109, 110, 112, 113, 114, 115, 131
DEWY, REUBEN (Tranter) 35, 43–4,
61, 62, 76, 77, 78, 93, 94, 95, 96, 100, 104, 106, 108, 114, 195
DEWY, WILLIAM (Grandfather) 44, 92, 93, 100–1, 104–5
Dickens, Charles 63, 83, 191; *Great Expectations* 140; *Our Mutual Friend* 129

Dogbury Hill 163
'Dorsetshire Labourer, The' 102
Douw, Gerard 82
Drake, Robert 181
Druce Farm 147
Dryden, John 180
Duke Senior (*As You Like It*) 9
D'Urberville, Alec (*Tess*) 172
D'Urberville, Tess (*Tess*) 68, 122, 127, 166, 176
Durbeyfield, John (*Tess*) 201
Dynasts, The 39, 89

Egdon Heath 61, 72, 91, 147, 157, 158, 171, 175, 201
Eliot, George 36, 46, 51, 52, 61, 85, 106, 186, 190; *Adam Bede* 55, 106, 182, 184, 187, 188; *Felix Holt* 51; *Scenes of Clerical Life* 107; *Silas Marner* 44, 50, 61
Eliot, T. S. 159, 196
Emminster 127
ENDORFIELD, ELIZABETH ('Witch') 45, 112
ENOCH (Geoffrey Day's Trapper) 44, 102, 114–15
Enstice, Andrew 15, **146–56**
Esther, Queen 67
Ethelberta (*The Hand of Ethelberta*) 127
EVERDENE, BATHSHEBA 8, 12, 14, 15, 21, 33, 47, 48–9, 52, 53, 54, 60, 61, 63, 64, 65, 66, 67, 68–9, 70, 71, 74, 78, 84, 85, 116–17, 118, 119, 120, 121, 123, 124, 125, 126, 127, 128–37, 138, 139, 141, 142, 143–4, 145, 147, 148, 149, 151, 154, 155, 157, 158, 166, 168, 177, 191

EVERDENE, LEVI 129
Examiner 28

Fairway, Timothy (*Return of the
    Native*) 32
FANCY *see* DAY, FANCY
FANNY *see* ROBIN, FANNY
Farfrae, Donald (*Mayor of
    Casterbridge*) 63, 68, 120, 177
Far from the Madding Crowd 8, 9–10,
    12, 13–15, 16, 17, 21, 27–9, 33–7,
    46–9, 50–5, 61, 62, 63, 64–82,
    84–5, 106, 116–28, 128–37, 137–
    46, 146–56, 157, 158, 166, 168,
    172, 177, 183, 189, 190, 191
Fawley, Jude (*Jude*) 68, 127, 182
Few Crusted Characters, A 25
Fielding, Henry 36; *Tom Jones* 182
FITZPIERS, EDRED 13, 17, 18, 57,
    58, 59, 158, 160, 163, 168, 170,
    171, 172, 173, 174, 176, 177, 178,
    179, 181, 184, 186, 187, 188, 189,
    190, 191, 192, 193, 194, 196, 197
Flaubert, Gustave 83
Fletcher, John 181
Floyer, Rev. Mr 31
Fontenelle, Bernard le Bovier de
    187
Fordington 34
Forster, E. M. *Aspects of the Novel*
    137
FRAY, 'HENERY' 46, 52, 85
Freud, Sigmund 143
Frome (Froom), River 147
Frye, Northrop 197
Furmity-woman, The (*Mayor of
    Casterbridge*) 62

GABRIEL *see* OAK, GABRIEL
Garland, Anne (*Trumpet-Major*) 63
GEORGE (Oak's sheepdog) 152
Gibbon, Edward 29
Gifford, Emma Lavinia *see* Hardy,
    Emma Lavinia
GILES *see* WINTERBORNE, GILES
Goethe, *Hermann und Dorothea* 43
Golden Treasury, The 98

Goldsmith, Oliver 61, 78; *The
    Vicar of Wakefield* 60
GRACE *see* MELBURY, GRACE
Gray, Thomas, 'Elergy Written in a
    Country Church-Yard' 9, 138,
    140
Graye, Cytherea (*Desperate
    Remedies*) 98, 114, 121
Greenhill Fair 34
Gregor, Ian 198
Grein, J. T. 39
Guarini, Giovanni Battista, *Il
    Pastor Fido* 181

HALL, CAINY 132
Halperin, John 143, 146
Hambledon Hill 30
Hand, Elizabeth 146
Hand of Ethelberta, The 61, 127
Hardy, Emma Lavinia 34, 36, 100
Hardy, Florence Emily 39, 169
Hardy, Thomas (father of
    novelist) 31, 32, 33
Hardy, Thomas (grandfather of
    novelist) 31, 32, 33
Henchard, Michael (*Mayor of
    Casterbridge*) 60, 61, 63, 68, 118,
    115, 158
Hercules 197
Hicks, John 169
High-Stoy 29, 30, 199, 200
Hintock House 57, 189
Hintocks, The 29, 30, 56, 57, 157,
    160, 163, 166, 169, 174, 180, 181,
    182, 183, 187, 188, 189, 191, 192,
    197, 200
Holst, Gustav 147
Homer 68
Hudson, W. H. 74
Hunter, Shelagh 19–20, **194–202**
Hylas 65

Ibsen, Henrik 39
Ilchester, Earl of 31
*Indiscretion in the Life of an Heiress,
    An* 111

'In Time of "the Breaking of Nations"' (poem) 99

Jackson, William (musical composer) 31
JAMES, GRANDFATHER 92, 93, 95, 101, 102, 108
James, Henry 9, **46–9,** 68, 83, 144, 191; *The Portrait of a Lady* 135
Jaques (*As You Like It*) 12, 101
Jefferies, Richard 60, 61, 74
Jonson, Ben, 'To Penshurst' 133, 134, 181
Jude *see* Fawley, Jude (*Jude*)
Jude the Obscure 89, 93, 127, 182, 201

Ken, Thomas 32
Kingsbere 32
Kingston, Higher 147
Knight, Henry (*Pair of Blue Eyes*) 61, 68, 115, 117, 122, 127, 130, 132, 133

Laodicean, A 61
Larkin, Philip, 'Lines on a Young Lady's Photograph Album' 132
Lawrence, D. H. 104, 142, 146; *Lady Chatterley's Lover* 188, 190; *The White Peacock* 186, 191, 192, 193
LEAF, MRS 44
LEAF, THOMAS 44, 77–8, 91, 100, 112, 115
Le Sueur, Lucetta (*Mayor of Casterbridge*) 68, 173
Lewgate 91
LIDDY *see* SMALLBURY, LIDDY
Life of Thomas Hardy, The 8, 16, **31–9,** 98, 107, 115, 195
Lodge, David 13, 17, 196, 197, 198
Loveday, John (*Trumpet-Major*) 61, 63
Loveday, Robert (*Trumpet-Major*) 63
Lucas, John 14–15, **127–37**

Macmillan (publisher) 97, 106, 107
Macmillan's Magazine 196
Maiden Newton 31
MAIL, MICHAEL 77, 91, 109
Manston, Aeneas (*Desperate Remedies*) 114
MARTY *see* SOUTH, MARTY
Marvell, Andrew 190
Max Gate 38
MAYBOLD, PARSON 12, 43, 45, 78, 96, 100, 104, 105, 112, 115
Mayne, Egbert (*An Indiscretion in the Life of an Heiress*) 111, 114, 121
Mayor of Casterbridge, The 13, 60, 61, 63, 68, 118, 120, 148, 151, 155, 158, 173, 177, 201
MELBURY, GEORGE 56, 158, 161, 163, 164, 165, 166, 169, 171, 172, 176, 177, 178–9, 181, 186, 191, 192, 193
MELBURY, GRACE 13, 17, 57, 58, 157, 158, 160, 161, 163, 164, 165, 166, 167, 168, 170, 171, 172, 174, 176, 177, 178, 179, 180, 181, 182, 183, 184, 185, 186, 187, 188, 189, 190, 191, 192, 193, 194, 195, 197
'Melia (in 'The Ruined Maid') 114
Mellstock 11, 77, 91, 96, 99, 104, 111, 114
Mellstock Quire, The 25, 26–7, 31, 35, 43, 62, 76–8, 90, 92, 97, 103, 104–5, 107, 108, 109, 112, 113
Meredith, George 68, 70, 106, 120
Millgate, Michael 9, 11, **97–106,** 111, 197–8
Milton, John, *Lycidas* 197; *Paradise Lost* 125
Mnasylus 65
Montacute 30
MOON, MATTHEW 48, 52
Morrell, Roy 14, 15, **116–28**
Moschus 196, 197
Moses 65
Moule, Horace 8, 34, **43–5,** 107

Murray, Rev. Mr Edward   31, 33

Napoleon Bonaparte   32
Nation   **46–9**
Norcombe   66, 81, 118, 147

OAK, GABRIEL   8, 12, 13, 14, 15, 21,
  33, 46, 47, 48, 49, 53, 54, 55, 63,
  65, 66, 67, 68, 70, 71, 73, 74, 75,
  79, 81, 84, 116, 117, 118–21, 124,
  125–6, 127, 128, 129, 130–2, 133,
  134, 136–7, 138–41, 142, 144,
  145, 147, 148, 151, 152–3, 155–6,
  157, 158, 160, 183
Odysseus   197
OLIVER, GRAMMER   58, 59, 173
Orlando (*As You Like It*)   98
Orpheus   197

Page, Norman   19, **106–11**
Pair of Blue Eyes, A   8, 10, 33, 34,
  50, 68, 71, 72, 73, 115, 117, 122,
  126, 127, 128, 130, 131, 132, 133
Paterson, Helen   36
Patmore, Coventry   17
'Paying Calls' (poem)   89, 97
PENNY, ROBERT   44, 76, 77, 91, 92,
  102, 103
PERCOMB BARBER   195, 200, 201
Piddle, River   146, 147
Plato   183
POORGRASS, JACOB   80
POORGRASS, JOSEPH   46, 48, 52, 53–
  4, 60, 65, 66, 78, 79, 80, 81, 82,
  85, 116, 134
'Poor Man and the Lady, The'
  111, 112, 114
Puddletown   31, 147

Randolph, Thomas   181
Reade, Charles   49
Rembrandt   14, 82
'Remember Adam's fall' (hymn)
  112
Return of the Native, The   13, 16, 20,
  32, 61, 69, 72, 73, 78, 82, 109,
  111, 117, 140, 153, 158, 160, 166,
  169, 172, 173, 175, 177, 192
Review of English Studies   111
Ridd, John (*Lorna Doone*)   63
Ridgeway, The   147
ROBIN, FANNY   14, 53, 54, 64, 69,
  78, 79, 84, 85, 122, 123, 124, 130,
  135, 139, 141, 145, 155, 189
Rosalind (*As You Like It*)   98
Rosenmeyer, T. G.   194
Rossetti, Dante Gabriel, 'The
  Blessed Damozel'   109
Roytown   150
'Ruined Maid, The' (poem)   114
Ruth   67

Saturday Review   8, 10, 33, 34, **43–5,
  50–5, 56–9,** 107
St Cleeve, Swithin (*Two on a
  Tower*)   63
St James's Gazette   17
Scott, Sir Walter   51, 52, 63, 83, 85
Scott-Siddons, Mrs   98
Shakespeare   36, 52, 68, 78, 85,
  100; *As You Like It*   9, 11, 19, 66,
  98–9, 101, 107; *Henry IV*   14, 76;
  The Merchant of Venice   134; *A
  Midsummer Night's Dream*   66
Sharpe, John Brereton   146
Sharpe, Martha   146
Shaston   30
Shelley, P. B.   183
Shelston, Alan   16, **137–46**
Sherton Abbas   164, 186
SHINER, FARMER   43, 45, 95, 98,
  100, 105, 112
Sidney, Sir Philip   190
Silenus   65
SMALLBURY, JACOB   65, 66, 129
SMALLBURY, LIDDY   125, 126, 134,
  154
SMALLBURY, WILLIAM   60
SMALLWAYS, OLD   144
Smart, Alastair   110–11, 195
Smith, Hallett   181
Smith, Stephen (*Pair of Blue Eyes*)
  68, 115, 122, 131

Somerset, George (*A Laodicean*) 63
Sophocles 200, 201
Sothern, Thomas 62
SOUTH, JOHN 166–7, 171, 180, 192
SOUTH, MARTY 13, 16–17, 18, 57, 157, 158, 159–60, 161, 162, 163, 164, 165, 166, 167, 169, 171, 174, 175–6, 177, 179, 180, 181, 182, 183, 184, 186, 190, 191, 192–3, 194, 195, 196, 197
Sparkes, Christopher 146
Sparkes, Henery 146
Sparkes, James 146
Sparkes, William 146
Spectator 36, 46, 107
Spenser, Edmund 190
SPINKS, ELIAS 91, 114
Springrove, Edward (*Desperate Remedies*) 111, 121
Squires, Michael 17–18, **180–94**
Stephen, Leslie 8, 33–4, 35, 36, 37
Stevens, Wallace 131
Stinsford Choir 31, 32
Stinsford Church 31, 33
Stinsford House 31
Stinsford Vicarage 31
Stour Head 30
Swancourt, Elfride (*Pair of Blue Eyes*) 61, 68, 69, 73, 122, 126, 127, 128, 130, 131, 133

TALL, LABAN 48, 52, 66
Tallis, Thomas 32
TANGS, TIM 172, 179, 188, 192
Tasso, Torquato, *Aminta* 181
Teniers, David 107
Terburg, Gerard 82
Tess *see* D'Urberville, Tess
Tess of the d'Urbervilles 68, 73, 117, 118, 122, 127, 147, 166, 167, 176, 201
Thackeray, Anne Isabella 36
Thackeray, William Makepeace 60
Theocritus 180, 193
Thomas Hardy Year Book **106–11, 137–46**

Thomson, James 99
'To an Impersonator of Rosalind' (poem) 98
Trantridge 172
Trollope, Anthony, *Barchester Towers* 187
TROY, SERGEANT 8, 12, 14, 15, 33, 47, 49, 53, 54, 55, 63, 64, 68, 69, 71, 84, 85, 116–17, 118, 119–20, 122–4, 126, 127, 129, 130, 134–6, 139, 141, 142, 143–4, 145, 146, 154, 155, 172, 173, 189, 190
Trumpet-Major, The 61, 63, 98
Turner, J. M. W. 19–20, 152, 195
Two on a Tower 25, 61
'Two Rosalinds, The' (poem) 98

Under the Greenwood Tree 8, 9, 10– 12, 14, 17, 19, 21, 25–7, 31–3, 35, 43–5, 50, 56, 61, 68, 69, 71, 76–8, 83, 89–97, 97–106, 106–11, 111– 15, 128, 131, 195–6, 201

Venn, Diggory (*Return of the Native*) 69, 72, 157, 158, 175
Vergil, *Eclogues* 180, 184–5, 195; *Georgics* 102
Victoria, Queen 27
Vye, Eustacia (*Return of the Native*) 68, 109, 173

Walpole, Hugh 68
Warren's Malthouse 15, 28, 35, 60, 80, 81, 120, 149–50, 153, 155
Waterson Manor 28
Weatherbury 28, 46, 65, 68, 69, 71, 73, 79, 120, 121, 124, 125, 126, 147, 148, 151, 157, 158
Weatherbury Farm 81, 148–9, 150
Weatherbury, Little 154
Webster, Thomas 108
Wells, H. G. 68
Wessex 10, 13, 14, 15, 20–1, 26, 27–8, 30, 37, 56, 58, **59–64,** 64– 5, 68, 72, 75, 78, 80, 85, 97, 127, 147
Weymouth 32

Wildeve, Damon (*Return of the Native*) 68, 172, 173
Wilkie, Sir David 107
Williams, Merryn 16, 17, **170–9**
Windy Green 30
WINTERBORNE, GILES 13, 17, 18, 57, 58, 69, 157, 158, 161, 162, 163, 164, 165, 166, 167, 168, 169, 170, 171, 174, 175, 176, 177, 178, 179, 180, 181, 182, 183, 184, 185–6, 188, 190, 191, 192, 193, 194, 196, 197, 198
Woodlanders, The 12, 13, 15–20, 21, 29–30, 37–9, 56–9, 71, 73, 111, 130, 157–70, 170–9, 180–94, 194–202

Woolf, Virginia **83–5**
Wordsworth, William 67, 81, 120, 189, 200
Wren, Sir Christopher 121

Yeobright, Clym (*Return of the Native*) 68, 72, 117, 158, 160, 166, 177, 192
Yeobright, Mrs (*Return of the Native*) 62, 68, 169
Yeobright, Thomasin (*Return of the Native*) 175, 177